The Event Manager's Bible

How to Plan and Deliver an Event

Second edition

Des Conway

howtobooks

Published by How To Books Ltd,
Spring Hill House, Spring Hill Road
Begbroke, Oxford OX5 1RX. United Kingdom.
Tel: (01865) 375794. Fax: (01865) 379162
email: info@howtobooks.co.uk
www.howtobooks.co.uk

First edition 2004
Second edition 2006

British Library Cataloguing in Publication Data.
A catalogue record for this book is available from the British Library.

ISBN 13: 978 1 84528 134 9
ISBN 10: 1 84528 134 2

Produced for How To Books by Deer Park Productions, Tavistock
Cover design by Baseline Arts Ltd, Oxford
Typesetting and design by Sparks – www.sparks.co.uk
Printed and bound in Great Britain by Bell & Bain Ltd, Glasgow

NOTE: The material contained in this book is set out in good faith for general guidance and
no liability can be accepted for loss or expense incurred as a result of relying in particular
circumstances on statements made in this book. Laws and regulations are complex and liable
to change, and readers should check the current position with the relevant authorities before
making personal arrangements.

The Event Manager's Bible

If you want to know how ...

Getting Free Publicity

Learn the secrets of successful press relations

Organising a Conference

How to plan and run a successful event

Headless Chickens, Laid back Bears

Scientific techniques to create more time and revolutionise your life and work

Producing Successful Magazines, Newsletters and E-Zines

Great ideas, practical help, and straightforward guidance ... a must-have for anyone planning their own publication

howtobooks

Please send for a free copy of the latest catalogue to:
How To Books
Spring Hill House, Spring Hill Road
Begbroke, Oxford OX5 1RX, United Kingdom
Email: info@howtobooks.co.uk
www.howtobooks.co.uk

Contents

1 Introduction

What is an event?

This book will help you to research, plan, organise, manage and deliver any event, match, show, tournament or function that will be attended by more than a handful of people. You may call your event a gymkhana, fun run, steam fayre, half marathon, carnival, school sports day, jumble sale, tennis tournament, car boot sale, or model aircraft show. The names change, but there are common requirements and considerations to them all. For the purpose of this book, we will describe your target function simply as the 'event'.

What will this book give me?

Many events have not been as successful as they could have been, because the organiser failed to adequately plan, and overlooked or under-estimated important things. Apparently insignificant mistakes can ruin a potentially successful event.

Events can be of any size, from huge pop festivals or Formula 1 car races attracting many thousands of spectators, down to primary school sports days attracting only a handful of people. No matter what their name or size, they all have an event manager, an objective, an audience and attractions. To deliver any of them, somebody had to investigate, research, plan, liaise with the authorities, obtain permissions and licences and then deliver the event to the public.

Anyone organising a large pop concert or other major event will almost certainly have professional assistance and previous plans on which to base their arrangements. This guide is therefore aimed at aspiring event managers, or the inexperienced who want to organise a smaller event attracting a few hundred, or a few thousand spectators.

More experienced event managers will read this book as a refresher, or possibly just to get a different view of some aspects of event management.

The objective is to offer four things:

- *guidance* – as to what to consider when researching, planning and running an event,
- *structure and method* – to use to plan and organise your event,
- *lists* – to help you to make your plans, and
- *outside agencies* – an indication of the agencies that you may have to contact to arrange a successful event.

Who wrote this book?

I have been involved in the organisation, planning and management of events and shows for about 20 years. For 15 of those years I have had a growing part in the police coverage of small, medium and large events.

During that time I made mistakes and have learned from the mistakes others have made. In event management, there is always something new. That is partly due to the introduction of new regulations or legislation and mostly due to the imagination and inventiveness of the population at large. As an illustration of that point, 20 years ago nobody had heard of bungee jumping out of a basket suspended from a mobile crane, so that was not a potential attraction that an event manager had to consider!

I am still learning. I welcome any input on problems that I have not experienced or covered in this guide.

I realised that at event after event I kept seeing the same mistakes being made and was constantly being asked the same questions. I began to give advice and hoped that my assistance would help others avoid known problems but there was a limit to the number of people I could speak to. To reach a wider audience I decided to produce a 'small pamphlet' summarising my method and advice. Over time, the original pamphlet expanded into this book.

Though your event theme, content, size, venue, target audience and objectives may vary, the methodology I propose remains basically the same. Using the sections of this guide will help you to consider logically the common aspects of event management, with the aim of validating and planning your proposed event so that it is ultimately successful.

What do you need?

To plan, organise and run an event, you will need time to investigate, research and plan; you will need methods to help you with that investigation and research, and you will need to possess or 'buy in' a variety of skills. Those skills include such diverse trades and professions as project management, sign writing, accounting and personnel management.

This book is primarily aimed at helping you to organise an event; I do not cover any of the specialist skills in any depth. For example, I simply touch on administrative and organisational aspects of event accounting that will contribute to the success of your event. If you need expert advice regarding event accounts, you should buy an accountancy book or, better still, consult an accountant or other relevant expert.

How long will it take?

The amount of time it will take depends on your event type, theme, objective, location, size and attractions, your skills and experience, the amount of time you have available and maybe a hundred other factors.

As an indication, I would suggest that organising and delivering the smallest event will probably take at least four months from first concept to when the gates are open to the public. On your first attempt to organise and deliver an event for an audience of more than 1000 people I would allow a *minimum* of 12 to 18 months. This includes time for your research and investigation, for staff recruitment and training and for waiting to receive written estimates and quotes from commercial suppliers. You must also remember that you will be dependent on the timetables of other organisations. For example, because many authorities have scheduled monthly or even quarterly committee meetings, you may find that you have to wait several months for their next scheduled meeting to approve or reject your proposals.

Different event – different emphasis

Working through this book, you will investigate and eventually arrange all of the requirements for your event, but *every event is unique*, so this book can only be a guide. The emphasis of different aspects of the investigation and arrangements will be different for everyone and I will remind you of that fact at appropriate places in this book.

To illustrate that point, you will accept that there is nothing complex about 'first aid' as a subject, but the effort needed to organise first aid cover for a primary school fête will be insignificant compared to the effort required to organise first aid cover for a Formula 1 car race. This shows that though both events require and organise 'first aid cover', at the primary school it will probably be a teacher with first aid skills and a small first aid box, for the Formula 1 race it involves several doctors, ambulances, hospitals on standby, paramedics and a helicopter for medical evacuation. Though all event managers will be looking at the same subjects, the content and delivery of their event will heavily influence how they organise, plan and manage those arrangements.

While working through this book, you must therefore be prepared to tailor the approach, amend the lists and vary the depth and scope of your investigation, to match your unique requirements. You will be helped in that as you work through by talking to and taking advice from local authorities, the emergency services and any other relevant groups or governing bodies. In some areas, these authorities have come together to form Safety Advisory Groups.

If you don't know how to approach the organisation and delivery of an event I suggest that you work through the chapters (stages) in this guide in numerical sequence. When you understand the concepts and issues involved, you might want to amend the sequence of your work to suit your event.

Your unique event might even lead you to change the order of some elements of your investigation and preparation. For example, there are two approaches to organising attractions – it depends on your starting point.

If, when you start, you have a specific attraction available, perhaps a steam engine, as the basis for your event, you will have to work towards attracting an audience that likes steam engines. Alternately, if your starting point is that you have an audience (members of your club), you could take the reverse approach and want to find and book attractions that your audience want to see and will find interesting. This illustrates the fact that you may wish to take a different path through your preparations. For example, in this case you may choose to change the order of your work in the areas of Chapter 8 'Defining your target audience' and Chapter 11 'Event attractions' – depending on your starting point. You can change the order to suit your needs, as long as you perform all of the stages.

You should also remember that some outside agencies might have jurisdiction over your event. For example, at higher levels of some sports the governing body may impose various rules and limitations. Government agencies may have some jurisdiction as well. For example, the Environment Agency may impose rules and restrictions on a fishing contest!

How to use this book

I strongly suggest that you read this book twice.

The first reading

During the first read-through, you will get an overview of the method and understand why you need to invest your effort in detailed investigation and planning.

As you work through this book, you will get a feel for the skills and expertise that will be needed at various stages and you will be able to identify areas where you need to get outside help, for example from an accountant.

The first pass will also give you early warning of decisions you will have to make and options you will need to take. You may even start preparing for those decisions. For example, you could ask your club committee to clarify why you are running the event, or perhaps start asking tent hire companies and other suppliers for price lists and brochures!

You will also begin to decide how to modify the depth and scope of your investigations to suit your unique event and circumstances. Where you do think you have a unique requirement, make a note in the margin or against the lists at the appropriate place in this book (see 'Is this your book' below), to remind you as you work through to deliver your event. For example, if your event includes animals, you may need to arrange for the presence of a veterinary surgeon and they will need an office or base of operations.

Finally, you will have a feel for the staff and resources you require and so will have extra time to start locating and arranging them.

The second reading

At this stage, you should begin working through the book, investigating, researching, documenting and making decisions as you work towards actually delivering your event.

'Dipper' warning

You may be tempted to simply dip in and scan a few selected chapters in this book, hoping to reinforce your existing knowledge, or checking elements of your planned arrangements where you are unsure or inexperienced. Alternately you may just want to check a few lists, for example in an attempt to satisfy yourself that you have prepared all the signs that you will need on your site.

I strongly advise you to *read the whole book* to fully understand the isues, concepts and potential problems before you look at illustrative lists. Reading small sections, or just reading a couple of chapters will not give you the 'big picture' and full understanding that you need.

More experienced event managers should also consider the changes that have taken place over the past few years. Not too many years ago, event planning and management had two basic functions: first, renting a big enough field; and second, collecting the money. That has changed in the last few years and the emphasis is now on health and safety, management and control, licences, authorisation and permissions.

If nothing else, this book will refresh your memory and I am certain that you will find nuggets of new information that you will adopt to improve your event and method of event planning and delivery.

In understanding the scope and depth of problems, you may discover a potentially fatal or costly flaw in your proposed approach to planning and running your event.

Though every effort has been made to ensure that the contents of this guide are accurate at the time of printing, events vary dramatically and rules and requirements change over time depending on the event content and format. It is important that you remember that *you* are the event manager for your event; *you* are responsible for everything. That includes checking current and local rules, national legislation and the current rules of other governing bodies to ensure that everything is right for *your event*.

Format of the guide

The format of this guide is simple and easy to follow. The process of defining, researching, planning and running an event is broken down into simple stages and each stage is described in a separate chapter. I have already stated that as your event is unique, you are free to change the order in which you complete the stages, as long as you do complete all of the stages. Beware of switching stages too much. As the output from one stage usually feeds in to the following stage, the sequence used in this book is carefully planned. If you wildly change the order of stages you risk losing the benefit of the method. You should also note that the illustrative lists are for guidance only, you may have to add non-standard roles, signs and facilities.

Where I consider a point of information to be worthy of a special mention, it is displayed as a boxed 'Tip', at an appropriate point in the text of the relevant chapter.

At the end of each chapter, I have listed the progress you should have made (during your second reading of the book). There is also a list of the 'products' that you should have completed and delivered after working though each chapter. You should remember that if you have created additional 'products' for your specific event, you should write them in at an appropriate place to remind you.

Writing style

I was once told 'never use three words when one will do', which is correct when you are dealing with a reading audience who knows the subject and has a common level of skill, understanding and experience. This book has been written to help 'any' reader understand the underlying concepts and procedures in event management. I have therefore included more explanation for two reasons.

I have tried to make each chapter free standing, so you will not constantly be referred to other pages, chapters or an annex. As some event management tasks and functions are linked, I have attempted to include all relevant details and explanations in a given chapter. This occasionally means that explanations are appropriately duplicated elsewhere in the book though different examples are used. Though you need to have read through the whole book to understand the approach, this inclusive style helps in your second working-through of the book, when everything you need to know about a stage should be contained within that chapter.

I have explained the reasoning behind my advice by including anecdotes and examples to help you to see and understand the underlying concepts and processes. With that 'deeper' understanding, you will know how and why decisions are made and be able to apply the concepts to your unique event, rather than having to blindly following a crude list that tells you to do some things and not to do others.

Is this your book?

Some books are expected to be read and then put down. If you follow my methodology, you will start to personalise the contents of this book. This book is a 'workbook' and as such it is an integral part of your event planning and delivery.

As stated above, my event planning and delivery method requires you to read this book twice. As you read through with your unique event in mind, you will identify areas in which you have unusual, specialist or non-standard requirements. As you identify them you should write them in at appropriate places in the book. You will probably amend lists, add comments and reminders, or write in the name and number of important contacts. For example, against the list of possible standard jobs and responsibilities in Chapter 20, you may know that for your event you need a hot air balloon pilot and an expert bee keeper. If so add them to the jobs and responsibilities list. You may also want to highlight sections that you think will be difficult or may give you problems in delivering your event. If you think it is worth writing it in, *do it!* All of these things will help you to deliver a successful event and this interaction with the book will turn it into a 'workbook'.

Writing these reminders at appropriate places in the book delivers two significant benefits:

- Important things will not be forgotten or overlooked later.
- The reminders are written into the sections of the book where they will be included in your planning and delivery.

But if this is a library book – please don't write in it! By all means take it out of the library and read through to see if you think that its methodology and approach will work for you. However, if you want to use the book and methodology as intended, you must buy your own copy of the book so that you are free to write in it as you see fit. Please remember, though my methodology advises you to write in this book, *only do so if you own the book*.

Overview of process

The approach and methodology I propose in this book are not new or ground breaking, they are simply the collected wisdom, trial and error and experience gathered over many years from a host of event organisers.

I propose that where possible you should work through the contents of the book in order (or in the order that matches your needs). Each chapter contains a 'stage' of the process, though there is a degree of overlap in some areas and checkpoint reviews may demand that you go back a stage or two to change or confirm some details. I know that life is rarely neat and convenient, but generally one stage should be completed before you start the next stage. I accept that, depending on circumstances, you may have to vary that approach. You will probably find that while working on Chapter 6, you may still be tying up loose ends and documenting elements of Chapter 5, and you or a deputy may just be starting to make calls and send emails in preparation for Chapter 7. Although that is acceptable, be warned that if you try to run some critical stages in parallel, you stand a huge risk of falling into an endless circle of review and reworking. It is possible that your findings and decisions for some stages could impact decisions and arrangements in other stages, causing yet another endless loop of review and reworking.

As you progress, you will gradually collect more information, refining your plans and arrangements. You will gain confidence in the viability of your proposed event, or it is *possible* that you could realise that there is a fatal flaw and that your proposed event will be too costly or too dangerous to run, so you may abandon the idea!

Generally, when finished, the output and results from each stage should be reviewed to reconfirm the viability of your proposals and then fed on into the following stages.

This logical progression with *checkpoints* at the end of some stages formalises your reviews and forces you to reconsider the event's viability in the light of the latest research and investigation. For example, if you discover that there is no suitable site available, you may feel it best to abandon the proposed event at that point, with least effort and resources expended. Alternately you may wish to check which aspect of the proposed event you would need to change so that you could fit it onto the available site! Whichever option you choose, you can be assured that if your research is valid, you are making decisions based on fact and not guessing or simply taking a chance.

Tip

As you work through this book, keep copies of all of your research, options, problems and decisions – it may come in handy later. If you encounter a problem with your plans, you may want to backtrack to an earlier stage; to revisit earlier research and decisions in an attempt to take a new direction bypassing the problem you encountered.

Progress and stepping back

Generally, you should work through one chapter at a time, but there will be times when you have to step back to amend and review elements of your investigations and plans. Though that is acceptable and expected, you should try to do so in a logical way.

For example, if while working through 'Staffing' (Chapter 20), you find that you have to revisit 'Permissions' (Chapter 17), you should take the following action:

- Slow or suspend work on staffing (Chapter 20).
- Return to Chapter 17 to resolve the problem relating to permissions.
- Realise that your new revision of investigations and decisions in Chapter 17 may have an impact on subsequent preparations.
- To check that there has been no impact on subsequent research and decisions, review, amend and reconfirm investigations and decisions made in the intervening chapters: permissions (Chapter 17), car parking (Chapter 18), radio communications (Chapter 19).
- Review, amend and reconfirm work done so far in investigations and decisions about staffing (Chapter 20) then carry on as normal.

Project management – a simple approach

In the past, event organisers have complained to me that they have become confused with, or lost track of, the dozens if not hundreds of different tasks that they have to complete to deliver their event. I have suggested that they treat the planning, organisation and management of the event as a 'project' and that they should adopt a 'project management approach' to planning and delivering their event.

Saying that has scared some people and worried most, because 'project management' is viewed as something mysterious, very technical and complicated. It can be, but fundametally, project management is simply a formalised and structured approach to planning and managing a group of tasks, to a given timetable, with a specified objective, within given quality standards.

At Annex A '*Project Management Supplement: Managing The Event*', I have described my simple approach to managing a project, using a simplified project management methodology.

Progress – Chapter 1

You should now:

- know that you are taking on a complex task,
- know how to use this book,
- understand the overall method.

2 The event manager

■ ■

This is the start of the process of investigation; research and decision making that will ultimately lead to the development of detailed plans for the successful delivery of your event. (Remember on your first reading you are only being asked to recognise the method and stages and to start thinking about the decisions you will be asked to make during the second, 'workbook' phase.)

What is an event manager?
■ ■

For anything and everything, there has to be one person with supreme authority. For our purposes we will assume that the person in charge of a proposed event is called the 'event manager'. Their primary duty is to make or confirm all decisions and act as central liaison, directing and controlling the activities of individuals to whom they have delegated responsibility for elements of the organisation and arrangements for an event.

Delegation – benefits and risk
■ ■

Except for the smallest of events, the event manager cannot possibly do everything, so they must learn to delegate. Delegating organisational responsibility for various elements of the event to deputies or assistants spreads the workload and takes advantage of specialist expertise that the deputies may have. It is, however, very important that the event manager retains control, in order to deliver the event on time and within budget.

Though delegation is one of the most important tools available to the event manager, it must be used with caution. There is a level of delegation beyond which efficiency and quality of arrangements made will deteriorate. Delegating down through too many levels distances the event manager from decisions, increases the number of 'managers' involved and increases the risks of errors and oversights due to misunderstandings and communication problems.

As a general rule, organisational and management authority should not be delegated to more than two levels below the event manager.

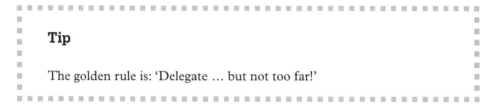

Tip

The golden rule is: 'Delegate … but not too far!'

Progress – Chapter 2

You should now:

- understand the need for and role of the event manager,
- understand the benefits and risks of delegation, and
- have taken the role of event manager or recruited somebody into that role and passed this book on to them.

3 The event objective

The event objective is a simple statement that encapsulates the reason(s) for running the event. It could be as simple as 'to raise money to repair the church roof', or more complicated – 'to hold finals of the Reading and Swindon football league and declare a winning team, while raising funds for a new team minibus'.

Your initial task is to give immediate thought to your 'event objective'. You may have to consult with a governing body, such as a sports league, club president, committee members, or an employer or senior officer who will work with you to establish and define your event objective.

How to define an event objective

This is a simple process – just think through what you are proposing to do and why you are thinking of running the event. Establishing the motivating factor will lead you to your event objective. There are many different motivations, some of which are listed below.

Where possible, make the objective simple and easy to understand. When it has been defined (and where necessary it has been approved by the management or other group), print off simple signs that state the event objective, and give one to everyone involved in planning and organising your event. I usually try to include the objective as a sub-heading on all event documentation as a further reminder. The objective should be kept in mind by all of the organisers and staff, acting both as the driving and controlling force.

But beware – it is very easy to lose sight of your event objective while trying to make the best arrangements you can. For example, if the purpose of the event is to raise funds for a small local charity, don't spend money on international advertising and don't offer free meals to competitors and exhibitors. Keep yourself tightly focused on the event objective, in this case proposing local advertising and volunteer staff.

Before making *any decision*, bring the event objective to mind and then review the decision at hand alongside the objective. Make absolutely sure that each and every one of your decisions supports and promotes that objective and/or the health and safety of all concerned.

Be ready to reconsider any decision, if you find or fear that you have drifted off your objective. For example, for our local charity event, do we *really need* to fly in an 'A'-list movie star from Hollywood to open the event? It would be more appropriate to get the local MP, mayor or sports celebrity to do it instead, especially as they are often quite keen to get the exposure, to be seen to be associated with a good cause and willing to come for free.

Tip

Once you have identified your objective, make up signs showing the objective in bold letters, stick one to the cover of your diary and display another over your desk.

Possible event objectives

- school/club socials
- local charity fundraiser
- national charity fundraiser
- local/county sports event championship/league
- national sporting event championship/league
- business promotion
- family fun day
- profit-making enterprise
- political event
- themed or traditional event
- seasonal event
- learning
- protest rally
- having fun

From this point on, I will assume that *you* are the event manager for your proposed event, so decide on your objective *now* and put one of the objective signs over *your* desk.

Progress – Chapter 3

You should now:

- understand what an event objective is,
- have fully accepted and committed to the role of event manager, and
- understand that everything you do supports and promotes that objective and/or the health and safety of all concerned.

Product completed

- Have defined your event objective.

4 Planning the event

For even the smallest of events (such as the primary school class 3A Easter Hat Show), the event manager should undertake a formal planning stage, including a risk assessment (explained in Chapter 5, 'Health and safety').

As event manager, you must ensure that you adopt a structured and logical method of planning and managing for every aspect of the event arrangements, in order to deliver a successful and enjoyable event. If you are happy that your qualifications and experience enable you to handle the dozens of things that need to be arranged, read on and start planning now.

If you are on your first read-through of this book and have little or no planning experience or possibly want a different view on how to go about it, you may wish to invest an hour in reading and understanding the project management supplement (see Annex A) at this point. It consists of a simple project management methodology that lends itself to the controlled management of multiple tasks in order to achieve a single goal, within defined costs, timescales and quality. After reading it you should return to this page.

Contacts with other people

As part of your investigation and planning, you will need to contact local authorities to confirm requirements, permissions and licensing for your event. You will also almost certainly need to seek advice from the local emergency services regarding any specific hazards there may be.

You may also have to seek advice from the health and safety executive to ensure that you meet their safety requirements, and depending on your event type and content, you may have to seek approval or advice from certain sports governing bodies.

During this process you will therefore be making a lot of contacts. You will benefit from an administrative procedure that formalises that contact. I suggest that the administrative procedure has two elements.

Contact details

This is a simple list of contact details, including name, number, address, email address, function/title, organisation and purpose (i.e. Council Environmental Health or Police Events Liaison Officer). I usually try to keep this list in a spreadsheet format, simply because it is so easy to update, print, sort and search the contacts.

Manchester Slug Breeders Society – Annual Show

Name	Number	Address	Function	Org	Purpose
Barry Worth	0701 564 272	Tents, 1 High St	Tent Hire Co	Tents City	Tent requirments
Joe Smith	01 626 3454	Council HQ	Planning Officer	Borough Council	Signs
Harry Williams	01 528 6547	Police Station	Events Liaison	County Police	Event permission
Sue Thomas	02 556 6574	Police Station	Traffic Depot	County Police	Event Traffic

Contact history

This section is more of a diary, in which I list the people I contacted and why, then move ahead to make a note of when a reply will be overdue. For example I might ask a tent supplier for a quote. My diary entry for that day might read: (Monday 13th June) 'Contacted ABC Tents (New York). Spoke to Mark Quay. He will send written quote.'

When I have finished making my entry for Monday 13th June I will turn ahead to the page for Monday 20th June and insert a reminder for example: 'Written quote from ABC tents should have arrived by now.' This insignificant record takes just a moment to make, but will be a valuable reminder to me. I will be prompted to think about Mark Quay, and will know if he has still not sent the promised quote – and, maybe if that is indicative of their efficiency and reliability, I don't want to do business with them!

Planning evolution

Planning is not a single isolated action! Your planning has already started because you have put some thought into your event and will be undertaking a lot more investigation, research and preparation.

You will soon realise that plans are never really finished. You will arrive at a fairly stable plan, with which you can decide if and when to run your event, but the plan will constantly evolve as new information comes to light and circumstances change.

Frozen plan

When you think your plan is complete (checkpoints and reviews indicate that following that plan you will be able to successfully deliver your event and the authorities have approved it), you will have to *freeze the main plan*. The plan at this point will be declared the final version and will be identified as being completed on a stated date, for example 'Wapping Working Horses Show – Approved Plan dated 29 August 2006'. This will be used as the basis on which you will build your event.

When you have 'frozen' the plan, *you cannot and must not* make any significant changes. You cannot decide that, for example, your model aircraft event should be 'hijacked' and turned into a caged bird show. Making major changes at a late stage will result in most, if not all, of your research, planning and arrangements and approvals being invalidated. Do not do it.

Gentle tweaking!

Though a plan is frozen, no matter how well researched, how detailed or how accurate it is, circumstances will conspire to make you constantly revisit and gently 'tweak' it, to make the event as good and as safe as it can be. Perhaps the event arena has to be larger to accommodate the surprise attraction of the world's largest steam engine, which means that the displays will all have to be moved west on the site. Perhaps an emergency repair to a gas main is going to block the competitor entrance to the show ground and you have to re-plan access and parking requirements accordingly. The only thing that you can guarantee is that the planning starts here and will never be quite finished! If circumstances do require you to make small changes, you should confirm with the authorities that they approve of the modified plans.

Progress – Chapter 4

You should now:

- realise that you will have to plan if your event is to succeed,
- realise that you will need to research and investigate and contact a host of other organisations and authorities to collect sufficient information to allow you to make decisions regarding your event,
- realise that planning is an iterative process and that even though your plan has been frozen, you will still have to make minor adjustments to deliver a safe and successful event, and
- possibly have read the project management supplement (Annex A).

5 Health and safety

The Health and Safety Act 1974

Health and safety is, should be and will be a critical and important element in everything you do. It is generally accepted that a citizen in the UK has an obligation to consider and protect the health, safety and welfare of other citizens. That general assumption is supported in law, including the Health and Safety at Work Act 1974 and the Management of Health and Safety at Work Regulations 1999. The law is complex and there is a further complex framework of regulations and codes of practice supporting it.

Health and safety is therefore something which you should be supporting and promoting throughout the investigations, planning and management of your event. Your objective has to be compliance with the law and the need to protect staff, visitors, suppliers, everyone in fact, from coming to any harm.

New legislation

Even if you ran the event last year, you have to check to see what new legislation has been introduced. For example the 'Control of Noise at Work Regulations 2005' are scheduled to come into force on 6 April 2006 – with a two year transitional period to full implementation

Tip

You must introduce a positive and proactive health and safety culture and promote this by insisting that 'health and safety' is the first and last agenda item for any meeting.

Safety

The event organiser, whether an individual, collective or local authori ,, responsibility for protecting the health, safety and welfare of everyone. That is everyone working at the event, attending or passing by, in fact anyone potentially affected by the event. You must remember that your responsibility for the safety of members of the public even extends to burglars and vandals! If a criminal breaks in and enters your site at night and is electrocuted by a partly completed circuit, it is your fault. If he falls down an unguarded hole and breaks his leg, or is injured when an insecure tent pole falls on him – you are responsible. Everything must be safe for *anyone at any time*.

Many events attract large numbers of people. From a commercial viewpoint that appears to be a good thing, because the larger the crowds, the more profit will be made. However, you have a duty to look beyond projected profit and exercise common sense and caution.

As has been seen over the years at some sporting events, surging crowds combined with bad crowd management can result in people being crushed to death against walls or railings. At the least, being caught in a surging uncontrolled crowd could lead to such high levels of fear and distress that in future the public will not attend your event or any other event you and your group organises.

Forget the cash incentive of attracting huge uncontrolled crowds – detailed investigation and planning is important. Plan and manage your event, know what the audience will be and ensure they are safe.

Remember, sometimes even small changes to the access routes, gates and barriers at an event can make a significant difference. With properly trained and alert staff you can gradually feed a sudden rush of people through, using different routes, ensuring that there is no pressure on them and that they all enter safely.

Tip

Trained and alert staff combined with effective risk analysis, planning and procedures *will* prevent accidents.

Management responsibilities

People are usually sensible. Several people together are often sensible. A crowd, however, can be a *wild animal*! I accept that something like a primary school sports day will probably not have any trouble, but staff should still read this chapter and investigate further to prevent or counteract crowd-related problems.

There are trained people who have studied crowd dynamics all their working life. All I can do is hope to point out a few things that will illustrate the potential problems you could encounter. Anyone proposing to hold events, especially sporting events, at an existing ground or arena *must* seek further advice through the stadium/venue owners and management, local authority, fire authority and health and safety executive.

All venues should have processes and procedures in place to monitor crowd levels, crowd status and to institute best practices of health and safety in crowd management. To achieve this, staff members must be trained to continually monitor the crowd status and to take appropriate and timely corrective action when and where necessary.

Their training should enable them to see problems developing, rather than to wait and react to a crisis that erupts in front of them. They should be alert and aware enough to identify and report problem indicators, as well as being proactive in preventing a situation from getting worse.

A busy escalator provides a simple example that everybody can understand. Suppose a man travels down an escalator with a large suitcase and then trips over his case at the bottom of the escalator. Before he can stand up, two people behind him trip over him and his case, and fall on top of him. The escalator efficiently and continually feeds more people into the tangle of fallen people and bags. Higher up on the escalator, people can see what is happening, but there is nothing they can do about it. They will be carried down into the heap of injured people until somebody pushes the escalator emergency stop button. An alert member of staff could press the stop button instantly, *if* they were present at the top or bottom of the escalator, *if* they were alert, *if* they had been trained in the use of the stop button and *if* they have been trained to recognise the risk.

At an event site or venue, alert staff and managers could use the equivalent of that emergency stop button, by closing gates, diverting pedestrian flow, announcing delays in the start of games or displays, etc. All of these actions will ease tension, divert the flow of people and overcome mounting problems, and, more importantly, reduce or remove the risk of injury. Once the urgency and reason to push is taken away, the source of fresh people pushing at the back is removed, so the crush of people at a gate, escalator or turnstile can be relieved.

Managing large numbers of people requires good teamwork, good communications and close co-ordination between management, staff and potentially the emergency services. While all appropriate staff should be trained and aware of procedures that have been set out, it is vital that in any situation managers and supervisors *must* continually promote a *positive and pro-active safety culture*. The event manager must make sure that staff at all levels are aware of the importance of crowd and individual safety.

To ensure that the visitors and site are managed effectively and safely as event manager you need to know that:

- there is a clear definition of roles and responsibilities (see C[ ] 'Staffing'),
- there has been (and will be annually – or following any incident) a review of the planning and operation of crowd/visitor safety,
- appropriate staff are properly trained, identifiable and properly supervised,
- by research and planning, the event organisers are aware of the size and type of crowd they will attract and so will be able to anticipate crowd behaviour,
- risk assessments are undertaken to allow you to arrange appropriate controls and management,
- they have visited and reviewed the event site and venue as part of the planning process, and revisited shortly before the event to ensure that circumstances have not changed,
- you have set understandable limits that can trigger remedial or emergency action among stewards and management (for example, the risk assessment may state that if the back of the queue at the pedestrian gate reaches the main road, another gate must be opened to relieve the pressure and keep members of the public off the main road), and
- you must check with the local authority and the emergency services to ensure that your risk assessments, plans, management and procedures are acceptable.

Risk assessment

What is a risk assessment?

A risk assessment is a formal review and consideration of potential hazards, their impacts and the likelihood that together they could cause harm, affecting the health and safety or welfare of people affected by your event.

What is a hazard?

A hazard is anything that has the potential to cause harm in any given circumstances! Take litter as an example, a simple plastic carrier bag left on a country path may seem quite harmless, but there are several ways it could cause harm. It may choke a lamb that tries to eat it, or, if blown into the face of a motorcyclist, it could cause a fatal accident. Just as under certain circumstances and conditions unsightly litter becomes a fatal hazard, almost anything can become a hazard in a similar way. The following list gives a range of examples, and should not be considered complete, but it will steer you towards reviewing and identifying potential hazards to your event:

- dangerous activities – bungee jumping or tree felling
- moving and manipulating heavy or awkward things by hand
- any machinery with or without guards
- any source of contained fire – glass blowing furnace
- accidental fire – discarded cigarette
- vision – dust or chips or other contaminants sprayed at eye level
- hearing – very loud sustained noise such as at pop concerts
- any chemicals in use – toilet bleach
- moving vehicles – especially if the view of the driver is restricted
- building features – slopes, steps, locked gates and doors etc.
- site features – such as icy, slippery paths, flooding
- trip hazards – guy ropes, electrical cables or hosepipes
- animals present – cattle, horses etc.
- contaminants – animal manure or sewage
- electricity – supply and equipment
- overcrowding – facilities unable to cope with crowd surge etc.

What is a risk?

The risk is the likelihood that the identified hazard will cause any harm and a measure of the severity of the harm that it causes. Let us say we are considering a hosepipe, which is a trip hazard. If, when tripping on that carelessly placed hosepipe, the person falls on your extensive collection of jagged broken glass there is a high risk. However, if we moved the hosepipe and the person trips and falls on your huge pile of super soft cushions the risk is dramatically reduced!

In simple terms, will anyone be injured by unsafe rides, or electrocuted by bare electrical wiring, which has not been installed by a professional? Will staff be injured operating equipment on which they are not trained, or where safety guards are missing? Will heavy trucks reversing blindly out of your site injure passers-by, or will passing traffic swerve and crash because they were distracted on a dangerous junction where your model aircraft flew over the hedge and across the road at head height?

The immediate common sense response is, 'Of course not, I wouldn't do that'. Unfortunately, without a formal risk assessment and review it is likely that you may not notice that safety guards are missing, or may not ask what is on the other side of the hedge over which you propose to fly model aircraft at head height.

Just as importantly – if there is an accident or injury, you must protect the scene and get treatment for the casualty, then undertake a new and urgent risk assessment of the accident scene. From your records you should be able to prove that in your original assessments you took every care to ensure that the event and site were safe, and the written records of the risk assessments and reviews will help you prove that.

The new emergency review will be to prevent the cause of the accident causing any more problems and that should be recorded as well.

What is likelihood?

The likelihood is the chance of 'it' happening, and has to be estimated by the assessor. For example, an invasion of your event by UFOs piloted by aliens intent on destroying the human race would be fatal in more ways than one. *But* – the chances of that happening are quite remote. Using our common sense and knowledge of that risk, we will probably decide to ignore the potential hazard of an alien invasion and carry on with the event.

What is impact?

The impact is the scope and depth that will result if an incident happens. In our example above, falling on an extensive collection of jagged broken glass would be fatal or cause grievous injury, so the impact of that is high. However, the impact of falling on a collection of cushions is very low. As they fall on cushions I will have the hosepipe removed, but I won't close the show until it has been done!

Why make a risk assessment?

There are many reasons why you should perform a risk assessment:

- to plan for safety,
- where possible to design out risk,
- to introduce and promote a safety culture among your staff,
- to implement control measures to remove or reduce hazards, risk and impact to acceptable levels,
- to reject or ban activities that impose too high a risk, and
- to design normal and emergency procedures that will enable staff to safely cope with all eventualities.

The bottom line is that you make a risk assessment to make your event as safe as it can be.

When to make a risk assessment

You must risk assess all of the time! To be sure, make health and safety a primary concern for all event staff by making 'Health and Safety' the first and last agenda item for all meetings. You should make a risk assessment:

- at the initial consideration of every action and proposal,
- in the detailed planning of each element, including an assessment of neighbouring and associated factors (for example, though a glass-blowing furnace and display may seem acceptable on its own, you may have a different assessment when you find that it is now expected to be located between the petrol station, the gas works and the hay barn!),
- whenever any of the proposed or expected circumstances change – those changes may be different accommodation, changes in staff, change in size or timing of displays, change in audience numbers, change in weather etc., and
- whenever a new hazard is identified or when there is a near-miss or accident. This assessment will enable you to take measures to ensure that nobody is injured by the hazard identified.

What to risk assess

As events vary so much it is impossible to produce a standard list of the things that need to be risk assesed. The simple answer is to risk assess everything! You know and understand your event and so you know where there may be potential hazards. Do not restrict yourself to jobs and activities that you know are hazardous; even activities that seem totally safe might have hidden risks. For example, a toilet attendant may be handling bleach or other chemicals and so there is a potential hazard that must be assessed and documented: they may be overcome by fumes, may splash some in their eyes, or may leave a bottle where a child could drink it.

For guidance only, I have compiled the following list, but you must remember that you are responsible for the safety of your event, with advice from the authorities you must make sure that you risk assess any potentially hazardous role, procedure or activity. You must risk assess any:

- job type you need to fill, for example people to erect signs, car park stewards, gatekeepers, night security, toilet attendant, or ticket sellers,
- activity you propose to undertake, for example erecting fences, constructing and staffing car park access lanes, mounting public address speakers, or counting cash,
- interface with machinery and equipment, for example cutting and clearing grass on the site, or operating an electrically powered radio base station,
- display, act or attraction, for example folk dancers, parachute displays, model aircraft flying, or a knitting display,
- activity that requires vehicles to move around or near pedestrians, for example carnival processions, roving car park supervisor, traction engine displays, or cash collection using an electric golf cart.

Brainstorming

Brainstorming is a popular technique that can be of great use thoughout the plan-ning and delivery of an event. It simply requires a group of people to gather together to openly and freely discuss a subject. During discussions, they can suggest options, raise doubts, ask questions, propose alternatives, or suggest improvements; in fact they can say anything that comes to mind.

One member of the group should take on the role of scribe, to record every idea, suggestion, question or other point raised during the session, for later consideration and review. (For accuracy and clarity the scribe must be allowed to slow the pace of the brainstorming session – to allow them to catch up and record everything raised – or ask questions to clarify what has been said, for example, 'Sorry – did you say *An aardvark?*'.)

If a manager presents their findings or proposes plans to a group and then 'brain-storms' them, the group can provide a quick and easy sanity check, as you will see in the 'Checkpoint' below.

It is vital that your brainstorming group knows that they are free to say anything that comes to mind and that the group lets their ideas flow.

How to risk assess

It is a simple process, but a lot of time, thought, investigation and consideration has to be invested in doing it right. A 'quick risk assessment' is a bad risk assessment and that is a hazard in itself!

Ideally to perform risk assessments, you should be familiar with all aspects of the event, so that you know the operating environment. For example, though the event is listed as an open five-a-side rugby tournament, the operating environment becomes important to your risk assessments when you know that the team members and potential audience is comprised of frail elderly people.

As with investigating and planning the whole event, risk assessments should be broken down into manageable areas. Attempting to undertake a risk assessment for the whole event is too complex to comprehend and the assessor(s) are unlikely to have the appropriate information, skills and experience necessary to do it properly.

There are various methods of undertaking a risk assessment and coming to an informed conclusion as to the risk that any given identified hazard poses to health and safety. I use a method that assigns a numerical value to likelihood and impact. For your event, you should take the advice of the experts, but in simple terms I propose the following approach:

- The event manager should assign the risk assessment of elements of the event to appropriately skilled individuals. For example, an engineer might risk assess temporary seating, or you might discuss fire hazards with the local fire service. Note – even though other members of staff may use their expertise to undertake the risk assessment, the assessment and any decisions arising out of them remain the responsibility of the event manager.

- The event manager should delegate risk assessments of each element of the event to appropriately skilled members of staff. For example, if a traffic manager is risk assessing car parks, the traffic manager should discuss plans, risks, threats and problems encountered in previous years. They should visit the car parks and look at the ground and hazards in place, then brief their staff on existing and known hazards and risks. They should consider numbers of vehicles attending, access and exit routes, the signs required and staffing. With all that in mind, they should then list the actual or potential risks and assess them using the tables below.

- When risks are identified, record them, list them, review them with the event manager or other staff, brainstorm them and add any new risks to the list.

- Review the identified risks with associated elements of the event and inherit or bequeath risks to those elements. For example, where cars and pedestrians use two adjacent gates, the car parking risk assessor, in consideration of vehicular access and dangers, may inherit 'trip hazards' from the pedestrian gate risk assessor. Similarly the pedestrian gate risk assessor may inherit 'car fire' as a hazard from the associated car parking risk assessor.

- Beware of and consider joint risks. That is an area where an assessment shows little or no risk in isolation. Be aware that surrounding activities outside the scope of the immediate assessment may introduce a new and highly relevant issue in your risk assessment. For example, a go-cart racing event has made provision to hold, store and issue go-cart fuel at the start/finish line. The risk assessment on that fuel storage and issue has indicated that all measures are sensible, adequate and safe and that these activities do not present any unacceptable risks. Now reconsider that assessment in the light of the news that the organiser is going to open the activities with a major fireworks display! Suddenly, the new dimension of fireworks, sparks, explosions and stray rockets puts a whole new light on the storage of our fuel and it has to be reassessed.

- Consider each listed risk against the likelihood and impact of that risk. Where the likelihood is an indication of how likely that risk is to happen and the impact is the extent of damage and or injury that would be caused if it did happen.

- Using the risk assessment scoring chart below, assign a risk value to each hazard you have identified. For example we have a hazard with a likelihood of 'moderate' (scoring 3 on the likelihood row). There is an impact that is 'severe' (scoring 8 on the impact column). Taking the two together, and reading across the likelihood row to its intersection with the impact column, we arrive at a risk vale of 24 (3 multiplied by 8).

● Record all hazards and their risk values in a hazard table such as the example below. This is just a list that will hold the results of all of your risk assessments in one place. This method is a suggestion only, but it will record all of the information you need in a convenient format. The ID number relates to areas of responsibility; in this example, a prefix of P for pedestrian hazards, C for car park, G for go-cart fuel etc. The hazard table will form part of the event manager's manual.

● For each hazard you have identified you must review its score and checking with the risk acceptability table on page 30, decide if you can accept the risk disclosed or if you must take measures to remove the hazard, or reduce the risks using control measures.

Risk assessment scoring chart

		Impact – damage/injury caused				
		Minimal	Slight	Moderate	Severe	Very severe
Likelihood	Minimal	1	2	4	8	16
	Slight	2	4	8	16	32
	Moderate	3	6	12	24	48
	Likely	4	8	16	32	64
	Very likely	5	10	20	40	80

Hazard table

ID no.	Hazard detail	Likelihood score	Impact score	Risk value
P1	Pedestrian trip at main gate	1	2	2
C1	Collision in elephant car park	2	4	8
C2	Car fire in elephant car park	2	4	8
G1	Go cart fuel store fire	3	8	24
A1	Model plane crash in crowd	2	16	32
	Etc.			
	Etc.			

Risk acceptability table

Level of acceptance	Risk score	Action required
Unacceptable	40–80	Remove hazard/reduce risk
Just tolerable	16–32	Contingency plan and control measures
Quite tolerable	5–12	Implement control measures
Acceptable	1–4	No action required

Control measures

A control measure is an action you take to remove or reduce the risk and impact of a hazard. For example, if the hazard in question is broken glass in the office window, a control measure could be to repair the window where new unbroken glass is not a hazard. An alternative might be to fix steel shutters over the window, because with steel shutters nobody will be able to touch the broken glass so it will not be a hazard. Finally, fencing off the area around the broken window will prevent anybody from getting near to the broken glass, so the hazard is removed.

I have used a few examples below to illustrate the use of this process:

Risk 1 = tent collapsing on small child

Likelihood – Minimal = Score 1 – We use experienced contractors who supply and erect tents to nationally accepted and documented standards.
Impact – Severe = Score 8 – If it happened, the injury to adults and children caused by heavy tent poles and canvas falling could be significant.
Overall result from table 1 × 8 = 8 – Quite tolerable.

Checking the risk acceptability table above, we find that a score of 8 falls in the 'Quite tolerable' range, with a suggested action of implementing control measures. The control measures would include the following:

- Check with the authorities to identify acceptable standards.
- Check with contractors to ensure their tents meet those standards.
- Check with contractors to ensure their staff erecting the tents are properly trained and supervised.
- Check with contractors to ensure that they will contract to safely supply and erect the desired tents on your site to a given and accepted standard.
- Check that tents are being delivered and erected in a safe manner, using safety equipment supplied.
- Invite the authorities to inspect the tents to review safety and compliance with standards.
- Check yourself that the tents appear to meet the safety requirements and standards.
- Make sure the deputy manager with responsibility for tents will inspect the tents supplied and erected before the event and at regular intervals during the event.
- Contract with suppliers to include on-call staff to rectify any problems, such as loose ropes and bolts, etc.

Though the impact could be 'Severe', as we use a specialist tent hire company, who are licensed and have trained staff etc., the overall score is only 8 ('Quite tolerable'). We don't have to spend any more time making the tents safer than they already are and so we can go ahead with the event.

Risk 2 = people tripping on litter – causing injury

Likelihood – Minimal = Score 1 – Litterbins placed all over site and emptied regularly. Litter patrols on site collecting any litter that is dropped. Signs requesting people to put litter into the bins provided. Hourly public address messages asking people to put litter into bins

Impact – Minimal = Score 1 – Level site, comprising well-tended grass. No sharp, rough or uneven hazards. Audience expected will comprise fit young men. If it happened no injury is expected as a result. St Johns and county paramedic on site in case of any injury.

Overall result from table $1 \times 1 = 1$ – Acceptable.

Checking the risk acceptability table we find that a score of 1 falls in the 'Acceptable' range and the suggested action is 'None'. We don't have to do anything else, the event can go ahead.

Risk 3 = rally car colliding with spectators

Likelihood – Very likely = Score 5 – The rally will attract novice drivers. The novice drivers will drive cars maintained on limited budgets. The rally route passes along private and public roads. Public roads will not be closed for the event. Spectators were a major problem last year when they often walked on the roads during the race. We can only get 12 marshals to cover the 18-mile route. The event will be run in winter on snow and ice.

Impact – Very severe = Score 16 – Inexperienced drivers tend to lose control easily. The route runs near three major towns. Hundreds of children came last year without parental control. No medical facilities will be available. Drivers and marshals will not be able to communicate with the controllers.

Overall result from table 5 × 16 = 80 – Unacceptable.

Checking the risk acceptability table we find that a score of 80 falls in the 'Unacceptable' range and the suggested action is to remove the hazard or reduce the risk.

To remove the hazard we might have to take huge steps, such as to erect barriers and man them with marshals for the entire route, introduce vehicle inspections to ensure vehicles are properly maintained, insist that drivers achieved a certain level of skill by a licensing system etc. That is beyond the means of the rally club and they could not do it in the time scale available anyway. As it stands the event *cannot go ahead*.

Example hazard table

ID no.	Hazard detail	Likelihood score	Impact score	Risk value
A	Tent collapse on child	1	8	8
B	Pedestrian trip on litter	1	1	1
C	Car rally	5	16	80

What to consider in a risk assessment

When assessing the risks to safety for a given event at a given venue both physical and behavioural factors need to be considered. Some of the more important considerations are described below.

Site/ground plan

The basic design of the event ground or arena is a significant factor, which must be considered in conjunction with the type and content of the proposed event. A school fair should be small and quiet, but a major horseracing event could have the potential for a disaster. Imagine people arriving in a trickle through the morning and being distributed through bars, restaurants and seating areas in the stands. Then in the first big race, the favourite horse spectacularly throws the jockey in front of the stands. It is likely that everyone at the meeting will decide to run to the front of the stands to see what is happening. The markings, warning notices, type, style and design of things such as handrails, steps, doors and ramps could, at that instant, be the difference between everybody seeing the fallen jockey, or hundreds being hospitalised and some being killed in the stampede. In those circumstances it would be easy for somebody at the front to trip and their fall could cause a crush that trapped dozens of people in a heap on concrete steps, killing some of them!

At fixed sites, you may not be able to change the design or layout of the grounds to improve safety, but you should always consider the site in view of *your event* and how you propose to use the site. You should at least consider what improvement could or should be made if it is possible.

Remember that a fixed venue is often designed with a specific use in mind. A racecourse grandstand is designed to allow people to safely watch horse racing. If the owners allow you to rent their site and part of your event is a precision free fall parachute display, will that generate new risks? Could spectators fall over low walls while looking up at the parachutists? Could the parachutists drift on to spiked railings around the perimeter? Always view the venue with your specific event, audience and attractions in mind.

Are they lost or do they know better?

Generally, if the public know their way around a venue, they will be more comfortable, more confident, happier and safer. They will know where the exits, ramps and stairs are. At the same event, a stranger will be lost and they will have to follow the crowd, or aim for different signposted facilities. Unfamiliarity with the venue makes it that much less safe for the stranger.

On the other hand, it has been seen that familiarity breeds contempt in respect of warnings and directions. In some disasters, even though the 'known' exit route was filled with smoke or otherwise appeared to be dangerous, ordinary people preferred to attempt to use the route they knew would take them to the exits, rather than trust a sign or member of staff directing them another way.

Apply the same degree of 'unreasonable' behaviour to simple events and you can see that just erecting a large sign saying 'Danger! Do Not Enter – Model Aircraft Take Off and Landing Zone' will probably be ignored. You *have* to erect barriers to force people to comply and you may even have to man or check the barriers regularly to make sure that they have not been moved and that the public don't ignore the barriers and climb over.

At the same time you must remember to design the site with the visitor in mind. Don't expect the visitors to make a lengthy and unnecessary detour around a fenced-off 'dangerous arena' to reach the toilets. Plan the site so that any 'dangerous arena' is on the edge or corner of the site, or that there are toilets available on both sides of the danger area and therefore it doesn't have to be crossed by anyone!

Information invites compliance

Most people mildly or strongly object to being 'told' to do something. However, if you take the time to explain to the same people what the circumstances are and then ask them to comply with a clearly sensible request, they are likely to comply without question.

Clearly in an emergency you don't have time for lengthy explanations. You wouldn't point out the smoke and flames, explain that the tent next door is on fire and then politely ask the public if they wouldn't mind leaving the tent now. However, supplying enough information to trigger sensible compliance is usually worthwhile. Generally as a rule of thumb 'inform and request' is better than dictatorial and unexplained orders.

Signs and announcements are key factors in getting people to move around an event or show safely. A lack of information will probably be the cause of disobedience, for example where a site is being evacuated, failing to say 'everyone will be evacuated *to the field on the opposite side of the road*' may cause parents to try to go against the flow to find their children and ensure that they are safe. Adding to the announcement the fact that 'everyone' will be evacuated to the same place will make people happier to comply, because they will meet their loved ones at the evacuation point. Informed compliance will make the process run smoothly.

Which crowd?

Crowds come in all sorts of different shapes, sizes and moods. Knowing what crowd you will have to deal with will be a big help to you and will make it safer for them.

A huge crowd in a car boot sale will mill about, intent on finding a bargain, with random individual movements around the site. A crowd at a cup final will all want to be on the terraces at kick-off time, going for a beer and to the toilet at half-time and heading for the coach park after the final whistle. All crowds have different motivations, rythms and dynamics. Understanding them, or at least understanding the crowd 'type' that you will attract, will help you to manage them effectively.

Knowing your event, you will research and define their size, sex, age range, social background, travelling plans, arrival and departure times, habits and interests etc. All of which help you to anticipate probable behaviour and make appropriate arrangements for it. Don't make assumptions about people and circumstances. For example, if you said that Sir Cliff Richard was signing autographs in the high street, a regiment of Marines couldn't stop my wife getting there at the front of the queue and I guarantee that the queue would be a long one!

What did last year's crowd do?

Knowing what the crowds did last year at a similar event, will help you enormously in planning how you will manage them this year. You still have to plan, review and risk assess to forecast and plan for your proposed event. Perhaps your event has doubled in size this year, or perhaps Sir Cliff is attending – review all elements of the event and take them into account when risk assessing and planning the crowd control aspect.

Individual versus mob?

People are usually sensible; several people together are often sensible; but a crowd can be a wild animal! Sensible adults will sometimes do what in retrospect is a really stupid thing when they are in a crowd situation. To see their pop idol or movie star, people may try to dodge through several lanes of fast traffic, climb along building ledges, or balance half way up an electricity pylon. Once one person does it, somebody else will have to climb higher or go further to get an even better view. Thus the crowd/mob mentality may provoke unbelievably risky ventures in normally sensible individuals.

In your risk assessment, remember to look at vantage points and make sure that your control measures prevent the bold or stupid from taking dangerous options for a better view!

Danger points

Some points can be listed as dangerous when large numbers of people are moving across or around an area, as they may be swept along with the flow and, at the same time, be unable to see where they are stepping. For example:

- steep slopes,
- grassy/slippery slopes,
- dead ends, locked gates,
- points where several routes meet and merge,
- uneven ground, floor or steps,
- damaged surfaces, cracked concrete, loose gravel etc.,
- narrow doorways/choke points,
- transition points – e.g. top and bottom of escalators or the ends of moving walkways.

Where these risks are identified, action should be taken to reduce or remove the risk. You should remember that the risks above may be compounded in some circumstances and these circumstances have to be foreseen and risks planned out, for example:

- where the busy and congested flows of people cross over, or conflict,
- where main access paths are obstructed or blocked by people gathered to watch a demonstration or even an accident, anything that will make them stop to watch,
- where the crowd has to cross, mix or merge with animals or vehicular traffic flow,
- where processions, or displays are designed to move through or among the crowd.

Recording accidents

If there is an accident or an incident that could have caused an accident or injury, you should report and record it. An outline accident recording form is included in Chapter 21, 'First Aid'. You should review the detail in that suggested form and create your own accident recording form and incident/accident risk assessment form. Your duties when responding to an accident or incident are:

- to provide medical assistance to any casualty,
- to prevent any other person suffering injury due to the same cause,
- to obtain details of the casualty,
- to record details of the accident,
- to record details of the circumstances leading up to it,
- to record details of witnesses and obtain short statements,
- to report the incident/accident to the landowner and your insurer,
- to risk assess the area and equipment or anything involved,
- to take remedial action to prevent further incidents or accidents, and
- to record the detail of the new risk assessment and remedial action.

What else to record

You should record anything that relates to health and safety. If you have cause to warn your tent supplier that his staff are not wearing hard hats or using safety harnesses, record it and ask him to make sure his staff are supervised properly and to inspect and approve all work done to date. If you have to ask a contractor to leave the site because their lack of skill, negligence or 'horseplay' is putting people at risk, record it. When you brief other supervisors and staff about their health and safety duties and responsibilities, record it and ask them to sign to show that they understand and are capable of complying. If staff or visitors report anything that they consider may be dangerous or could potentially deteriorate and become dangerous, record it *and act on it*. If there is any incident, record it and record the actions that you took to remove that threat to ensure that there were no other incidents.

Check with the experts

This book is intended as a guide only and cannot contain detailed instructions on all of the skills and detailed knowledge needed to plan, organise, manage and deliver every type of event.

Though I have attempted to give some guidance on health and safety matters, the local authority, police, fire service and health and safety executive should be approached for up-to-date advice on the specific event, site and hazards that you will be dealing with.

Remember the complications, as you may be 'employing' staff to run the event, you may have to comply with the Health and Safety at Work Act 1974 and other associated Acts and Regulations. You must check and confirm your obligation to your 'employees'.

Keep in mind that Health and Safety is an important and complex issue and you should take appropriate advice to ensure that your event is safe and successful.

Iterative process

You will now understand how important risk assessments are to the delivery of a safe event and hopefully will have realised that more than any other task you will undertake in planning and delivering your event, the risk assessments will need to be revisited.

As circumstances change you will have to reassess the risks of various elements of your event. For example the tent hire company you had previously selected may have gone into receivership, so you are faced with either a new company or running your event in the open. That change in circumstances means that many of your assessments will have to be revisited and assessed under the new conditions and circumstances. In the example we have used above, a risk assessment of the go-cart race confirmed that it was acceptable to keep and issue their fuel at the start–finish line. When they were told that the promoter wanted to start the event with a huge fireworks display, circumstances had changed. It is vital that all risk assessments are reviewed now that that new information is available. Reassessing the risks associated with the fuel storage and issue, we now think that there is a risk that a stray firework spark might ignite the fuel, so some control measures have been suggested. They have asked for the fuel to be stored under shelter and in a secure location.

Have we met our obligation to risk assess the fuel storage and issue? It depends. It seems sensible to store the fuel under cover. However, looking further we find that to meet the requirement to provide covered shelter for the fuel, the promoter has suggested that we store the 5000 litres of high octane fuel in the event manager's office. He stated that it meets the suggested control measures, being 'secure' and 'under cover'!

Obviously that solves his fuel problem, but just as obviously we now have to reassess the risks associated with the event manager's office. The new information states that the event manager smokes; 5000 litres of fuel will fill three-quarters of the event manager's office; there is only one door to the office and that amount of fuel will obstruct the entrance; lastly some of the fuel cans leak a little too! Hopefully, you will agree that the fuel cannot be stored in the event manager's office, and that alternate storage will be needed for the fuel.

This is a perfect illustration of the need to realise that as you change something to resolve one problem, there may be knock-on effects to other elements of your arrangements. Just as in the example above, the opening fireworks display demanded that the fuel be moved, the proposed movement of that fuel to the event manager's office endangers the occupants of that office and the cashier's and the first aid office, all of which are clustered together. You must continually check to ensure that a small change to make one thing safer will not invalidate the risk assessment of other elements of the event.

Event health and safety policy document

To make sure that your health and safety aims are fully understood, you should (and may be legally obliged to) draw up a health and safety policy document. In England and Wales if you have five or more 'employees', you *must* provide a written health and safety policy, which details your health and safety procedures. This document should be simply stated, easy to understand, and in plain English.

Progress – Chapter 5

You should now:

- accept that you have a legal obligation under the Health and Safety Act, as well as a moral duty to protect the health and safety of anyone affected by your event,
- be aware of the risks associated with crowd dynamics and have taken steps to remove or minimise risks to an acceptable level,
- take all precautions to ensure that your event is as safe as it can be made and be aware that you have to continually monitor and assess safety and risks during the event,
- know how and when to undertake a risk assessment, record the details and act on your findings,
- understand the application of control measures and be aware of their effect on the hazards and risks under investigation, as well as associated hazards and risks,
- be ready to identify and eliminate danger points from your plans,
- ensure that rolling risk assessments are carried out as your plans evolve and you near delivery of the event,
- draw up an event health and safety policy document, and
- define and publish standing health and safety rules.

Product completed

- Have defined a standard meeting agenda for your event where 'health and safety' is the first item.
- Have produced a health and safety policy document.
- Have produced a hazard table form to assess your event.
- An event health and safety policy document.
- A list of standing health and safety rules.

6 Type of event

You may think that you already know what type of event you want to deliver, but you must be sure! It is important that you read this chapter, even if you are absolutely certain about the type of event you propose to run. There are an infinite number of event types, themes and classifications. One thing remains constant: the event type, in conjunction with your objective, will heavily influence every aspect of the event that you research, plan, organise and deliver.

Just as importantly, when you have decided what type of event you are going to deliver, you must not change your mind half-way through. Even a small change to the emphasis or theme of your event at a late stage will affect dozens of your decisions and arrangements. When you reach the end of this chapter on your work-through of the book, you must formally decide and define what type of event you are proposing.

After that, you must be aware that any late changes will have a major impact on the success of your event. The later those changes are made and the larger those changes are, the greater the negative impact will be, because late change will invalidate much of your earlier investigation and research.

You may currently be in one of three states:

- You have already decided what type of event you want to organise.
- You are considering several different options.
- You have no idea of the type of event to run.

This chapter will lead you through some considerations, which should allow you to either choose or confirm your event type.

How to decide

Start at a fairly high level and for now avoid getting pulled down into too much detail. List a few possible candidates for an event that you could run and would like to run, then discus them with friends or other club members, etc. For example, as president of a model aircraft club, you may start with three options:

- a model aircraft show,
- a tour of the local slate quarry, or
- a weaving demonstration.

To deliver a model aircraft show, the club will already have premises, arrangements for an area to fly, club members, plenty of models and detailed knowledge of the subject. In this example, as president of a model aircraft club you have a head start in delivering a model aircraft show. You should also have contacts with other model clubs, enthusiastic exhibitors, an established target audience and knowledge of associated crafts, subjects and suppliers.

The manager of the slate quarry is a member of the club and he suggested the tour. Your wife suggested the weaving exhibition and the club secretary only added it to the list to please her. So, as president of a model aircraft club, your event type seems to have been defined for you!

With that basic type and theme established, working through the following stages, you will gradually refine your idea and confirm your ability to deliver it.

Obvious choice

Often the event type will be obvious. In the example above the members of a model aircraft club would probably not be advised to attempt to run a weaving show. As with anything, you will have more success if you stick with what you know.

However, even though your event type might be self-evident, you should still run through this high-level review process just to confirm that the 'obvious choice' is the 'right choice'.

To illustrate the point using the example model aircraft club above, the model aircraft show is of course the obvious and top choice, *except* that during preliminary discussions you find that during the year there are 27 different model aircraft shows in the vicinity. After further discussion you discover that none of the shows attract more than 100 spectators, which is not going to raise the funds you need!

Having discounted the weaving show, a conversational risk assessment shows that the quarry is far too dangerous, with heavy machines, deep holes and deep water, not to mention daily explosions.

You are now stuck, because all of your options have been discarded. Using my method you will openly discuss the possibilities with a small group of club members. After further discussion, you find that when asked, every single club member remembers that several people have asked them in recent weeks if they knew of anywhere that offered courses in building model aircraft!

After a 30-minute discussion and some phone calls, the 'obvious choice' of a model aircraft show has been discarded in favour of an option that still uses the contacts, clubs, facilities, skills and experience of members, but for which there appears to be a very strong demand. Model-building classes now becomes the favoured option to meet the objective of raising funds, but further work is still necessary.

Keep records of research and decisions

Remember to keep records relating to your investigations and decisions as you work through this book. If during your research and planning in later chapters you discover a fatal flaw that will prevent you from delivering your proposed event, your records will allow you to return to any stage in your planning and research, allowing you to select different options and start your research and planning again from that point. For example you may want to come back and look at that weaving idea that we dismissed so quickly earlier on!

Tip

Remember to be honest with yourself. After a lot of research and planning that uncovered a potentially fatal flaw, it has been known for an event organiser to be unwilling to start all over again to research a new event type. Instead they ignore the flaw they put so much effort into discovering and 'risk it' by trying to run their event and hope the flaw goes away. If your research shows that there are flaws, trust it. Remember that discovering and resolving hidden problems and flaws is why you put effort into the research and planning in the first place, so that your final event will be a success!

Review potential event types

Bear in mind your skills experience and knowledge. Remember that at this stage your aim is to simply identify and select an event type that you think you can deliver. The list below contains some possible event types. Take a few minutes to look through the list, with your first thoughts on a possible event type and your objective in mind. The list isn't exhaustive, so don't feel that you have made a mistake if your proposed event type is not listed.

Sporting competitions

- football leagues
- cycling
- marathon, half-marathon
- rugby
- golf tournament
- tennis tournament
- gymkhana, show jumping or other equestrian event
- new wave sports – skateboarding, snowboarding, rollerblading

Specialist/commercial

- dog (and other animal) show
- trade show – engineering, IT etc.
- recruitment fair
- steam rally/agricultural show
- model railway/aircraft/cars
- car boot sale – auto jumble etc.

Teaching/skills

- sports coaching
- training course such as model-building
- money-saving skills – home/car maintenance
- DIY skills – decorating, plumbing

Fund-raising

- charity group
- schools
- club
- political

Meet and greet

- Parent–Teacher Association
- interest groups
- business
- political

Public relations

- company greeting customers
- trade show
- local authority

Pure profit

- making money by finding something the public wants – e.g. latest fads and trends!

Fun

- having safe fun at least cost

How to choose

List and review your experience, knowledge, contacts, resources, staff, known exhibitors, suppliers etc. To be able to organise and run a successful event, you will need them all, or have to obtain them quickly if you want to succeed. Be realistic. If you don't have them, it is possible to 'buy-in' appropriate skills, experience and knowledge, but it can be expensive and is generally only viable at major commercial events. Just as experience and contacts etc. will help you in organising an event, the less you know about the theme, type or content of the proposed event, the greater your chance of failing!

Limitations and restrictions

Before you finalise your decision, you should consider external factors and circumstances that restrict or limit your range of choices. Remember all events are unique, so the restrictions listed below are only included to illustrate the point. This is not an exhaustive list. You must consider other likely or possible restrictions, bearing in mind your own circumstances. For example you might be limited by:

Objective

Sometimes the event objective almost dictates the type of event you will run. Whether the objective is imposed on you by a club, committee or other governing body or you define the objective yourself. If your objective states that 'the club will run a golf tournament with a final on 3rd August', you will be running a golf tournament with the final on 3rd August! If your objective is less restrictive, for example 'to make money', or 'to organise our company fun day', you have greater choice and scope for innovation and diversification.

Skills and experience

Sometimes the event type is restricted or limited by the available skills and experience of the people proposing to run it. For example if girls from a remote village pony club decide that they want to put on a pony show, their limitation is that they only have one pony, their only audience is three girls in the village who are not members of the club and the only venue they are allowed to use is the village school field.

Circumstances

Sometimes the circumstances dictate or severely restrict the type of event. For example, if the inmates of a prison ask for permission to put on an event involving escape equipment, I think the answer would be no!

Financial/time constraints

Time or financial constraints may dictate or severely restrict your options. For example, if your office manager asks you to organise an event for 200 people – by lunchtime and with a budget of £150 – it looks like it's going to be cheap beer and Karaoke!

Season

Though the concept may be sound, you may be seasonally restricted. For example you will fail if you attempt to organise an ice-skating display on the local lake in summer, or a golf tournament in January in 3 feet of snow.

Club/legal rules

Club rules and legal restrictions may dictate how funds or premises are to be used. For example legal restrictions may prevent a charity from spending funds on hiring a hall and advertising a fund-raising caged bird show, even though you forecast a huge profit will be paid into the charity funds.

Investigation

You may find that your research and investigation places a limit on the type of event that you can organise. For example if you are located in a major city and you want to run an event in your clubhouse where the maximum door size is 7 feet high and 5 feet wide, your event is restricted to what you can get in through that door.

Audience

It is possible that your audience is fixed, so you have to present an event that they will want to see, where and when they want to see it. For example if your local school has retained you to deliver a Christmas show for 350 children aged 11 to 17, no matter how enthusiastic, interested and skilled you are in engraving milk bottles, a milk bottle engraving show will probably not be acceptable.

Checkpoint

Write up a one-page event outline and present your decision to a small group of people. Explain what the objective is, what event type you have chosen and why you chose it. Explain why you think that that event type is your best option, perhaps by running through your knowledge and experience of the subject, and the existing facilities available to you, such as premises, members, models, knowledge, contacts and suppliers. If they agree – well done, you have selected an event type. If not go back and start again!

Progress – Chapter 6

You should now:

- realise that there is an infinite number of event types,
- know how to define your available skills etc. to decide on an event type,
- be keeping records,
- have reviewed the basic event types and be aware of possible limitations and restrictions,
- be aware that to confirm the viability of an 'obvious choice', will need as much investigation and research as for any other possible event type,
- have decided on an event type to aim for,
- have drawn up an event outline for your selected event type, attempting to keep that outline to one side of an A4 page, and
- have made a checkpoint presentation and had your selection approved – delivering your event type.

Product completed

- A one-page event outline.
- Records of your research and decisions.
- Checkpoint review – authorisation to continue.

7 When to run the event

■ ■

The crucial factors
■ ■

The day, date and time of the event are crucial factors, but they are factors that are sometimes lost in the drive to deliver an event or show. It is common sense that a summer fair will fail if it is run in early January and a skiing demonstration will probably fail if run without snow in high summer. Read this chapter and consider the factors that could affect your event day, date and timing.

Day

Many events are centred on leisure activities and as such will attract an audience only if they are held during leisure time. This automatically restricts the days on which leisure events can be held to days when most people are not working – Saturday, Sunday or an occasional Bank Holiday Monday or Friday. Similarly, a work-related event such as an office furniture show will probably attract a better audience if it is run on a weekday.

Date

The date is quite significant as well. Some events will be limited to a specific period, e.g. the football or cricket season, while others will be limited for other reasons. For example running an event on Friday the 13th will probably not attract as big an audience as it could have on another day, because the superstitious will stay safely at home.

Similarly, any event on the day of a football cup final match, or another significant national sporting fixture or occasion, will not attract as many visitors as it could on another day.

Season

Some occupations and pastimes are seasonal. Generally, flower shows can only easily be held in the growing season, so not many flower shows will be organised for the winter months.

Weather

Another consideration is the weather. A severe drought may make a river level drop to the point where a canoeing display and event cannot be held. Heavy rain may simply flood an event site, or make the field a quagmire, preventing an agricultural show from being held.

Clashes with other events

This consideration is often ignored! As most events are held during good weather, there is by default an 'events season', which generally runs from about April to September, peaking during July and August. Many event organisers will aim to set their event on a bank holiday weekend, which gives them a chance to run a three-day event, gives the public a longer leisure period and so makes them more likely to attend.

The problem here is that event organisers often fail to take into account that several, if not dozens, of other event organisers are probably arranging events for the same bank holiday weekend.

I have seen many events fail because there are simply too many other events running at the same time, or that there is one major event running in competition and visitors fail to appear.

During your research and discussions with the police and local authorities, try to find out what other events are being organised in your area. Also keep an eye out in the press, or on notice boards. Find out the location, type, size etc. of other events and use that information in deciding when to run your event.

Time

The time you expect to open and close the event is important. You must take into account the size and type of the event, the time it will take stallholders and exhibitors to travel in and prepare their displays, the geographical distance you expect most of your audience will be travelling, access to the site and the availability of public transport etc.

You should choose your opening hours to maximise the period during which the paying public can gain access and spend money. You must balance this with the need **49** to allow yourself time to set up the attractions and sufficient time to clean up and strip down afterwards.

Event type

Not surprisingly a night fishing competition/event will be held at night and in the fishing season. For best effect there may be other factors that need to be considered, for example the presence or absence of a full moon and tidal movements etc. Knowing what event you want to organise and having the appropriate expertise will be a huge benefit to you in planning and organising it. If you don't have the appropriate skills and knowledge you must have access to people who do and you must constantly check with them to make sure that your proposed arrangements are suitable for the event being proposed.

Target audience

Your target audience may well contribute to your consideration as to when to run the event. In the simplest case, a primary school sports day will be run during a weekday, in term time and during school hours. Similarly, an archery competition will have to start early enough for all competitors to be able to compete in the heats, while still allowing the finals to be held during daylight unless you have an expensive floodlit arena!

Take everything into account

Specific event themes may well impose variable limitations on the day, date and time the event can be run. Make absolutely sure that you have taken everything into account, thoroughly investigated and considered every aspect of the event you have in mind, as well as reviewing any rules, regulations and limits on the running of that event.

For a new event, it is worth presenting your findings to the deputy event manager and a few invited guests (perhaps members of a similar club or group from the next city), to get a sanity check on your assumptions, decisions and arrangements.

Progress – Chapter 7

You should now:

- be aware of the limitations and restrictions that day, date, time, weather, season etc. may place on your event,
- have reviewed the restrictions and limitations, having taken the opportunity to discuss other events with the police and local authority.

Product completed

- A day, date and time when you propose to run your event.

8 Defining your target audience

You now need to start considering your target audience. Sometimes, defining the objective by default defines the scope, size and audience of the event. If your objective is to run a three counties five-a-side rugby tournament, you know exactly how many teams are arriving, how many motor coaches need to park and how many rugby pitches and changing rooms are necessary. You also know that your audience will be 80% male, many of whom will be young, sporting and fit.

Who will attend?

Some events are run annually. So it should be possible to make fairly accurate estimates based on the attendance the previous year. If your event has been run before (as with, for example, Round Table fireworks displays), don't be afraid to talk to past organisers and ask to see any accounts books and reports they may have. Don't be afraid to approach people who have organised similar events to the event you are proposing. By looking at their plans, reports and accounts, you should see how much gate money was charged, how many hot dogs were sold, how much the tent hire company charged and a host of other details. This will give you a base line on which to base your investigation, research and planning. Don't be afraid to ask anyone you think may be able to help for information, advice and guidance.

This list of potential audience members is not exhaustive, but it does indicate the sources of potential audience members:

Club

- members only
- prospective members

- families
- friends

School

- parents
- families
- friends
- the public

Company

- existing and prospective staff
- existing and prospective customers
- existing and prospective suppliers

Special interest groups

- e.g. steam engine enthusiasts, cyclists

General interest

- those wishing to learn something
- the public at large

Defining your audience

When defining and profiling the target audience, several variables come into play. For example you know your event type and have an idea of the proposed attractions, so one of the considerations to be taken into account is the age range of the audience you want to attract. The objective and event type may slant the age range of the target audience and this will be an important consideration in planning different aspects of the event.

If you are targeting pensioners, you probably should not book 'bar-fly' or 'bungee jumping' attractions. If the target audience is primary school children, don't book a stripper.

You must refine the content and range of your attractions to suit your identified target audience. A beer tent at a primary school will probably not pay for itself – unless the teachers are particularly thirsty!

Take advice from the suppliers of rides and attraction, because they know the target audience that appreciates their attraction and they know what prices to charge. More importantly, they know the size of audience that is needed to pay for the attraction and make a profit.

Similarly, the age range of the audience will have a bearing on the entry fee. Adults at a steam fair will probably be willing to pay £6 each in gate money, but a school sports day will almost certainly have free entry.

Effects of diversification

Remember that if you have diversified in arranging the content of the event, the complexity of estimating and attracting the target audience will be increased. The more you diversify, the harder some elements of the planning will become.

Although it is possible that a 'brass rubbing' event will fail to attract sufficient numbers to cover costs, a combination brass rubbing, horse brass and rural metalwork show could attract sufficient fee-paying members of the public to make it viable. Unfortunately, this additional complexity increases the effort required to plan and run the event, and can cause more serious problems. For the combined event example, you now have to consider advertising in three different special interest publications, trade papers and clubs. The advertising expenditure will now be considerably higher, so the entry fee may have to be raised to cover the cost, and that may put people off coming.

Tip

At all stages balance your enthusiasm with a large helping of common sense and a dollop of caution. Take a long look at your event objective before doing anything.

Progress – Chapter 8

You should now:

- realise that you need to profile your target audience and that you have two options – you can start with a pre-defined audience (school, club members, etc.) and then try to find and book attractions that they want to see, *or* start with an event theme and attractions and try to find an audience that will come to see them, and

● recognise that if you start with a pre-defined audience, a major worry is resolved because you have the audience, but you still have to deliver an event they will come to and possibly pay to get in to. Profiling a captive pre-defined audience is easier, because you know them, know where they come from and what their interests are and as a last resort you can go and ask them what they want to see at your event.

Product completed

● You should have drafted a written audience profile, stating such things as age range, sex, source, interest, likely mode of transport, etc.

9 Audience size

We are now moving into a more detailed phase of the investigation, where we need to define the size of the event in terms of expected audience numbers.

Estimating audience numbers

Many of your event arrangements hinge on the size of the audience; get this wrong and you get an awful lot wrong. Think of the services and facilities that are based on the event size: the number of toilets available; the car parking space; the number of gates in use; the number of gate staff; the amount of cash float; and the number of burgers you may have bought in for resale.

You must concentrate on generating an accurate estimate of the number of people who will attend. The larger the prospective event the more imperative it is that you invest time and effort in getting this right.

> **Tip**
>
> Don't rely on only one method of estimating audience size, in case there is a flaw in your method or errors in your calculations. Use several methods to independently calculate the projected size and compare the results to confirm that you are on the right track.

If you derive an audience size using three separate methods and two methods indicate your audience is going to be around 3000, but the third method indicates an audience of 20,000, you must look further. One or more of your approaches is wrong. You must get the estimated target audience right, to make the event a success.

Making your estimate either too high or too low will almost certainly cause you problems and cost you money.

Underestimating attendance

Underestimating attendance could cause major problems. If too many people arrive, your event site may not be large enough to accommodate them. There could be insufficient facilities and it may be unsafe (or even illegal) to allow more than the specified number to enter the event site. This will alienate your audience (so don't bother running the event again next year because nobody will come) and you will grossly aggravate logistical problems. You are then also denying access to people who have come a long way to give you money to visit your event. You will have to close the gates, ruining your reputation and that of your event too.

Overestimating attendance

Similarly overestimating attendance will also cause you problems. If less than the planned number arrive, you will have wasted money on unnecessary and unused facilities and staff and all too easily will have made a significant financial loss.

> **Tip**
>
> Don't skip or rush this phase. Get the projected audience size wrong and it will cost you money. If you make a financial loss, *you* will be liable.

Accurate estimates

How do you arrive at an accurate estimated attendance figure? There are a number of methods, some of which are more accurate than others. You should use three or more appropriate approaches to give you confidence in the accuracy of the figures that you derive.

Previous years' attendance

Some events are run annually or at least on a fairly regular basis. It should be an easy matter to check on the attendance from previous years to arrive at an estimate of the numbers that *might* attend the event you are planning.

If previous event records are available, refer to them. Better still if the people who organised the previous event are available, don't be frightened to consult them for inside knowledge, things that went well, things that went wrong, price levels, attractions booked and attendance etc.

It is important that you do not simply assume that you will get the same number of people attending your event this year. Perhaps at the brass rubbing show last year, there was a passing fashion or trend for brass rubbing that boosted their figures. Alternately, the weather may have been terrible last year, suppressing attendance – that is an added bonus of talking to the people who ran the event last year. They can interpret the statistics and fill in missing information! Make sure you read any reports from last year's event, talk to staff and check by using other methods to estimate event size.

Similar event attendance

You may be able to gather information on attendance figures at similar events. This method is simple, but wide open to misinterpretation and error. If a recent bicycle-racing event at your site attracted 3000 people, can we really assume that 3000 people would be interested in a trick cycling event on the same field?

The answer is no and perfectly illustrates the need to use more than one method to independently gauge the size of the attendance, to help you make some decisions.

All we know from the attendance at the bicycle-racing event last year is that there were 3000 people who were interested in bicycles – or maybe 3000 people interested in racing. Or could it be that perhaps a local first division football match was cancelled that day last year and 3000 people came to the event because they wanted something to do before the coaches came at 6pm to take them back home? Alternatively, was it held on a bank holiday and everything else for 20 miles in any direction was closed? Perhaps a local holiday camp was evacuated due to a fire alarm or flood. Or… or … or … well, *or* any number of other external factors that can totally reverse the projected and planned audience and attendance numbers.

All we *really know* is that there was a figure of 3000 people on that day, simply an indication. If the event staff and or accounts and reports are available, there may be additional information that could help you to understand this attendance and allow you to apply that to your proposed event with an increased degree of accuracy or confidence.

Club/team entries

Some events require that players or team entries have to be made in advance. For example, players in a football league or tennis tournament will have come up through the club leagues, so all potential participants will be known and expected.

The participants will know the non-team members they will bring (they are doing a similar but smaller exercise and arranging their own transport etc. so they know quite accurately, e.g. managers, teams, coaches, reserves, supporters etc.). Once the information is gathered, it is a quite simple matter to collate numbers and arrive at a fairly accurate total attendance figure.

Registrations

Some events may require competitors to register their interest and attendance in advance and they may also be required to pay an entry or registration fee in advance. Where competitions are part of the event, for example a half-marathon, runners may be required to register and pay say a £5 entrance fee that will pay for first aid cover and insurance etc. If this is the case, by the time of the registration deadline you should know fairly accurately how many people will probably be coming. As an indication of their commitment to attending, you have their £5 fee in the bank. If some do not come on the day, there is no loss because they paid their non-returnable registration fee.

Fixed capacity

It is possible that the venue may dictate the maximum audience that an event will be allowed to attract. Football grounds, theatres and some other venues have a legal maximum capacity. Some events require safety certificates from the local authority and/or emergency services. The certificates and authority to hold the event are issued when the organiser has proven that appropriate regulations and necessary safety obligations have been met.

In such events, once the venue is decided, the seating capacity is then known. Remembering that it is possible that some seating may be taken out of use to accommodate equipment (such as flood lights and sound control electronics at a pop concert, or partitions separating opposing fans at a football match). It is a simple matter to then calculate the maximum number of attendees.

■ ■

Tip

Don't fall into the trap of assuming that every seat at a fixed venue will be purchased. Even though a stadium may have a capacity of 10,000 people, you may not sell all 10,000 tickets.

Time/venue limits

Some events will be limited by time. For example, referring again to the football league example, if there is only one pitch, you cannot invite 50 teams to a knock-out tournament on a single day. With only one football pitch, there is insufficient time to arrange and play enough games in a single day to arrive at a winner.

Restricted and prescribed attendance

Some events by their nature very strictly define and restrict the attendance. These include investitures at Buckingham Palace, reunions for holders of the Victoria Cross etc. At these events the organiser closely specifies and invites the attendees, so he or she knows exactly who is coming and can even tell them when and how to arrive.

Effect of current circumstances

You have now arrived at a figure that is your best estimate of the numbers of attendees you will be expecting, *but beware*. You must also consider current and imminent changes in circumstances. You must remember that your investigation, planning and preparation will take some months and during that time there could be significant changes that will or may affect your event. Your potential audience could change considerably over two or three months and depending on circumstances may change radically within hours. You may get ten times the expected attendees, or one tenth of your estimate. You must allow for this in your planning and arrange matters suitably. What could cause such a change?

The economy

Such problems as a sharp rise in interest rates, or the closure of a major local employer will almost certainly cut the numbers attending. At times of economic crisis, 'the public' counts every penny they spend and disposable income plummets. They may want to come, but they have to spend the cash they have on rent and food and save any surplus for a rainy day, so there is little or no money available for entertainment or charity etc.

On the other hand, favourable interest or exchange rate changes, the opening of a new factory locally, or unlimited overtime in the local factory making electric fans in a hot summer, will put money in people's pockets, give them confidence and almost certainly increase the size of attendance.

The weather

A huge storm will keep all but the most hardy and dedicated enthusiast away from almost any event. You may even find that the exhibitors you have booked will stay away in very bad weather. Apart from the travelling difficulties, a vintage car owner will not be too keen to park their pride and joy in a storm-swept muddy field for your event! Even the helpers and staff may stay away during a severe cold spell, or gale force winds.

However, an unexpected Indian Summer, when an October weekend is suddenly very dry, warm and sunny, will increase the number of people looking for outdoor entertainment, deciding to take one last unexpected day out in the sun before winter drives them indoors.

Transport problems

Everyone who wants to attend has to get to the event. If there is a train or bus strike, or a protest demonstration gridlocking local roads, or severe weather making it dangerous to drive, or a signal failure or flu epidemic severely curtailing services, people just won't come!

It is just possible that transport problems could increase your attendance, but highly unlikely. If, for example you propose to hold your event on a bank holiday weekend, it is just possible that the public will prefer to come to your local event, rather than fight the bank holiday traffic. Another example may be that unscheduled engineering works on the main railway line will prevent locals going up to town for the day and they may look for alternative entertainment locally, boosting your audience and income.

Terrorist activity

A well-publicised terrorist attack will severely reduce the number of people willing to attend an insecure public event, hence attendance and interest will almost certainly fall, if not vanish. (This illustrates the need to show that your event is professionally managed and run and is safe.)

National emergency

An outbreak of foot and mouth disease or other similar national emergency will impose legal restrictions on travel, meeting and use of land. Such an outbreak would kill an event.

Season/fashion/craze

A tennis-related event would naturally attract significantly increased numbers if it were held at or around Wimbledon fortnight. Similarly, any craze or fashion could potentially increase the number of attendees at your event. During your investigation and planning, keep an eye on changing circumstances to get a feel for trends and be prepared to consider adding a new fashionable and crowd pulling attraction, *but only if it is economically viable.*

Similarly, don't expect to succeed if you are basing your whole event on last year's summer sensation – it may have had its time and now be defunct. Beware, nothing is more changeable than teenage trends and fashions.

You *could* deliberately organise an event that was totally out of season if you had strong demand. For example, the summer skiing event might work if you can appeal to the dedicated snow junkie who is suffering summer withdrawal symptoms being away from skiing for the summer months. You might also take advantage of holding the first such event before the new season begins, especially if you can advertise it well and it become known as 'the event' that sets the trend and exhibits all that is new for the coming season. Hard to do, but possible.

Start small

In starting a new event, with no track record available to refer to, all your plans are based on estimates and interpretation of data. Don't try to jump in and arrange the event of the century. Start small at a size you can handle and the objective will not be hopelessly missed if things don't turn out as planned.

If you have planned properly and managed your event well, you have lost nothing by starting small (unless you were hoping to cash in on a passing trend). In subsequent years you can increase the size of the event to the point where you arrive at the optimum size.

If you were trying to take a quick profit from a passing trend – consider your actions carefully: that will be a gamble and unless you are confident that you have the skills and knowledge to jump in and deliver what the public wants quickly – do not risk it.

How many can you handle?

Now you know how many people you are expecting you must seriously consider how many people you can successfully and safely handle, bearing in mind some legal limits and rules imposed by the authorities.

Don't get carried away. More visitors may mean more money coming in, but it also means that your problems increase. Ten thousand extra visitors paying £5 each to get into your event sounds good, until you look at the logistical problems that may present. For example you may find that the last 500 visitors will have to park 7 miles away (in the only field in the county you have not yet assigned as a car park). Even then, because of a lack of space on the event ground, the last 300 people will have to stand on each others' shoulders, just to get onto the site!

There are many aspects of the organisation and logistics that are either drawn from the numbers attending, or where numbers have a direct bearing on every detail of how the event is planned, organised and run. Get this right; spend as much time on it as you need to. Keep going until you are happy and confident of your estimates.

Checkpoint

When you think you have finished, check your results. Organise a brainstorm session with some colleagues, particularly those who have an intimate knowledge of the club, sport or event type. Give a presentation of your work on your estimated attendance.

Answer their questions; tell them where the figures came from. Can they see a flaw in your assumptions, decisions or calculations? Remember that if there are any significant changes at later stages, you must go back and start this audience estimation process all over again. For example, if you have now decided that your tennis tournament will have a 'Flossy Doll' theme – since they were introduced two weeks ago, every child in the country wants a Flossy Doll – go back and rework the audience figures.

Your work will be quicker the second time around, but it will reconfirm and reinforce your confidence in the research you have undertaken and the plans you are making.

Progress – Chapter 9
■ ■

You should now:

- realise the critical importance of making an accurate estimate of audience size and be ready to use at least three methods of calculating that size to give you confidence in the resulting estimate,
- know that different circumstances may affect attendance at your event and so you should monitor external circumstances to track and, if possible, minimise any detrimental effect,
- accept that you may wish to start small if it is your first event, but remember that grand ideas may result in grand profits or grand losses,
- realise that there is a limit to the number of people your event can handle, due to venue, legal or space limitations,
- realise that audience size will feed in to calculations about car parks and size of site, and
- give a checkpoint presentation to a new group, to confirm your results are ready to move on to the next phase.

Product completed

- An estimate of attendance (from at least three methods of calculation).
- Checkpoint review – authorisation to continue.

10 Advertising

Advertising is a specialist area and the intricacies of advertising are a whole new problem. If at all possible use a professional to advise you on every aspect of advertising, including the wording to use, where and when to advertise, as well as what colours and art work you need for maximum benefit. They will arrange for that artwork, insert the advertisements on the most effective days and pages, and negotiate very good rates.

Should I advertise?

Advertising may not be strictly necessary, depending on the type and size of the event, but it is always, always, always beneficial. Especially when you remember that advertising doesn't have to cost money!

If the event is limited to members of a small club and their friends, an announcement at a club meeting may be all the 'advertising' that is necessary to inform the potential audience of the event. As event manager, you must decide if you could attract a larger audience if you also advertised the existence of the event with surrounding clubs as well? Larger events, particularly those trying to attract members of the general public, especially if the event is being run for the first time, must advertise or die.

Many events have failed not because the public didn't want to come, but simply because the public did not know that the event was taking place, where it was and what the attractions were. When you have gone to the trouble of investigating, planning, organising and running the event, avoiding clashes with other events and pitching the costs and prices at the right level, it would be a shame if nobody came because nobody knew it was on!

Is it worth it? Yes it is – *if* your proposed target audience and income justify the costs, and only you can decide that, probably in consultation with an advertising professional.

Did you know that an advert on the right-hand page of a paper or magazine often gets more response than the same advert on the left-hand page? Positioning on the page is also important in the level of response, as is the day on which the advertisement is run.

Putting an identifiable code in the advert lets you know which ad the reader is responding to; knowing that allows you to see which advertising was most effective. For example including a code in the reply address such as '*Reply to London Steam Show – Room LP1*' tells you that they replied to your first (1) advert in the Local Paper (LP), i.e. LP1.

Changing just one word in the text of an advertisement can have a remarkable effect as well. For example 'Free Car Parking Available' may get a vastly better response than 'Car Parking Available'.

Advertising and publicity is nowhere near as easy as most people assume. Response can be doubled or tripled by using appropriate knowledge and experience, just as the price of advertising can be halved using knowledge and experience.

Forms of advertising

Newspapers and magazines

Which publication you use to place your advert will depend on what you can afford, but more importantly will relate to the profile of your proposed audience. If you are running an over-80s knitting event, even the cheapest rates and largest advert in *Punk Rock Weekly* will have little if any benefit. Place your adverts in the publications that your expected or target audience will be reading.

The rates in even local newspapers can be shockingly high. As with any other trade or profession, if you know your way around you can get cheaper rates and squeeze good deals out of the publishers. For example find out what the deadline is for the insertion of adverts, then talk to the ad sales department just a couple of hours before they close the books. It is possible to push the price down and arrange for a bargain advert, but it's a lot more complicated than that, so consider using a professional – especially if you can get one to volunteer their services.

Free coverage

You may be able to talk the local paper into doing a small item about your event, particularly if it is raising funds for a charity or local crafts and local residents are the stars.

Don't overlook the possibility of arranging for an article in the local papers or special interest magazines a few weeks before you plan to run the event. People will note it and hopefully mark it in their diary and social plans. Later when you start advertising, people will hopefully recall the interesting things they read in the article and be more willing to make the effort to get to your event.

Some special interest magazines will accept free listings of events that wholly or partly cover their particular interest. It is worth investigating this possible source of free advertising and making additional or further enquiries through the side-show and attractions' suppliers that may give you additional coverage.

Let's face it, how many times have you seen a local newspaper with a front-page article about a turnip shaped like a duck or some other trivia? If that's all they can find for the *front* page they may well be interested in filling some column inches with an article on your forthcoming 40th anniversary model aircraft show!

Radio

Local radio can give free mentions, but more often than not you will have to pay for radio exposure. Depending on the event type and size it may be possible to attract a radio or television road-show. This gives multiple benefits, attracts the young, gives free advertising and helps to attract additional side-show owners, who want to cash in on the expected audience.

Members

Your club or society members are good sources of free advertising. Distributing handbills and notices to them so that they, their friends and relatives can pin them up in shops, offices, clubs etc. will give you greater coverage. Additionally, you can mention the event in the club newsletter and make agreements with surrounding and affiliated clubs to advertise the event in *their* newsletters, and even get their members to distribute handbills etc.

Handbills

You may wish to consider the possibility of getting handbills printed up. They could be delivered to all of the local homes and businesses by club members or possibly they could be distributed for a fee with the local newspapers, or even hand-delivered by the post office, though the last two methods are quite expensive.

With clubs or societies, you may call on the support and good will of members to keep the cost of handbills down. With so many people having home computers, you could consider emailing, or circulating to club members a handbill document on diskette or CD. Then you could ask them to copy the handbill file onto their machine and pass the diskette or CD on. They could print as many copies as they require to distribute themselves, or to hand out for circulation through relatives and other contacts.

Public transport

If you are proposing to plan, organise and run a major event, you may be able to interest the appropriate bus coach and rail companies in co-operating with you. Depending on the location, target audience, event type and event attractions, they may be interested in offering a combined travel and entry ticket. The benefit of this is that they will help in advertising the event and could attract members of the public from a much wider area.

Internet

You may well already have a club website, or access to a person who can supply a site for you. Again depending on the type and size of the event it may be worth generating a few web pages to advertise the occurrence of the event.

For some larger events you may wish to attempt ticket sales over the web. Using the right key words in the site description and keeping your site current with the search engines will give you better web exposure.

It can be profitable, but common sense has to prevail. If you are organising the village primary school, class 3b, under 7's Easter Hat Competition, are you really expecting to get interest from Australia and America?

Chain email

Though chain letters have had a bad press, you could use an electronic equivalent to advertise your event. Compile a short email equivalent to a handbill, and email it to any interested parties you may know, asking them to forward it to interested parties that they know etc. In this way, your event details can be circulated to thousands of people in just a few days.

Please remember to include at the top of your email a note asking people not to forward the email after the date of the event, there is enough junk email in the world already and nobody wants to see an email advertising your event months after it was

run.

Hoarding/signs

You could erect signs or hoarding to advertise your event, but this will introduce a few new headaches as it involves issues of planning permission, permission of the landowner, costs, health and safety, erection and accidents etc. A large sign on the proposed event ground next to a major road, saying 'Model Aircraft Show Sunday 23rd August' will warn passing public that the event is coming. (See Chapter 16, 'Sign posting'.)

> **Tip**
>
> Promotion and advertising is not simple. It is possible to waste a lot of money and time, mounting a totally misdirected and useless advertising campaign. The most important point to remember is that advertising in the right places, at the right times, with the right advert, at the right price *will* increase attendance and income. The secret is to get it right – easy to say but very hard to do!

Fly posting

That is when cheap advertising signs or leaflets are made up and then simply stuck onto phone boxes, bus shelters, shop windows, in fact any vacant flat surface. Some people find the low cost of this advertising method to be too tempting and paste their signs everywhere. Do not do it! You must have seen the notices around – 'Bill posters will be prosecuted' – and you may be.

If you are caught fly posting, you may have to pay for the posters to be removed and/or the local authority or owners of the fly-posted property may take action against you. Fly posting is unwarranted, spoils the environment and cheapens your event. Make sure that members of your club or friends and relatives are not fly posting as well. It is your event and you will be the one held liable for any damage.

Additional information

Though not strictly speaking advertising, you should consider additional information that you want to pass on to the public. This information could be printed on the tickets, handbills or posters as a service to the public. Wherever it appears, make the best use of the space. For example if you are arranging a fireworks event in November, you will have to display all the usual information regarding venue, date, time and price, but there is other information that could be of use.

It will be dark when the event begins. Frequently fireworks events are held out of town, which means they are off unlit roads. Using one side of a ticket for helpful information and advice, or just using the last few lines of a poster or handbill could save the lives of spectators, or at least avoid inconvenience.

I would suggest, for example, that you note for a fireworks event that people should wear some light-coloured clothes so that the drivers of passing traffic can easily see them. Ask them to be particularly careful with excited children while approaching and leaving the event. I would also include a reminder to bring a torch, simply so that they can see where they walk and find their way back to the car after the event! A lot of people forget that they will have to get out of their car and cross fields and tracks to get to the fireworks site and then go back again to find their car, which is one of over 300 in a huge and unlit field.

Selling advertising space

Do not forget that it may be possible for you to sell advertising space. Perhaps the local pizza restaurant would want to pay you for the privilege of putting an advert on the back of every ticket, or at least sponsor the production of the tickets. They may want to erect a banner at the event, at the main entrance and exit. They of course hope that after the event, the public will want something to eat – and the first thing that will come to their minds is that juicy pizza they saw on the back of their fireworks ticket or on the banner at the gate.

Other advertisers may want to put advertising signs and hoarding on the local site. Would a local four-wheel drive garage supply patrol and cash collection vehicles as long as they could have a stand on the site? Explore every avenue.

Removal of signs

Erecting signs to help people at your event is important, but don't overlook the importance of removing them as well. You have probably seen shabby signs advertising something that happened weeks or even months ago. You don't have to walk very far in most areas before you find the remains of signs, or bare plastic cable ties festooning poles along our streets. When your event is over, remove your signs and any fixings or posts. Do not ruin your reputation by being a cowboy who leaves these signs to rot and litter the pavement. Take them down and dispose of them yourself, safely and quickly.

Progress – Chapter 10

You should now:

- accept that advertising will always be beneficial,
- recognise that advertising can be complicated and expensive and may not be appropriate or justifiable,
- recognise that inserting 'response codes' into advertisements will allow you to identify the most effective adverts,
- realise that specialist advice regarding publications, day and date of publication, the wording and even colours used can increase the effectiveness of an advertisement,
- accept that you need to apply common sense to your advertising strategy in selecting publications and setting an advertising budget,
- realise that it is possible but difficult to get free 'advertising', through members, handbills and press coverage,
- recognise the opportunity of putting additional information on handbills and tickets, and
- recognise the opportunity of selling advertising space at your event as a revenue stream.

Product completed

- Advertising schedule – stating what advertising you propose to undertake, where, what format and for what cost.
- Schedule of potential income from advertisers and sponsors.
- A plan showing the activities necessary to attract sponsors or organisations wishing to advertise at your event, attracting revenue.

11 Event attractions

You have collected sufficient information during your investigation and research and have defined the objective, type of event and the expected audience. You are now able to more closely define the specific attractions you need or desire.

Selecting event attractions

You need to research the proposed attractions in more detail. Why are the public going to come? What are they going to want to do at your event? What are they expecting to see at your event? What will bring them out of their homes to attend your event and pay a sum of money for the privilege of getting in? What will make them spend more money while on site?

Generally, the event type and your objective quite closely restrict the attractions. If you are advertising a 'steam fair', but have no steam-related equipment, stalls, rides etc., the public won't stay, won't spend money and will almost certainly demand their entrance fee back. If your objective is to run a tennis tournament, 'tennis' will be the main attraction at your event.

The simple and basic list of what the public can or will want to do at an event is:

- eat,
- buy,
- go on rides,
- see,
- listen,
- learn,
- try,

- photograph,
- join,
- compete,
- collect the experience (to say 'I was there' or 'I saw it'), and
- possibly just be out together as a family or couple.

Audience-led attractions

The audience may closely define the attractions that are required and expected at an event. For example, if the event has been tailored for members of a model aircraft club, the theme will almost certainly be model aircraft. This 'default' method of selecting event attractions is the one most commonly used. In this approach, the known audience of model aircraft devotees at an event defined as a model aircraft show dictates the attractions that the event manager will provide.

Attractions-led audience

Under different circumstances, the attractions and rides arranged could define the audience who will be attracted and drawn to the event. For example running an autojumble will attract people interested in vehicles and engines. In this approach, the theme of the event and the engine spares and petrol junkie attractions will only attract that type of person to attend.

Attendance patterns

An event can attract different people at different times of the day. For example in a fun fair, the fair is likely to attract families between opening time and about six in the evening. After six, the bulk of attendees will probably be teenagers and young adults. At weekends, the fun fair is likely to attract families, or grandparents giving their grandchildren a treat, but again during the evening the bulk of attendees will be teenagers. You should investigate and be aware of attendance patterns appropriate to your proposed event.

Variety

Whatever your theme and objective, you must consider variety. Even the most ardent fan will want a little variety at the event. At a model aircraft event, you might include a number of model cars or ships. You may even include a model steam train, which can provide rides for adults and children.

Another consideration is that some of the audience will not be particularly interested in the main theme of the event. You will attract members of the public who were just passing. There will also be enthusiasts who have been accompanied by a friend, children, wife or husband who has no interest in the event theme.

There is a potential to increase income by providing entertainment, ice cream and toy sales etc. for the junior audience and diversions for adults who have only a passing interest, or no interest at all in the main theme.

This increases profits in two main ways, a) providing something that those not interested in the main attraction can spend money on, and b) increasing the likelihood that anyone interested in the main theme of the event will feel able to attend without alienating their partner or children. All of which makes it more likely that they will come, stay and continue to spend money, without being dragged away by bored partners.

Depending on the target audience and objective for running the event, you should very seriously consider arranging for the presence of diversionary attractions. Target groups could be for example, motorists (car rally – grand prix), vintage car enthusiasts (car event, vintage car spares and sales), pop music fans (concerts), or gardeners (flower shows). Diversionary attractions could be a fair ground, food stalls, or even milk-bottle engraving!

Sources for attractions

Generally attractions come from three sources.

Your group

Members of your group may voluntarily supply some of the attractions. For example in our model aircraft event, members of the club would supply dozens of static models, exhibitions of model-making and exhibitions of flying models.

This is the best and cheapest source of attractions and totally within your control.

Other groups

Members of associated or affiliated groups may voluntarily supply some of the attractions. Using our model aircraft event again, other clubs can exhibit their best models and the local model ship and model car clubs could supply diversionary attractions.

This is a cheap source of attractions, but you do have less control over other groups and so less control over the quality and supply of these attractions.

Commercial sources

The final source of attractions is through commercial sources. For example you may want to hire a 'bouncy castle' or a roundabout as an attraction. This option gives you the widest choice of attractions, but costs can be significant, when factoring in insurance, operators and attendants, delivery and collection etc.

You may rent the attraction from the owner and keep all income, or rent a plot to the owner of the attraction and contract with them to pay you a fee or a percentage of their takings.

A commercial contract gives you control over the owner of the attraction.

Select and define attractions

You should by now have a good feel for the theme of the event, the target audience and the attractions that are available. Working with a small group you should discuss and select the best options, bearing in mind the audience profile, costs, safety, potential income and popularity.

This is another task that for all but the smallest of events will take a few attempts to complete. Brainstorm the attractions with a small group and compare the list of suggestions to what you have available. Consider looking around for some diversionary attractions and begin to enquire about cost and availability. Make sure that the attractions you are listing are compatible with your organisation, your event objective, your site and funding level. Leave the resulting lists for a few days and then revisit them and work through again until you think you have a good schedule of attractions. Above all do not forget that the attractions have to 'attract' the public – you might still be enthralled by that milk-bottle engraving but nobody else will be!

You must also remember that you are responsible for the health and safety of anyone attending your event or affected by it (see Chapter 5). If the event requires safety barriers or specialist safety certificates, it is your responsibility to ensure that they are obtained and available for inspection.

Liability

Though you have insured your show, members of staff and the public, you should consider your liabilities in relation to attractions. I strongly suggest that you take advice from your insurers and insist that all exhibitors, displays, bands and any other attractions should have their own insurance. This insurance should cover them for the activities they perform while on your site and cover them and any damage or injury they may cause.

Ensure that you and the managers of each specific attraction or exhibit know what is required and expected. Review their act and or exhibits and agree and write down what they are expected to do. If during the review you consider their sword-swallowing trick to be inappropriate or unnecessarily dangerous, tell the performer and get them to sign to acknowledge the fact that they have been told and will remove any identified dangers and risks.

To make your safety ethos clear to them, I also suggest that you make it a clause in your agreement with them that they will abide by your health and safety rules, and that any breach may result in fees being withheld and them being asked to leave the site. You will have to supply them with a copy of your rules and procedures and also monitor them while on site.

Tip

Get a firm commitment from any attraction or stallholder you want to book. I have known stallholders and mobile concessions to simply abandon a commitment because of a better offer, without even having the decency to let the event manager know that they are not coming. This often happens with things like ice cream vans at small school fetes etc.

Sponsorship

Don't forget the benefits of sponsorship. You may get sponsorship on any aspect of the event. For example *The UK and North West Europe Model Aircraft Magazine* (if it existed) might advertise your event for free and even sponsor prizes for the model aircraft event we have been using as an example. The local sign writer might produce the main signs as long as their details are prominent and they can have a free stall on the event site. A pet food manufacturer might sponsor prizes at a pet event and will profit from selling thousands of cans of dog or cat food at the event themselves.

Explore every avenue of sponsorship and don't forget to make this an early task in the planning and arrangements. Remember though, some organisations allocate their sponsorship funding a year or even two years in advance, so remember that you have to get in early!

The larger and more successful the event, the more likely you will be to attract sponsors. Sponsorship can significantly benefit the balance sheet for the event, so early commitment to sponsorship should be sought. Sponsorship funding is very limited, but it's always worth trying to find it.

Review and refine site size

In Chapter 14 you will be reviewing and defining your site requirements. As you finalise arrangements you may need to return to review and confirm site plans and requirements. For example, a review may be necessary if you had previously booked and confirmed the presence of the South Of England Fun Fair. Then the new owner calls two weeks before your event to confirm his presence, but he also states that under new management they have relaunched themselves with 10 extra rides. They will require more site space and though you may have a neat and tidy site plan, you now have to re-draw the plan to accommodate the new larger fun fair.

Tip

When you eventually begin to take bookings from attractions and exhibits, you must confirm their access and parking space requirements. They may bring a low loader containing a huge traction engine, which needs tarmac access and parking to prevent it bogging down or sustaining damage. They may bring a truck with a trailer, a supporting van and a caravan, all of which require off-site parking during the event. When you know what they intend to bring, you will have to calculate and reconfirm the space required for exhibitor parking and confirm your other plans and arrangements.

Checkpoint

When you have a finalised list of attractions and your enquiries tell you that the cost and availability is acceptable, hold a checkpoint presentation. Present the list of attractions and any explanations of why they were selected, then throw the meeting open for questions, answers and suggestion. After the meeting you may have to return to further refine the attractions list, in the light of suggestions made during the checkpoint meeting. The new revised attractions list must now feed into the next stage.

At this stage you should book any free attractions, that is anything that you do not have to pay for. For example the model car club may have agreed to come and demonstrate remote control cars, if you will attend their show and demonstrate radio-controlled helicopters.

Progress – Chapter 11

You should now:

- be aware of the variety of activities that are possible at the event you are planning,
- have refined your event type and theme after researching attractions,
- be aware of the sources of attractions you require,
- have identified and approached potential sponsorship targets especially where sponsors offer big names, displays and attractions,
- have brainstormed and listed your required attractions, taking into account popularity, costs, space requirements and availability,
- given a checkpoint presentation to a new group, to confirm your results are ready to move on to the next phase, and
- possibly have returned to review audience size and profile in light of investigations into attractions.

Product completed

- Have produced a list of proposed and required attractions based on cost, availability and suitability investigations.
- Have provisionally booked any attractions for which there is no fee and possibly pencilled in bookings with commercial attractions, depending on possible cancellation fees etc.
- Have scheduled health and safety reviews of all proposed event attractions.
- Checkpoint review – authorisation to continue.

12 Event requirements

You know your proposed 'event type' and have produced a one-page 'event outline' as a starting point. You broadly know the format of your proposed event and have some fairly firm outline ideas for the main stream and diversionary attractions and other content. You must now undertake a review of the detailed requirements needed to deliver that event.

Brainstorm the requirements

Working from the event outline, you must discuss, review/brainstorm and list in detail everything you think you need to deliver your event. These are 'the requirements'. Whether the requirements are a model aircraft runway, football pitches, tents, a cycle racing track, 75 gate staff, an accountant, four sheep, or ski jumps etc., you must list everything that is raised. This review method attempts to identify the detail of your proposed event, extracting and documenting every possible requirement of any description.

For the requirements brainstorming session, the 'scribe' should note down each requirement idea on a *yellow* Post-it® note (the yellow-coloured notes will be useful later). *Anything* that is raised should be noted on one of these notes. Don't dismiss or ignore any suggestion or idea during the brainstorming session. It may not be kept in the final list of requirements, but for now it may trigger a new thought that could later on point at a missing requirement. For our example event, our brainstorming list of requirements might include the following:

- tents
- food
- money

- exhibits
- collecting bins
- bank account
- players
- transport
- good weather
- rubbish skips
- brass band
- hire van
- celebrity guest
- double-decker bus
- team uniform
- loudspeaker
- ice-cream van (attract the kids, and mum and dad will come too).

Note – If there is a need to clarify why an item is listed (as in the ice-cream van above), do it now. The explanation alongside the ice cream van clearly shows that somebody thinks the ice-cream van will increase attendance. Better to explain why it was raised now while it is fresh in your mind, than try to remember some time later, why somebody thought having a tightrope-walking aardvark at the event was so important to its success!

Apply common sense

This is an opportunity to reconsider and decide if it is worth continuing. In the worst-case scenario, if while brainstorming your proposed event you find that you have *no idea at all* – stop now.

For example that festive idea of an 'Xmas Reindeer Rodeo' sounded exciting and profitable when it was discussed in the pub after the last club meeting. Unfortunately, having brainstormed it, all we came up with were questions and doubts, with no answers at all!:

- Are there any reindeer in the UK?
- Can you rent a flock of reindeer?
- Come to that – do reindeer come in herds or flocks?
- Do reindeer bite?
- Could a reindeer gore a spectator with its antlers?
- Are reindeer expensive to buy and feed?
- Do I need a ministry licence to keep reindeer?
- Do I need a local authority licence to train reindeer?

- Would the animal welfare groups let us have the rodeo?

In this example, the brainstorm result clearly shows that though it sounded like a good idea to begin with, team members don't have sufficient experience, knowledge and contacts in this subject to organise the event and make it a success. Stop here and start again with an event type that you are more familiar with. Not all cases will be as clear as this example, but you will soon realise if you don't have the skills, knowledge or funds to organise a proposed event.

The bottom line is that if you find now that to run your event you *just have to have a troop of 20 performing elephants* – it may be time to start thinking of an alternative event, or at least taking another look at that event objective!

'Classes' of requirements

When no new ideas for 'requirements' are forthcoming, move on to the next stage. Change to a pad of new *blue* Post-it® notes and brainstorm the separate 'classes of requirements' you might have. Write each classification on a blue Post-it® note. Thus in our example we might have generated the following classifications:

- staff
- tents
- site
- transport
- equipment
- cash float
- exhibitors
- food sales.

Collate and sort

Take some large blank flip-chart pages and stick them around the room. You are going to assign one flip-chart page to each 'classification' of requirements (or assign more pages if it is a large classification). Select each blue 'classification' Post-it® note and stick it at the top of its own clean flip-chart page. When that has been done, start working through the requirements (yellow Post-it® notes) and stick them on the appropriate classification page.

Working with the examples above you may find you have the groupings below. Note that at this point some classifications have few or no requirements and some requirements do not seem to really fit into any of our classifications!

Staff	Tents	Site	Transport	Equipment
	Tents	Rubbish skips	Transport Hire van Double-decker bus	Loudspeaker

Cash float	Exhibitors	Food sales
Money Collecting bins Bank account	Exhibits Players Brass band	Food

Unclassified Requirements??????
Good weather Celebrity guest Team uniform Ice-cream van (attract the kids, and mum and dad will come too)

Revisit and rework

When we finished brainstorming the requirements, we thought we had listed every possible requirement. When we looked at the classifications we thought we had identified all of them too. However, the simple act of collating them and bringing them together on the flip-chart pages has shown us a lot of gaps already:

- The 'staff' classification has no requirements shown, but we clearly need staff with different skills and abilities.
- The only requirement listed under the 'site' classification is 'rubbish skips', but we need more than a few rubbish skips to provide the optimum site!
- Under the classification 'transport', we have transport, double-decker bus and a hire van. Do we need a van and a bus? Do we need a van at all? Perhaps we should have explained why we wanted them at the time we listed them? Further discussion is necessary.
- Under the 'equipment' classification we only have loudspeakers and we surely need more equipment than that?
- Under the 'food sales' classification we have 'food'. Do we want to get involved in food, or are we only really interested in getting some mobile food sales vans

to come onto the site, so we don't have to worry about food and cooking? More consideration is needed.

- More interestingly we have the requirements of good weather, celebrity guest, team uniform and the ice-cream van left and not assigned to any classification. Do we need more classifications?

You must now discuss the requirements and classifications again and start filling in the gaps. For example under 'staff', we need people on the gates, people in the car parks, people for first aid, somebody to count the money etc.

Looking at the wider picture, we can also question what we have at the moment, should we have an 'accommodation' classification, which will include tents, trailers, Portakabins™ etc?

After further discussion, under the 'site' classification, we need fences, car parks, signs, electricity, toilets, good road and rail access, wide gates, etc.

Perhaps we even need a new classification of 'pre-requisites', which will include a celebrity guest and good weather?

Repeat and add things

You must rework this process now. Don't expect to finish it in one day. Having the requirements for each classification on a separate flip-chart sheet allows you to put the sheets away easily and safely, without losing or mixing up the Post-it® notes. (Don't roll the sheets up if you don't have to – it works a lot better if you store them flat.)

Come back and repeat the process when you are fresh, and even invite a few new members to review and brainstorm with you. Remember your option to diversify, and the possible benefits of doing so. Check with specialists, until you think you have listed everything you will need.

Search the Internet, library or telephone books for 'reindeer rentals', if that is still outstanding, and keep looking until you get the answers to your questions. Discuss the requirements with the local authority, emergency services and the health and safety executive, heed their advice and make the additions to your requirements and classifications that they will almost certainly raise.

When you finally have a complete list of classifications and requirements, make some lists. These lists will form a basic building block for your event. They are important and will be more useful if they are created using a word processor so that you can cut, paste and amend them at later stages.

Remember, too, that some aspects are critical, while others are incidental. If you can get everything other than a site – there is no event. If you have everything but not enough exhibitors, who wants to come to a wonderful well-staffed site with no stalls or displays? If you have everything except an ice-cream van – does that really matter?

Confirmation of your event type

When you started reviewing your event requirements, you had an event type in mind and a one-page event outline. On completion of this process of defining requirements and classifications, you should have compiled a substantial list showing what you need to deliver your event. Though that proposed 'Reindeer Rodeo' might have attracted the crowds, your analysis and discussion showed you that you could not organise and deliver it. If you find yourself in this position – go back and select a new event type and start the process again.

Checkpoint

Before finally confirming the event type, make absolutely sure that you can meet all of the requirements to make it happen. I usually organise a checkpoint meeting and invite a new brainstorming team.

I initiate a short brainstorming session after showing them the proposed event type, event outline and event objective and wait for input – noting what they say and checking against my lists and plans to make sure I have already considered those points. If not I add them to my lists for further consideration.

When nothing new arises within a reasonable time, I present the team with the raw list of requirements from the earlier session. I allow another period of free discussion, noting any worthwhile suggestions and resolving any doubts or questions.

When the checkpoint group generates nothing new or significant, I switch to the final lists of classifications and requirements by issuing or presenting my final lists and once again allow them to study and comment on them.

If again they come up with nothing new, I have more confidence in the work so far and am glad that their sanity check has proved the value of the work so far. Remember, if during a checkpoint they raise nothing new, we have succeeded. Remember as well that if they do come up with something new, *we have still succeeded*! The whole idea is that they take a fresh look and confirm or add to our detailed requirements and plans.

Don't book anything yet!

Remember that this is only an investigation at the moment. *Don't commit to anything.* Don't spend any money yet, because at a later stage there may be major problems that prevent the event from taking place. If that happens and you have started ordering things and making bookings, you may find yourself liable to pay cancellation fees. Wait until you are quite sure that it will be possible and/or profitable to run the event.

Progress – Chapter 12

You should now:

- knowing your proposed event type, have brainstormed your event 'requirements' and applied common sense to the feasibility of your proposed event,
- have brainstormed your event 'classifications',
- have collated and sorted the results using coloured Post-it® notes and flip charts,
- revisited and reworked this until you feel that you cannot expand or improve the lists, but be ready to amend and extend them as your understanding of your event increases,
- remember to consider the benefits of diversification,
- give a checkpoint presentation to a new group, to confirm your results are ready to move on to the next phase, and
- though you have started making enquires and asking for quotes and availability from suppliers, you have still *not spent any money or ordered anything*, as you might have to change your plans.

Product completed

- Have produced a list of requirements and classifications.
- Have brainstormed and worked through the loop several times until you are quite satisfied that you have identified what you need to deliver your proposed show.
- Checkpoint review – authorisation to continue.

13 Accommodation and services

No two events are the same, but there are some factors that seem to be common to all events. Whatever accommodation and services you require, you must make sure that the suppliers have:

- good references that you have checked and confirmed,
- a safety policy which they can prove – for example by showing you copies of their safety policy and safety training and procedures,
- risk assessments in relation to the equipment and or services they will be supplying to you, and
- public liability insurance – they should be able to produce a certificate to prove that they have it.

Event manager's office

It is important that there is one recognised central control point and that should be the event manager's office. Though the office does not have to be central to the site, it should be easily identified, known to all staff and hopefully readily accessible from the main entrance on the main road.

The event manager's office should have power, heating (depending on season), water supply, tea- and coffee-making facilities. It should also have a quiet, private section or office for the event manager to use. For larger events there should be radio or other communications with event staff. A supplies area will be required, which holds first aid materials, sign writing equipment, staff badges/tabards, reflective/fluorescent jackets, writing material, pens and forms etc.

Depending on event size and duration, the event manager and their staff may need the use of a telephone. There will be a need for some furniture – chairs, desks, etc.

There may be a need for windows looking out over the event ground, with window shutters to protect the windows if the office is to be unattended overnight.

For a larger event it is good to have a large dry wipe board, or white gloss painted sheet of hardboard available, on which the event manager can write key details. This board contains the names of other managers, radio call signs, mobile phone numbers etc.

It is likely that the event manager will want to be near to the cash office. The event manager's office may need its own toilet, or could share the cash office toilet.

Cash office

This is the event 'bank' and must therefore be secure and protected. This is where float cash will be held and distributed and where incoming cash will be collected, bagged and dispatched for banking. Though any accommodation will do, bearing in mind the security consideration, I suggest that either a good sturdy Portakabin™ or an existing lockable building should be used.

To protect the cash from prying eyes, any windows on this office should be shuttered or otherwise screened. Electricity should be supplied for lighting and for heating or air conditioning, depending on season. Remember the doors and windows will be shut all day so the cash office will get very hot in summer – air conditioning is not a luxury.

The cash office will also need calculators, furniture, possibly a safe or lockable cabinet, cash bags, accounting forms, radio or other communications to the event manager's office, secure and discreet parking for cash collection, a separate reception area or window hatch for visitors, water and refreshment facilities and sufficient toilets.

When locating the cash office you must remember that it should be convenient for cash to be brought there from the gate and car parks, without undue risk and without collection vehicles driving around the event site unnecessarily.

It must also be possible to despatch cash safely to the bank. Locating any police control office near the cash office gives it additional security and protection.

Public address system

At any event you must be able to tell the public what is happening. Even the best-programmed event timetable can go awry and the visitors may (or should hopefully) have lost track of time as they enjoy themselves. You do not want them to miss the one attraction that they attend the event to see, so you need a public address (PA) system. This will also be used for the usual lost children, 'Will the owner of the white van please move it' and lost sunglasses messages.

The people setting up and running the side shows will probably appreciate a warning such as 'the gates open in 15 minutes' and will ask you to make announcements such as 'all burgers at half price' before the stall shuts down each night.

It is likely that on a very small primary school event, public announcements can be made using a megaphone, but any larger events will need to either borrow a PA system from somebody, or call on the services of a commercial organisation to install one. It is likely that the PA system can be sourced from the same organisation that rents you any pocket radios for the event.

Emergency PA messages

I strongly recommend that you adopt a 'code' for emergency messages. Rather than alert troublemakers and unnecessarily scare members of the public with emergency messages such as 'All security staff to main arena to stop drunks fighting', use a code.

At an event where not all staff have radios, many events and venues broadcast messages to an invented person to pass emergency messages, e.g. your security staff will be briefed that any message for Winston Churchill is an emergency message for security staff. Thus the apparently normal message, 'Will Winston Churchill go to the main arena' has the same meaning and effect as the first message, without frightening the public.

Of course if there is an immediate danger, e.g. a tent on fire, broadcast the warning in plain language, to:

- clear the area of members of the public,
- ascertain from the tent staff if everybody is clear,
- make sure that the fire and rescue service has been called,
- take any safe action to prevent the spread of the fire, and
- begin clearing a route from the main gate to the seat of the fire to allow easy accesses for fire engines.

If you do select a name for an emergency message code, make it an obscure name – one day somebody will come to the event manager's office and say 'Hello, I'm Winston Churchill, who wants me?' You could decide on a message that uses no names, for example your emergency message might be, 'Message for the site plumber. Will the site plumber go to the main arena'!

More importantly, the member of staff operating the PA system should be aware of the emergency messages to avoid making innocent announcements from a real Mrs Churchill, who turns up asking for a message to be put out for her husband to meet her at the candy floss stall!

Electricity

Power for the event manager's office was covered in the first paragraph of this chapter, but you will almost certainly need an external power source to run a radio base station and PA system, though the rental companies also provide appropriate generators for an additional fee. Power will be needed for all event site lighting, offices and equipment, kettles and other catering equipment, etc.

Only professional electricians should undertake the connection of these electricity supplies. Also, whether you are required to or not by the local authority you should demand that any electrical equipment used on site, from the fair ground generator, to the event manager's kettle, should have a current certificate of electrical safety.

Water

Mains water

Depending on the services you are offering you may need a supply of mains water for catering outlets and toilets. If possible the catering outlets you use should operate from self-contained water supplies. You may also rent toilets that operate from a reservoir of water held within the equipment.

In your discussions with the fire and rescue service you should also establish the location of fire hydrants and stand pipes, so that you can ensure that during your planning process you leave them clear and available for effective use.

Drinking water

You are obliged to provide a clean source of drinking water that is signposted and easily available to everyone on site. I usually try to make drinking water available for animals as well, because even if no pet dogs are bought onto the site, you may have a guide dog or two that is thirsty. A simple plastic washing up bowl underneath the drinking water tap will provide drinking water for any dogs.

Telephones

At larger events, the event manager and cashier should have ready access to telephones. Though mobile phones would be sufficient, for larger events it could be worthwhile getting British Telecom in to advise on and arrange for a few payphones to be temporarily installed for public use.

I have never seen an event where there was not a long queue at the available payphones. As you can 'rent' them and set the call charge rate yourself, this is not just a convenience and service to the public; it pays for itself as well and, better still, may subsidise and pay for the event manager's and cashier's phones.

Give the telephone company sufficient warning. For simplicity and security the telephones should be located near the manager's office, but away from the cash office. (Don't give suspicious people an excuse to hang around near the cash office. Screen the office off if possible, and certainly keep crowds and queues away from it.)

Stalls

At the smallest of events, for example at school sport days, you will be expected to supply some sort of tables for the stalls. That is quite simple because you can use school tables.

On larger events the stalls are not your worry. You will supply the plot and it will be the responsibility of the stallholder to supply, erect, staff, protect and remove his or her own stall. There are some concerns that you will have to be aware of.

Safety

You have a responsibility for the safety of members of the public attending your event, staff, stallholders and members of the public passing by. The quality and style of their stalls may vary, from wallpaper pasting trestles, through scaffold planks and poles, to quite sophisticated custom-made enclosed and covered market stalls and tents. Your concern is that they are safe and will not injure members of the public or event staff, due to unsafe construction, use or materials.

Beware of dangers from stalls – for example:

- collapse/overloading,
- splinters,
- protrusions (eye, head, and knee collisions),
- trip hazard, (guy ropes, stabilisers etc),
- electric shock (via metal frames and bad wiring),

- cuts (sharp edges and ends).

Size

Depending on the type of event you are running, the size of a plot or stall may vary. For example, a steam fair may require a stallholder's plot to be large enough for a traction engine, a generator, a tent and three tables, while a school fête plot may be one small desk and a chair to sell raffle tickets.

You must ensure that you provide plots of the appropriate size for the stallholder's requirements.

Toilets

Where large numbers of people gather, they will want access to clean toilets, where and when they need them. Depending on your target audience you may also need to make provision for baby-changing and toilet access for the disabled or infirm. Without clean and available toilets, most members of the public will stay away and the few who come to your event will not stay long.

Rental/hire

There are commercial companies that supply temporary toilet units. These units range from trailers containing blocks of toilets with built-in cubicles, wash basins and towels, down to decidedly second- or third-hand single toilets. It is worth contacting a range of companies and asking for advice, while you shop around for availability and the best price.

Numbers

From your estimated crowd size, the company should be able to indicate how many toilets you will need and give you a firm delivery date and price. From your audience profile, you should be able to agree with the suppliers on the percentage of male or female toilets. If you require it, for an inclusive or additional fee, they will usually put an operative on site with a tanker. The operative will patrol and service the toilets, ensuring that all toilets remain clean and available for use. They are also responsible for ensuring that they are supplied with toilet paper and water for flushing and hand-washing etc.

Remember to allow enough room on the site for the sewage tanker to get in, drive around to collect waste matter and then leave the site.

Most single portable toilet units are unisex now, but reversible signs can be used to specifically assign them to either exclusive male or female use. Toilet trailers with multiple blocks can also be assigned for male or female use.

Location/distribution

Rather than make a 'toilet city' in one corner of the site, where possible arrange for blocks of toilets to be placed at convenient locations around the site. That is for the convenience of the public and stallholders, but also to be convenient for the servicing staff and vehicles.

Depending on the toilets supplied, your location choices may be restricted if they require mains water to operate properly. Remember that for all but the smallest event you will probably require separate toilets for the exclusive use of the event manager, police, first aid, cashier etc.

When to deliver them

Depending on the size of your event and when you are going to start setting up you may need some toilets in place a few days before the event opens. For a large event you should begin marking the site and setting up as much as a week before the event opens (see Chapter 30, 'Setting up'). If that is the case you may have staff, contractors and exhibitors on site anything up to a week before opening day, and they will need access to toilets.

Sometimes it has been convenient for the toilet hire company to deliver and set up all of the contracted toilets a week early at no extra charge, but usually I have arranged for a few toilets to be delivered at the beginning of the week. I usually arrange for the event manager's/cashier's toilet, the police and first aid toilet and one central cluster of toilets to be installed first – the agreement being that the contractor should deliver the bulk of the toilets the day before opening and also service those already on site so that they are clean and ready for opening day.

When to collect them

In my experience the contractors have been in no rush to give the toilets a final service and remove them. Depending on your strip down and clear up schedule you may want to negotiate for a few toilets to be available for use on the morning after closing day for the comfort of people present. You must make sure that your contract and agreement with the toilet suppliers includes their removal to a schedule that meets your and the site owner's requirements. It has been known for a busy toilet supplier to leave toilets on site for several days after an event, until it was convenient for the company to collect them.

Queuing

To avoid disputes and problems, you may wish to install simple rope walkways that form the public into single 'post office'-style toilet queues. In that way there is one queue and the next person in that queue gets the next available toilet. Using this method means that no unfortunate person will suffer discomfort, with their legs urgently crossed, because somebody in the toilet they happen to be waiting for has fallen asleep! If you use the single queue system, erect signs that say, 'Toilets – Single Queue Here'.

Private toilets

Remember – if possible, as a courtesy, provide separate appropriately located toilet(s) for the event manager, cashier, police and first aid staff.

Tip

If you are not going to pay the toilet suppliers to patrol to ensure that toilets are clean and usable, you must somehow arrange for a member of your event staff do the same job. They will not have the same skill, equipment, experience and enthusiasm, so consider this 'worthwhile' expense very, very carefully.

Waste disposal

You should make your contractor responsible for the emptying and removal of the toilets. On no account should contents be emptied into ditches, streams or other watercourses. The slurry should be disposed of properly at licensed sites, in accordance with the regulations.

Checkpoint

To check your decisions, hold a checkpoint review meeting where you present your selection of accommodation and services to a small group. Discuss the facts and the reasons behind those decisions. Note the responses, make any adjustment and finalise your accommodation and services plans.

Progress – Chapter 13
■■

You should now:

- (based on your event type, size, audience and attractions) know what accommodation you require,
- ensure that where accommodation is to be rented it is placed at a point convenient to you,
- ensure that key activities such as the event manager and cashier are supplied with appropriate and appropriately located accommodation,
- ensure that services such as electricity, water, possibly telephones and sewage mains are available,
- have contacted all relevant suppliers to ask for at least three quotes for the supply of appropriate accommodation and services, giving availability and delivery times,
- have made a checkpoint presentation and had your accommodation and services selection approved, to ensure that they are necessary and justifiable,
- be aware how important clean and available toilets are to the success of most events,
- have researched among the commercial toilet hire organisations to establish numbers, queuing and signs for your toilets,
- have requested quotes from at least three suppliers, inclusive of delivery, set up, on site attendant, collection and removal,
- have got the supplier to include availability and to state if they can supply your requirements for your proposed dates,
- have assured yourself that the favoured supplier will conform to all relevant legislation and that the company and their staff operate under their own risk assessed health and safety procedures,
- have assured yourself that the favoured supplier is covered by appropriate insurance, and
- have added the location and distribution of toilets to your site plan.

Product completed

- A list of required accommodation, equipment and services.
- Lists of known and proposed suppliers.
- Requested and received quotes and references from suppliers.
- A note of the requirements to define locations for the delivery and set up of accommodation, services and equipment.
- Checkpoint review – authorisation to continue.

14 Event site

Clearly the event site is of utmost importance, because almost all other event arrangements relate or link in to the site. This chapter attempts to highlight the considerations and requirements specific to the site and the impact the site may have on other decisions and arrangements.

Site safety

Your site must be inherently safe. Chapter 5 'Health and safety' has illustrated the depth of attention you must pay to the health, safety and welfare of everyone affected by your event. At all stages for all aspects of your event planning and preparation you must consider health and safety first.

As an example, when looking at an appropriate site, no matter how convenient and ideal it may be, if the only access point is on a sharp, blind bend, or over the brow of a hump back bridge, use of the access gate may be so inherently dangerous that permissions to use the site may not be given. Don't despair, though. In exactly these circumstances, I know of one event manager who discussed the problem with the site owner and the local authority and they agreed to share the cost of moving the access gate to a safer location, after which the event was allowed to run. Your goal must be safety, but you are not alone in trying to achieve this; the authorities will help where they can. But they won't do the work for you!

Site size

You have to know how big a site you need in order to accommodate your event, and if you have been conscientiously investigating, researching and recording, you should now be able to estimate that with little more than some simple arithmetic.

- *Attractions* – You know the attractions you want to book (for example a fun fair). You need to work out the approximate area taken up by each attraction and then calculate the total area needed to accommodate them all. Add 30% to the calculated total, to include contingency and required fire gaps and spaces. This gives you Total A.
- *Stalls/plots* – You should have a feel for the number of stalls or plots that you will be able to sell, more simple arithmetic gives you the area total stall/plot size required. Add 30% to calculated total, as above. This gives you Total B.
- *Display/arena* – You know what arena or display space is needed. In some circumstances this will be strictly defined. For example you might need at least three football pitches for your knockout tournament finals. If your event is a steam show you will need an arena, or if it is a model aircraft show you will need runways. If it is a half-marathon you will need an acceptable and safe route but there will be a start/finish area, with marshals, timing equipment, staff, first aid, areas for clothes and equipment to be left and of course refreshments etc. Whatever your event, you should be able to calculate any 'display or activity' area that is needed and allow enough space for the public to stand or sit to watch those displays. Add 30% contingency and audience space. This gives you Total C.
- *Services* – You know the management and facilities accommodation required, event manager's office, cashier's office, cash collection vehicles turning and parking area, toilets, first aid, police post etc, so you can derive a total area required for that. Add 30% for contingency and required fire gaps and spaces. This gives you Total D.
- *Access* – Your site will also require access lanes wide enough to accommodate the emergency services and to allow the free flow and circulation of your visitors. I try to draft a sketch plan of the proposed site to roughly draw in access lanes and paths to calculate this. As early as possible when talking to the police and fire service, I have my sketch of the site plan available, to check that my ideas will be acceptable after further and more accurate drawings and discussions. Calculate the width and length of access lanes required. This gives you Total E.
- *Estimated site size* – Now add Totals A, B, C, D and E. This is your estimated absolute *minimum* event site size (excluding visitor car parking space).

Make sure that you are not double counting, for example including a set of displays under 'attractions' and 'stalls', so counting them twice. There is also a chance that you could undercount, by assuming that traction engines for example were only to be counted in the display/arena space when, although they will be displayed in the arena, they will need 'attractions' space as well.

As a checkpoint, I suggest that you should get your cashier to separately estimate the size of site that you will require. When the cashier has done that, compare your results and talk them through. Hopefully they will be fairly close. If not, work out why and correct your estimate.

This estimation method is only a guide, based on experience and relating to 'normal' events. Your event may have unique characteristics that you will need to take into consideration in estimating and then refining the size of site required. For example, if your model aircraft show will include radio-controlled model jet aircraft, you might need to guarantee a space of at least 30 metres between members of the public and the flight line for those jets.

Even when you have arrived at a first estimate of the site size, you must continually review it, as you confirm and refine your arrangements. For example, people buying pre-paid tickets may demand that you include a 'Grand Parade', where all steam engines on site enter the arena, allowing fans to photograph them in action. The arena will now have to be much larger than you had planned, so you will have to recalculate the site space required. Another example might be where your half-marathon has been asked to introduce a wheelchair class, so you will have to recalculate the site space required (due to a considerable increase in disabled parking at the start/finish).

Car parking space

The calculations above indicate the size of the actual central event, including the arena and facilities. You also need to know how much space you will need to park vehicles.

Vehicles will belong to three groups: staff, exhibitors and the public. You will have to make arrangements for sufficient space for them to park safely and within reach of the central event site. (See below for advice on how to calculate the parking space needed for a given number of cars.)

Staff

You have an idea of the number of people you will require to manage and run the event, so you can calculate how much space you will need for their car park. Remember that, depending on the layout of your site, this car parking area may also be used for disabled parking, judges, a celebrity guest opening the event, first aid, police and any other requirements such as a vet.

Exhibitors

You have an idea of the number of exhibitors and the attractions attending your event. This may be a football or hockey team in their team minibus or coach, plus equipment vans, bands and any other supporters they require. Some exhibitors will arrive in a large truck containing their stalls, tents, goods and materials, where the truck will be unloaded on the event site and then driven off and parked elsewhere. For some exhibitors, such as a mobile steam organ, the vehicle might be their transport and their exhibit, so they will have to park up and remain on the event site.

When booking attractions, you will have to ask for confirmation of their transport arrangements and ensure that your arrangements will be adequate.

The public

From your audience profile, you should have an idea of the number of people who will attend your event and how many of them will arrive by car or coaches etc. All you have to do then is to calculate the amount of space required to park the vehicles you expect to arrive.

Calculations

You can either work out how many cars you will fit into a field you have been offered, or you can work out the space needed to park the number of cars you have estimated will attend. The mathematics is similar and simple. All you need is a baseline and surprisingly you can get that at your local supermarket!

The supermarket system

As a courtesy I suggest you explain what you want to do and ask permission from the supermarket manager or security staff before you start. Depending on how busy the car park is, you may also wish to seek permission to come back when the store is closed so you can safely work in an empty car park to avoid being run over by a speeding shopper.

- *Select an area* – Select an area of the car park that is just used for parking; that is, it shouldn't contain large trolley parks or gardens. Select a section that includes several lanes of cars and access roads and is of a suitable size. The size is important because it must be appropriate to your proposed event. If your event will only attract 100 people you are wasting your time if you count and measure the car parking space at a major out-of-town shopping complex. On the other hand, if you are expecting 5000 people at your steam fair, counting 25 cars in the pub car park will not give you an accurate baseline.

- *Remember the size* – To help you cross-check your calculations later, you should visualise and pick an area with which you are familiar. For example it may be an area the same size as your school playground, or twice the size of the green in front of your house, or the size of a football pitch. Keep this in mind for the cross-check later.

- *Measure the area* – You have to measure the area you have selected, and it will be easier and safer if you measure it when the car park is closed or early enough to find a remote, unused area. You will not be able to measure easily or accurately if you only have a 3-metre DIY tape measure or hope to pace out and estimate the distance. I would prepare a 50-metre length of string or rope, measure it and mark it in advance using a felt-tip marker pen or sticky tape. I place a black band every metre and a red band every 10 metres. With an assistant it is then easy to get them to hold one end, while you pull the string taught to the 50-metre mark. If you want to measure 100 metres, you can get your assistant to stand at a corner of the car park while you walk to 50 metres, stretching your measuring rope, then stop. Your assistant then overtakes and walks past you to the 100-metre point, thus marking an area either 50 metres by 50 metres or 100 metres x 100 metres, or 27 metres x 34 metres etc.

- *Count the spaces* – When you have selected and measured your area of the super-market car park, you must count the number of marked car parking spaces in that area. Remember that cars using your car park will have to get into and out of your car parking spaces, so you must also include turning places and roads between the rows of parked cars in your calculation of the number of cars that can be fitted into a given area. Tracks in a marked car park are usually about one and a half to two car-lengths wide, which gives facing rows of cars enough space to manoeuvre into and out of individual parking spaces. Check the width of tracks and roads in your car park.

- *Lost space* – In an unmarked field used as a car park, because the access lanes tend to be wider and there are no marked bays, drivers tend to park further apart than they have to in supermarket car parks. You must also accept that there are always areas of a field that cannot be used, because they are uneven, steeply sloped, marshy etc., so you will lose space. Generally in an unmarked field you will park a maximum of 75% of the number of cars that could park in an equivalent marked car park area. To emphasise and confirm that point, assuming the supermarket car park is all car parking and no fancy gardens, where the supermarket fits 100 cars in a given space, you will probably only fit about 75 cars in an equivalent unmarked area of a field. Using experienced marshals may improve this, but using inexperienced marshals or insufficient numbers of marshals will reduce the number of cars you will be able to park in a given space even further.

- *Calculate* – Calculating your parking requirements is now a case of simple mathematics. If your selected supermarket area contained 100 cars and your proposed car parking field is 5 times that size the sums are:

  Supermarket marked area = 100 cars

  Field area = 5 times supermarket area

  = Field is 5 × 100 = 500 cars

  At 75% utilisation = 500 × 75% field = 375 cars

- *Cross-check* – In the instructions above I asked you to remember the size of your selected area and to fix it in your mind by comparing it with an equivalent area with which you were familiar. We can use that and a different approach to the calculations to cross-check our calculated vehicle total.

If for example the selected car park area that you visualised and remembered was the same size as your school playground, you can stand in the field you are thinking of using as a car park and look around. From your memory and looking at the field you make an estimate of the size of the proposed car park field compared to your visualised area. In this example we think that the proposed field is about four or five times the size of the school playground.

If the field is four times the size of your visualised area, you know that in your visualised area you will fit 100 cars, the field could therefore fit 400 cars. If the field were five times the size, it would fit 500 cars. Split the difference and call it a maximum of 450 cars.

We know we will lose 25% of the space when drivers park further apart than marked car parking spaces would allow, and we do not use spaces next to a barbed wire fence etc., so using mental arithmetic we calculate that one quarter of 450 is about 110 cars. From the 450 maximum, subtract that lost 25% of 110 cars, giving us a total of 340 cars.

Our cross-check gives us a total that is sufficiently close to our original estimate that it confirms the number. Round it off, with good car parking marshals we will park at least 350 cars in that field.

You can practice your estimating ability quite easily. Do your baseline visit and count at the local supermarket, so that you have that area in mind and the number of vehicles it will accommodate. When you have that feel for space and numbers try it out. For example view your office car park, or the local cinema car park. How does it compare to your notional space? Same size? Twice or three times as big? When you arrive at a decision, do the mental arithmetic to calculate how many cars you think are parked there and then count up to check. With some practice, you will even be able to make an accurate estimate by allowing for trolley parks, gardens and other obstructions. Extend your estimating to larger car parks like hypermarkets, but don't bother counting – just ask a security man or car park attendant how many car parking spaces there are – they should be able to tell you. As you practice and refine this skill your accuracy will improve, until you can look at a field and fairly accurately say how many cars you would be able to park in that space.

Traffic patterns

Note that some events will also have to cope with traffic patterns. For example I have attended a large dog show, run over a Saturday and Sunday, where heats are held during the day for different breeds, culminating in a best-of-show competition before closing on the final day. The result was that though 9000 people attended, there were rarely more than 2000 on site at any one time. Competitors arrived for the heats in a steady trickle through the day and departed if they were knocked out. Usually only winners stayed for further knockout heats. Those on site at the close of the day all left at closing time so there was a peak departure at closing time, but through the day there was a steady flow of arrivals and departures.

Unique

Always remember that your event is unique! I was caught out once when I was asked to calculate the required car parking space for 'an event'. I hadn't been told and didn't ask what the event was. I simply estimated the space required for a given number of cars to park. Unfortunately the event happened to be a grounds staff exhibition; everybody arrived in large vans or trucks, consuming my car park and the overflow parking in a twinkle. Nifty footwork and a friendly farmer opening a new car parking field and another lesson was learned. Know the event and know if visitors will arrive in little neat saloon cars, or huge trucks and vans!

Choosing your fields

The site must be large enough to accommodate the number of people and attractions you are expecting, with sufficient additional space for pathways, emergency vehicle access, offices, tents, on site parking and storage. From my experience, *if space looks tight on a plan, it will cause you major problems on the ground*. On the other hand, if you have any extra space you will *always* use it.

Keep in mind that with events, you usually rent space in terms of 'fields' rather than square metres or hectares. It is therefore important to calculate the space you require, and then find a field or fields that meet or, better still, more than meet those requirements.

You must also keep in mind that there is a difference between total area of a given site and the usable area of that site. Odd-shaped fields, slopes, swampy areas, areas inside and around gates and other access points, ponds and slopes are problems you will have to contend with. Though on paper an odd-shaped field may have the total space required, the shape may prevent you from making efficient use of some areas. Similarly, any areas that slope or are muddy or uneven will have limited use, which will reduce the amount of space that is available to you.

Your site inspections should allow you to measure and calculate the available area, excluding slopes, swamps, ponds, etc. You should be viewing and imagining the field as whatever use you have in mind for it – either event site or car park. Imagine the main gate and offices there, the fun fair in the far corner (taking the noise and nuisance away from the houses), steam engine display area there, arena on the central flat area, etc. You should be able to build a fairly clear mental picture of an initial site plan, as well as gauging the suitability of the site and the usable space available to you. A huge area covered in prickly gorse bushes or brambles, or the steeply sloping side of a hill would be of little use, no matter how cheap or convenient the location. It also almost certainly needs to have electricity, water and possibly sewage connections available.

Site location

The location of your event site is very important. It must be near enough to allow you to make constant visits during planning and preparation and it must be near enough to a centre of population from which you can draw the public to attend your event.

The largest, most luxuriously accommodated site is useless if you and the public have to travel the length of the country to reach it and then trek across five miles of bog to get onto it. The public will go a long way for a good event, but there is a limit to the time and money they will invest in reaching a distant event, no matter how good it promises to be.

Remember that the further away the event site is, the greater the logistical problems become and the wider the area you will need to cover with your advertising.

Road, rail and bus access

The attractions, supplies, tents, equipment and the public all have to reach the site. More than that, the majority of them have to reach and then leave the site at nearly the same time on the same day(s). That means that roads access and public transport serving your proposed site must be good.

Preferably the site will be served by inter-linking road, rail and bus services, so that no groups of the public are excluded from access. Such a site is rare, but you must try to get the best site you can. It may be worth including details of the easy and inexpensive access to your site in your advertising, or even paying a local coach company to run a park and ride service to the event, if that is viable or beneficial.

Depending on the location of your site and the audience you are expecting, it might be also be worthwhile to include simple outline maps on tickets and posters showing the best access routes!

Tip

If large numbers of people are likely to use public transport to reach your event, you should discuss it with the local bus and train companies. They may wish to lay on extra services, warn bus drivers of delays and route changes, or even offer discounted pre-sales event and travel tickets to their own passengers in a deal with you – and that could involve them advertising your event as well.

Secure perimeter

Many sites will need a secure perimeter, as without one, members of the public will be able to gain access free of charge. By giving free access, but putting a small surcharge on all sales and activities on site you can overcome this problem, but there is no substitute for a stout fence or hedge and an entry fee.

When negotiating with the landowner for a site, pay attention to the boundaries. For example a farmer may offer one field to you, with good secure, dense hedges on three sides, but open to another field on the remaining side. During negotiations, point out the access problems you will have with the open side of the field. Don't make problems for yourself, by planning to rent the field and then pay for the erection of a temporary fence. If the adjacent field has good solid fences and hedges, make use of it and simply negotiate to use *both fields* as the event site, taking advantage of the existing natural secure boundary hedges. This will leave you with a more than adequate area (if you did your sums right) with the benefit of an existing secure boundary. Though it may strictly speaking be larger than you originally required, the benefits outweigh the costs.

While checking the size and condition of the site and boundary, make sure that you also check for and consider access points. Having a strong, prickly hedge backed with chain link fence is wonderful, as long as there are sufficient gates at the right points to allow access by the public, exhibitors, deliveries and service trucks.

Tip

A secure or easily secured boundary, is one of the most important attributes a potential site can have. Assuming the price is acceptable rent an area larger than you really need, if there is a secure boundary around it.

Negotiations

When viewing a site for the first time and even during negotiations you must keep your event type and programme in mind. For example if the site has no secure perimeter, you will need to spend considerable sums of money to pay somebody to erect a temporary fence. For that reason, the amount you can afford to pay to rent that field is greatly reduced.

Once you have found the site you will have to negotiate for the use of it, which will probably involve payment of a fee. During negotiations, establish what responsibilities the landowner is placing on you. Remember that some sites may not be suitable for your event. It is likely that the site owner will demand that the site is clean and tidy when the land is handed back. Some landowners demand a deposit that is returned if the site is clean when the event is over, or used to clear the site if it is not.

The landowner may insist that you agree to repair all damage to turf, fences and hedges after the event. If this is specified, you will have to inspect them to establish the existing condition, which must be accurately recorded and agreed.

I propose that you should walk the boundary inside and out and record it on videotape, to preserve an accurate record of the existing state. If you do so, try to walk with the landowner or their representative and include them and their voice on the inspection videotape, as additional proof that it was filmed during the initial inspection.

After the event, another inspection must be made to agree on any damage, for which the landowner claims you are liable. You must agree what action is necessary to make acceptable repairs and how and when it will be done.

All of this could subject you to considerable unknown costs and could easily consume all of your profits and more, if for example a hedge has been set on fire and needs to be replaced.

If not offered, suggest to the landowner that you make an inspection and lodge a returnable repair deposit with him. The deposit will cover any potential damage 'for example ruts in the grass from delivery trucks, broken branches, or a spillage of cooking oil' – ensuring that the cost of any damage repair is limited to that deposit.

During the event ensure that all staff are on the alert for damage being caused by whatever means and that actions causing damage are halted immediately.

The ideal site

If there was an ideal site it would probably:

- be a large, flat, level, dry, firm, field – providing an ideal event ground,
- be located near and equi-distance from several large towns – providing a huge potential audience,
- be located at a point where two or more motorways meet – providing superb, fast access, to high volume traffic and a high-profile motorway junction or intersection landmark for the public to find the site,
- be on several main bus routes – for people attending by bus,
- be a short walk from a main line railway station – for people coming by train,
- have a high fence, backed by a thick, prickly hedge – providing a secure boundary,
- have three huge, good quality, flat, dry, level fields nearby all owned by the same landowner, with gates on both sides – providing ample car parking and a ready-made entrance and exit route, and all having access and exits to different main roads (for ease of traffic arrival and departure),
- have a large tarmac car park – providing parking for heavy trucks and caravans,
- have a farm building and an electricity sub station, which could supply mains power and water – providing simple access to both, and
- have a farm building that could be used for the event manager and cashier – providing a manager's and cash office.

But, there aren't many like that around!

The above ideal site would be perfect for most standard events and shows. If your event is unusual, for example that 'Xmas Reindeer Rodeo', or a shooting competition, you may benefit from taking a little time to amend or add to the above list to define the perfect site for your event. This will concentrate your mind on the key attributes that you must have in your site.

Accommodation

Tents/buildings

Accommodation requirements will vary, depending on event size, type and time of year. In Chapter 13 'Accommodation and services', we cover some standard requirements such as an event manager's office and a cash office. It is possible that depending on the site these offices can be located in existing buildings. For larger events, if existing buildings are not used for key services, sturdy Portakabins™ or mobile huts should be used for security reasons.

Almost every other requirement can be met by using tents where required. Some sporting shows and events such as a steam show, or car rally, where the attractions are exhibited outside, moving around the site or parked in exhibition enclosures, will probably only require minimal accommodation.

Whatever the decision, remember that tents and Portakabins™ are quite expensive and should only be used where necessary and where the cost can be justified.

Fire regulations

Seek advice regarding the layout of the site and proximity of tents, buildings, sheds, stores, etc. I am not qualified to give fire and safety advice. You *must* seek the advice of the local fire and rescue services.

As an example of the complexity, the following advice was taken from a discussion with local fire and rescue service staff, discussing a specific event. It is listed below as *an illustration only*. These points merely indicate the considerations and requirements you will have to meet.

- The fire and rescue services had to be supplied with a site map, highlighting all access and exit routes, water tanks and ponds, fire hydrants, generators and stationary vehicles.
- Fuel supplies had to be highlighted.
- Access had to be made for fire and rescue vehicles and equipment to be able to drive to within a maximum of 50 metres of any structure, store, tent, shed, cabin, building or display etc.
- Where stalls or similar displays were constructed in rows, any one row was not

allowed to exceed 45 metres in length. In each 45 metre row there had to be a minimum of two gaps, each gap being at least 2 metres wide.

- There had to be a clear space of a minimum of 5 metres between any rows of stalls.
- There had to be a clear space of a minimum of 6 metres between 'structures' such as buildings, caravans and Portakabins.
- All grass and vegetation around structures such as buildings, stationary caravans and trailers etc. had to be cut and the dead grass cleared away and removed from the site.
- All access routes had to be a minimum of 4 metres wide with a minimum head-room of 5 metres and able to take a loading of 12.5 tonnes in weight.
- All tent fabric had to meet appropriate British Standards in being flame retardant. (Note – a certificate of compliance had to requested from the tent rental company before permissions and licences were issued.)
- No accommodation was to have dead ends – that is, any areas from which exits were not immediately available.
- In all structures with multiple exits, the distance from any point to an exit had to be no more than 18 metres.
- Structures designed to house or attract more than 15 people had to have no fewer than 2 exits and still comply with the no dead-end and distance-to-an-exit rules.
- All exits had to be at least 1.1 metres wide.
- Where a structure was designed to house or attract 50 people or more, internal layout and use plans had to be submitted to the fire authorities for approval.
- All exits had to be marked with appropriate fire exit signs, conforming to require-ments.
- Where the exit was fitted with a door, the doors had to open outwards and be operated by a panic bar with the sign 'push bar to open'.
- Where the exit was fitted with tent flaps, the flaps had to be folded back and tied back in the 'open' position during opening hours.
- Provision had to be made for disabled people.
- Suitable fire extinguishers had to be made available (up to 15 people one extin-guisher, larger structures at least two extinguishers for every 200 square metres of floor space and sited so that nobody was more than 30 metres from an extin-guisher).
- Common sense rules also applied, such as smoking bans, storage of flammable liquids, rubbish accumulation, dry grass and brush, displays with naked flames, gas bottles, etc.

Remember, these points are only an illustration of the complexity and rules that may be imposed on your event. Also remember that they are imposed to protect life, *not*   **107** merely to annoy you. These points are included to illustrate the considerations and complexity of requirements, you must seek advice from your local authorities, fire and rescue and police services in relation to your own unique show or event.

Tip

Fire is a major hazard and must be the subject of serious consideration and planning. Seek out and take the advice of your local fire service and local authority.

Race start/finish

Where an event site is the start/finish point for a marathon or other race, additional considerations come into play. The site must be positioned at a place where the surrounding roads, pathways and tracks will be available and accepted as the route for the race.

Your site plan will have to allow for the safe departure of runners or cyclists at a mass start and be available for an extended period as an access point on return to the site. The finishers will be stretched out as competitors attain different paces due to different levels of fitness and different ages and abilities.

It is likely that vehicles, such as those listed below, will be included in the race order:

- pace car,
- timing car displaying time elapsed since the start,
- draft-buster motorcycles (for a cycle race),
- mobile judges and stewards,
- first aid patrols,
- marshals transport.

Your arrangements at the entrance and exit gates will then have to include vehicle *and* competitor access, *which introduces risks!* You will have had to risk assess the hazards and have designed a process that will easily and safely separate competitors from returning judges, stewards and first aid patrols, while still maintaining crowd safety at the gates.

There are also implications for sign posting (Chapter 16), permissions (Chapter 17), radio communications (Chapter 19), staffing (Chapter 20), and emergency and normal procedures (Chapter 24).

Site layout/planning

The layout of the site is important. For one thing you want to arrange the stalls etc. so that the public are drawn into the middle of the event site and then encouraged and allowed to circulate freely. The layout of stalls and access paths must meet the regulations imposed by the fire and rescue service. It should also be wide enough to allow cars and trucks through during set up and strip down, as well as allowing free circulation of the crowds attending when the gates are open to the public.

If any stalls are running displays, remember that crowds will tend to gather in front of those stalls to watch the displays. The access paths will therefore need to be wide enough to allow the public to circulate around and past any crowd that does gather to watch a display.

Similarly, any central arena space will have to include areas for members of the public to gather to watch the events in the arena while still allowing for free movement around the site.

Draw up a scale plan of the site and discuss the proposed layout with stallholders, local authority, first aid staff, the police and fire and rescue staff etc. Make sure that everyone is in general agreement with the design/plan.

Tip

When planning a site, in the first instance, I use a large-scale site plan and trimmed to scale Post-it® notes, representing stalls, offices, etc. Though it takes some time, this method allows a first cut site plan to be arrived at quite easily and quickly. Post-it® notes representing displays, Portakabins™, offices and stalls can easily be moved around the site plan and pencil lines representing arenas and roads can be re-drawn until you arrive at a plan that is approved by the authorities and will work.

Stalls/plots

A key consideration is the size of the stalls/plots that you are going to supply to stall   **109** holders. The size they require will vary depending on their purpose and the type of event you are running. While a school fête will require most stalls to be the size of one or two school tables, at a steam show a stall will almost certainly be considerably larger.

An autojumble stallholder may well require sufficient space to lay out and display a lorry full of car parts and spares. They may also wish to keep their lorry on their plot to act as a base of operations, shelter and store for more valuable or fragile items.

You may wish to consider 'selling' different size plots to stallholders at your event, with sizes ranging from 3 × 3 metres, up to 6 × 12 metres. You could then allow stallholders to state their requirements and lease them the plot(s) that meet their requirements. It is possible that a stall holder will want to 'buy' two adjacent small plots or possibly a small and a large plot side by side, to accommodate their goods and displays.

Another option often used for travelling funfairs is that they are assigned a designated measured area of an event site and set themselves up in the space allocated.

Tip

Remember that varying stall and plot sizes and configurations will make your site layout and planning task a little harder. However the use of a scale plan of a reasonable size and Post-it® notes cut to represent different stall/plot sizes will allow you to juggle plots to fit, while maintaining stated goals relating to co-location (vintage car classes = blue Post-it® notes) and separation (animals and food stalls = orange and yellow Post-it® notes respectively) etc. The more sophisticated you get, the more work you have to do, but potentially the higher the rewards will be.

Emergency access

However you design the access paths, gates and layout of the stalls, make sure that there is sufficient space to allow emergency service vehicles to reach every part of the event ground. If they are needed, they are needed in a hurry and nobody wants to stand around and wait while a cattle pen or burger stall is dismantled, before they can pass through.

Make sure that a burger bar, for example, does not rent a 10 ft x 10 ft plot and then use the whole access path to set out picnic chairs and tables for the use of their customers. If they want an area of tables and chairs, that should be included in their plot and they must rent sufficient space to do so.

Early consultation with the local fire and rescue service and the licensing authorities will be to the advantage of everyone involved, will reduce your workload and eliminate a host of potential problems.

Stalls, attractions and displays

Consideration should also be given to the grouping and location of stalls, attractions and displays. If there is an arena for the display of steam engines for example, it is sensible that the parking area for the steam engines is located near to the arena, or at least with free access to the arena. You don't want to accept the increased dangers involved with steam engines travelling the whole length of the site, weaving in and out of the stalls to get into and out of the display arena. (You almost certainly wouldn't be allowed to do that anyway.) Some displays may hold inherent dangers, such as the boiler fires and hot steam in steam engines.

In other displays, restricted access may be required for another reason. For example with highly polished and expensively restored vintage cars, the owners will not want the public to be climbing all over their display vehicles, so you must give consideration to erecting fences around displays, to exclude the public and where necessary provide marshals to keep the public out.

You may wish to consider grouping certain types of stalls, or putting all rides in one location. On a larger site, this will help the public to orient themselves, so that they can locate those things that are of particular interest to them.

An outline site map on the programme or ticket will also help, or you could sell a site map to the public for say 50 pence – proceeds minus costs to a local charity.

Food outlets need water, power, food stores and waste-food bins, so it could be argued that they could all be located together in one area of the site. However, owners of burger and ice-cream vans would probably prefer to be scattered throughout the site. That would have multiple benefits for them. They can spread their enticing aroma over the whole event and hopefully entice the public to 'browse' their way around the site, from burger van, to beer tent, to ice-cream van, to cold drink stall. Wherever they are the pubic will have access to fast food. Being located individually, the stallholders also have less immediate competition.

For obvious reasons a food outlet would almost certainly not want to be placed next to the dung heap from an animal event. Similarly, a choir would not want to be located next to a very noisy fair ground ride, or loud generator engine.

Though you won't be able to please everyone, at the planning stage you can make sure that simple mistakes are not made. Remember that during the planning stage, it is really easy to rub out a section of the plan and redraw several stalls. It is a **111** different matter if you find you got it wrong when the event is open and the sewage tanker can't get through so you have to move a burger bar and dog grooming studio or leave the toilets to flood!

Central offices

Remember that both the event manager's office and the cash office need to be in a fairly central location to make them conveniently available to everyone. You must ensure that vehicles can gain easy access to the cash office for cash distribution, delivery and collection. You must also remember to allow sufficient space for cash collection vehicles to enter, turn and leave safely and easily.

Because of the need for vehicular access, these offices are probably best located near a main vehicle entrance. Your walk through, on the draft site plan, will highlight problems with your planned location.

The first aid station also needs to be conveniently located in a fairly central location to make it easily available to everyone and if possible near a visually identifiable landmark on site, so it is easy for members of the public to find it. There is a possibility that serious casualties may need to be removed in an ambulance. To facilitate this, the first aid point should also be located near a vehicle access point, with sufficient space to allow ambulances to enter, turn and leave safely, with easy and potentially fast access to the main road.

Emergency helipad

If your event involves potentially risky pursuits, such as car racing, motorcycle racing, horse-riding etc, you may wish to consider setting aside a secure area for helicopter evacuation of seriously injured casualties. Consult the local health authority, fire service, police and air ambulance organisations for advice on the size and location of such an emergency helipad.

You must also make sure that appropriate information is available to the crew – such as longitude and latitude, landmarks (such as a motorway junction) and nearby risks (such as radio masts or power lines). The helipad itself should also be clearly marked to help the crew find it in an emergency from 600 metres.

Remember that the helipad will have to be staffed to keep it clear for use and to protect the helicopter and equipment from nosy and possibly 'souvenir collecting' visits while the crew are working on the casualty.

Police control room and parking

If there is a police presence on the event ground, they will probably require a site where they can locate (or you can supply) a temporary control room. Depending on the size of the event and the police presence on site, this room may need to have power and water supplies connected. As mentioned elsewhere as a courtesy you should try to provide separate toilet facilities for police officers, near their control room (or possibly shared with the event manager's and cash offices).

The police will also require parking for a number of vehicles, such as crew buses, patrol cars and the vans and any trailers used to distribute and collect signs and no parking cones. (Check with the police liaison officer to agree how much if any parking is required.)

The police control room should be located near a road gate to allow quick and easy access to police vehicles. If the police control room is located near the event manager's and cash offices, you gain multiple benefits, including increased security and a simplification of the power supply to the services that need it.

Tip

Once you have arrived at a first-cut site plan, walk through the scheduled show events, from first arrival to final clean-up, to see if the site layout proves problematic. By physically following through your proposed schedule on the draft site plan, you will discover things you may not have considered. For example, did you place the model aircraft runway under overhead power lines? Does the proposed plan expect traction engines to cross a narrow pedestrian bridge to get from the static display area to the arena? Do vehicle access gates require motorists to drive through queues of pedestrians waiting to get in? This sort of problem becomes clearer if you walk through the programme with a draft site layout and allows you to refine and finalise your site plan.

Vehicle-free zone

Once all of the stalls and displays have been set up, declare the event site a vehicle-free zone. There will be children around, and remember that even adults don't always look where they are going when they are deep in conversation and fascinated by the wonderful event you have arranged. Before the gates open to the public, remove all vehicles and ban vehicle movement on the event site.

With emergency services and necessary vehicles such as cash security vans and sewage tankers serving portable toilets etc, you may have to allow access. If so drivers should be instructed to keep to walking pace, have their hazard warning lights and other lights on and may even have to be escorted by a spotter to help the driver negotiate the crowds – especially when reversing.

Tip

If you only impose one rule on your event site, *make it a vehicle-free zone.* Pay particular attention to enforcement of that rule at opening and closing times, which are the times when stallholders are likely to want to be on site late or early to erect or strip down their stalls.

Progress – Chapter 14

You should now:

- be aware of the importance of the site size, location, suitability, convenience, accommodation, availability of services and transport links,
- be aware of the critical importance of a secure perimeter for most events,
- be aware of the importance of your inspections and negotiations for site use,
- have in mind the event schedule and be considering the planning of your event site before completing negotiations,
- be aware of the need for different stalls and plots, access paths, display arenas and static parking,
- be aware of the need to group or otherwise arrange some stalls and plots,
- recognise the need to estimate the size of site you need to accommodate the event you are proposing to deliver,
- keep in mind emergency access routes, widths and headroom,
- be aware of the attributes for the ideal site for your event,
- be aware of the accommodation requirements for offices, for the event manager, cashier, first aid, police liaison etc,
- have completed a successful walk-through of your event programme on your proposed site and plan,
- have located an appropriate site and begun discussions with the landowner.

Product completed

- Site selected with suitable car parking space.
- Site address, size, services, map reference etc. listed.
- Schedule of site transport links and expected event traffic patterns.
- Schedule of proposed accommodation and services with reference to proposed site map.
- Proposed site and car parking plans and maps.
- Proposed emergency exit and access points and routes.
- Health and safety review of site and proposed use, list of any known hazards and proposed control measures, list of vehicle-free zone times.
- Note proposed on-site sign schedule (see Chapter 16, 'Sign posting').
- Listing of event manager's, first aid, police post, and other offices and services such as public and private toilets.
- Report showing estimated attendance, number of cars expected, car parking calculations and arrangements.

15 Traffic management

If you have never managed the flow of traffic, you could be in for a shock. Sitting in their cars, most drivers are very critical of the arrangements for getting large numbers of vehicles into and out of a site. Most assume that they could easily do better. Think again. It is a major headache and takes considerable skill, co-ordination and effort. If it is to work, it also requires the co-operation of drivers, or at least an acceptable level of common sense and intelligence on behalf of your average car driver. (No – don't laugh, some drivers are quite clever – almost human really!)

Traffic manager

The importance of traffic management cannot be over emphasised. For all but the very smallest events, the event manager should give serious consideration to appointing a traffic manager at deputy event manager level. The traffic manager will be tasked to concentrate on planning the safe and timely arrival, parking, security and departure of vehicular traffic, in close co-operation with the local police and other authorities.

If this aspect of the event goes well, the event will go well. To highlight the dangers vehicles present, I make a point of telling everyone involved that my watchword is, 'Cars *live* on the road, people *die* on the road.'

Numbers attending

At the planning stage you will have estimated the numbers of people attending the event and you will know how they will arrive. If they are all coming by train or on foot there is little problem, but the likelihood is that most of them will be arriving by car. They will require help in finding the site and getting parked, after which they will need help getting out of the site and finding the road home.

Contigency plans

While the estimate of the number of people who are attending is quite critical, unforeseen circumstances, such as the cancellation of a neighbouring major sporting event, or a particularly clear and sunny late autumn afternoon can as much as double attendance.

The organisers must make allowance for greater numbers than originally planned for, by arranging for overflow car parks (with appropriate signs available), or be prepared to shut the event gates and see all those angry motorists and the lost revenue drive off along clogged roads.

The traffic manager must know what is going to happen if it rains and the car park field is flooded. They must know if the landowner is likely to ban you from using the fields because the fields are soft due to heavy rain and he doesn't want them cut up by heavy use. What happens if the main car park site is unavailable because there has been a fire at the farm? Try to cover all eventualities and make sure that your contingency plans will still allow the event to continue under most circumstances. (For more information on contingency planning, see Chapter 24, 'Emergency and normal procedures'.)

Emergency access route

The size and type of event is an important consideration when deciding on specific, dedicated emergency routes. For large events, if there is the likelihood of significant or critical injury such as in some sporting events, or drug-taking and physical collapse as in some types of pop concerts, just as you have considered introducing an emergency medical helipad, you should consider introducing an emergency access route.

If required, the emergency access route *should only be used* for the arrival and departure of emergency services vehicles. Consultation with fire, police, ambulance and local authorities will help you to decide if this is necessary and if so, what the route should be. It should allow the quickest and easiest access to the main road network. It should be clearly signposted. And above all, it should be manned and available at all times. For example the emergency access route may bring fire police or ambulances from the bypass, along a private farm lane, in through the farmyard and directly into the site, with signs showing them how to enter by 'Main Gate', 'North Gate' or 'Arena Gate'.

Approach routes

The cost of arranging for approach signs may be justifiable for major events. For example motorists coming from outside the local area may know the approximate position of the event ground, but will need help in finding the right gates. Indeed, to the traffic manager, it is beneficial if they simply follow the routes laid out. If all coaches use one particular car park and approach along one particular route they can be catered for. If it is a free-for-all, chaos reigns, car parking will be disorganised and space will be wasted as tempers wear thin.

Signs such as these could be invaluable:

- 'Coaches Next Right'
- 'Disabled Parking (Badge Holders Only) Turn Left'
- 'All Cars Turn Right'

The presence of approach signs will ease the flow of traffic and reduce stress levels for miles around, but the laws and rules relating to temporary event signs are complex (see Chapter 16, 'Sign posting' for information on off-site signs).

The traffic manager should check with the event manager (who will be able to pass on information gathered during the research and planning phase) on the mode of transport the public will use. Checking with the people responsible for group ticket sales will indicate how many people are coming by coach, because coach companies buy blocks of tickets for major events and sell them on to the public. Consultations and regular meetings with the local authority and police and studying the local and regional road layout will give prior warning as to the direction of approach of most traffic.

On most occasions you can 'read' the local roads to decide which way most of the traffic will come. For example, if the event site is out of town and a mile from junction 17 of the motorway, it is likely that the vast majority of the traffic coming to your event will come along the motorway. You will then know that most traffic will approach your site from the direction of junction 17 of the motorway and so you can plan accordingly.

It is also possible to deliberately direct traffic by a longer route that is served by better roads. So if there are two choices of route from junction 17 to your site, one of which is two miles along back lanes which can only take single file traffic, or a four-mile route along dual carriageways, depending on circumstances a case could be made to use either route. The authorities can give advice as to which roads are best used and where any approach signs can be located.

Take into account existing traffic flow to work out the best access points for vehicles and the best access routes to overflow parking etc. You will also be able to specify the inbound routes, whether segregated for coaches and cars, or not. The routes selected and signposted should be the roads that can best cope with the volume of traffic and with least disruption to through traffic, local life and business as you can.

Remember that on a map, a route may look perfect, but check it, drive it with the date of the event and expected vehicles in mind. Make sure for example that your nice easy exit route does not run past the local football stadium exit on a match day, or similarly run into conflict with another event, or obstruct a level crossing etc.

Car park location signs

If the event is large and/or the car park vast, you should consider ways of helping the public remember where their vehicle was parked. Simple things like naming car parks, fields and gates will help, so 'Red Car Park' or 'Elephant Car Park' will stick in their minds, where they may not remember 'Car Park 2A' at the end of the day. At least by naming car parks and marking them on the site maps, you can direct them to the right field at the end of the day, when they ask the way to their car.

Even if you are not going to charge for parking, it may be beneficial to hand out raffle tickets to each car as it arrives. So you will know that pink tickets came from Pink Car Park on the field beside the motorway and blue tickets came from the Blue Car Park to the north of the farmhouse etc. You may also be able to make double use of the tickets by having a prize draw on them, as an extra attraction to members of the public and to make them use the car parks and not to use surrounding roads and verges.

You may not have witnessed the distress on a young couple's faces when after five hours at the event they realise they don't know where their car is. Have you seen the despair in the eyes of parents who have spent two hours trudging around the fields looking for their Fiesta, dragging screaming, hot, tired and temperamental toddlers with them? I have seen it. If the car park names and coloured raffle tickets don't work and all else has failed, it may be worth having a vehicle available to take them around to look for their lost car. Consider extending the insurance of the roving car park supervisor's vehicle to cover them for taking those lost and forgetful members of the public to search for their car.

The roving car park supervisor will be in charge of car parks, their staff, money collection, security and the use of the car parks. I suggest that this supervisor be issued with a radio and a minibus which is insured to carry staff, signs and equipment, plus members of the public looking for lost cars.

Tip

If a motorist reports that they have lost their car, good, sensible *investigative questioning* can help you to find it again. Knowing the site will give you an advantage. For example the answer to a simple question like, 'After you parked, did you walk up hill or down hill to the event site?' will allow you to narrow the choices because you know Penguin Car Park is above the event site and Elephant Car Park is below the site. They walked uphill so they are in Elephant Car Park. 'Did you pass a pond when you drove in?' will narrow it further, because you know that if they drove past the pond they used the west gate. Similar questions, based on a knowledge of the site and car parks usually allow you to identify which car park they parked in – then all they have to do is find their car in the appropriate car park. Even when you identify which car park field they are in, simple questions can help to locate their car. 'Was your car facing the pedestrian gate?' if the answer is yes, then their car is on the right-hand side of the field, because all the others are parked facing the other way. Simple but effective.

Exit routes

Getting all of the cars in is easy; getting them out is a lot harder. They arrive in a steady stream, but they all tend to want to go at about the same time and they all think they should go before everyone else.

If at all possible make several exit routes available, but only as long as the traffic from those additional exits can run directly out to main roads leading away from the site. If you open three exits, which all lead to a small roundabout half a mile down the road, you will simply move the delay from the manned car park exits to a free-for-all at that roundabout, as well as inconveniencing local residents, businesses and through traffic.

Consult with the police about this and take their advice. For a really big event, introducing a temporary one-way system will help to keep the traffic flowing and get the cars out simply and cleanly. If this is going to be introduced, make sure that you have plenty of directional signs erected at the exits (see Chapter 16, 'Sign posting').

Late arrivals

All points must be manned during the event. When a car park has been filled, the bulk of your traffic management staff and car park marshals can be moved off to the car parks currently being filled, possibly in the roving car park supervisor's minibus. But you must keep skeleton staff on duty at all car parks while the event is still open.

There will always be late arrivals and if you pull all of your staff off to a remote car park, the late arrivals will park or more often 'abandon' their vehicles, wherever is most convenient to them.

It is likely that without the skeleton staff on duty, these late arrivals will block gates and emergency access routes. The skeleton staff should be aware of the 'danger' areas and so attempt to remain at or near those points to redirect stray motorists to the correct parking points. Skeleton staffing also adds an extra element of security to car parks, giving the public more peace of mind.

Motorists are funny people! I worked at a large cage bird event one year. An elderly lady, who was not a judge and who was driving a brand new car approached the Judge's Gate far too fast. She aimed at the huge gatepost and was going too fast to turn into the gateway. She rammed the large concrete post, wrecking her car. I stopped to offer her assistance, while asking one of the gate staff to call an ambulance. The elderly lady was very agitated and on being offered assistance said she was late and demanded that somebody take her canary into the event, because it had a chance of winning its class. Was that dedication?

Mature staff

Erecting 'Car Park Full' signs works with most drivers, but there are always the lazy ones who think that they should be allowed to do what they want to and they are the ones who cause the problems.

Ensure where possible that the more mature staff are selected as skeleton staff; they are better able to deal with argumentative motorists. A few 'Unauthorised Cars Will Be Clamped' signs help a lot at this stage.

Skeleton staff should also be left with a radio or other means of communicating with the event manager's office, in case any problems arise for which they need assistance. They may have to deal with various events, such as:

- breakdowns – call motoring organisation or mechanic (may be on site),
- car fires – call the event manager to contact the fire and rescue service,
- people who have 'lost' their car – if unable to reunite them with their car by

investigative questioning and common sense, contact the roving car park supervisor for eventual reunion with their car,

- medical emergency – call the event manager/medical assistance,
- persons tampering with vehicles – call the event manager and police.

Vehicle passes and permits

For various reasons, some vehicles will be allowed access to areas where the public is not allowed. The police, car park attendants and marshals must be able to quickly and easily identify any vehicles with special parking and access permissions.

For larger events, the simplest way of arranging this is to issue clearly visible passes that those drivers can display in their windscreen. The passes can have printing on them, but colour, shape and size are more important than the printed contents.

Just as disabled badges are orange or blue for simple identification from a distance, your car passes should be in similar bright colours. Instruct all drivers issued with them to display them clearly, in say the top corner of the passenger-side windscreen (as long as it does not obstruct the driver's vision). Make sure that they understand that without the pass displayed they will be refused access and directed to the public car park. Then it is a simple matter to know that red passes are judges, blue passes are stallholders and green passes are staff etc. It is then even easier to wave them into their allocated entrances without any delay or obstruction.

Tip

It is imperative that when passes are issued, holders are clearly instructed that they *must* display their pass as stated, or they will be refused access. It is surprising how many clearly intelligent members of the public assume that instructions to display passes are not directed at them and that their pass, in its envelope in the glove compartment or boot of their car, is of some magical use!

Traffic plan

After consultation with the local authorities and the police, the traffic manager should produce a 'traffic plan'. This short report will outline the traffic arrangements and refer to other more detailed documents that contain the details of investigation, and research that support the final traffic plan, which will be developed in consultation with the police. The traffic plan will be presented to the local authority and the police as part of the request for permissions and licences to hold the event.

Checkpoint

The event manager can move on, but the traffic manager must complete their investigations and draw up a schedule of routes, signs required, car parking plans etc. These should be presented and discussed with the police and then the traffic manager should give a checkpoint presentation to review and check the proposed arrangements.

Progress – Chapter 15

You should now:

- understand the role and importance of the traffic manager, especially for larger events,
- be aware of the estimated audience numbers, profile, transport arrangements, exhibitors etc. and so be aware of proposed traffic,
- have identified and recruited or appointed a traffic manager,
- have brainstormed expected traffic flows and drawn up appropriate contingency plans,
- for larger events, identified emergency traffic access routes,
- be aware that you should select the best most appropriate traffic routes, not necessarily the shortest,
- have planned to manage late arrivals and early departures,
- by written and verbal instructions insisted that anyone attending with special car park passes should display them in their windscreen, or *without exception* they will be treated as a member of the public and directed to a public car park,
- produce a short traffic plan,
- have held a checkpoint meeting to review and discuss traffic management issues,
- if you need to confirm your decisions, hold a small checkpoint meeting to present everything to either your governing body, or to a few deputy managers (when you are satisfied following formal presentation and approval (Chapter 25, 'Formal

presentation') you can start placing orders, spending money and booking your requirements), and

- when formal approval has been given and licences issued contact those suppliers above who offered and quoted the best deals for you, ask them to confirm their quotes and start placing orders (if you have done your research and planning thoroughly and conscientiously, you should now have eliminated all doubt).

Remember – if you have skipped any stages, or failed to investigate properly, it's your event and you will be liable for any legal problems or financial loss.

Product completed

- Nominated and recruited a traffic manager.
- Have agreed and drawn up a contingency plan.
- Have agreed and drawn up emergency access routes.
- Listed all approach and exit direction signs required.
- Listed all car park location signs required.
- Have estimated and listed staff requirements.
- Have designed appropriate bright colour and shape vehicle passes and badges.
- Have ensured that all pass and badge holders have been clearly instructed to display them in the windscreen of any car or expect to be directed to public car parks.
- Have drawn up a summary traffic plan.

16 Sign posting

Safely, quickly and efficiently getting large numbers of people on and off a site in a short time, with minimal interference for local residents, or to the free flow of local and passing traffic, is a complex operation. Similarly, ensuring that large numbers of people can find their way around a large event site is not easy. A critical part of the logistical process of moving large numbers of people and their cars on, off and around a site is the design, positioning and erection of appropriate signs.

The law

The law relating to signs is complex and strict. To complicate matters further, under UK law, by definition a sign may be a 'sign' or, depending on purpose, content and positioning, it may be an 'advertisement'.

At your earliest opportunity you should approach your local authority and discuss your proposed sign-posting requirements with them. They will view your proposals against current legislation, to rule on, agree, amend or refuse permission for your temporary signs, possibly imposing strict restrictions on any signs that will be permitted. Some of the legislation that governs the display of temporary signs is listed below to illustrate the complexity involved.

- Road Traffic Regulation Act 1984.
- The Traffic Signs Regulations and General Directions 1994.
- Traffic Signs Regulations and General Directions 2002.
- Temporary Traffic Signs (Prescribed Bodies) (England & Wales) Regulations 1998.
- Town and Country Planning (Control of Advertisements) Regulations 1992.

In my experience there are differences in the way local authorities deal with requests for temporary event signs. Most are helpful but some are actively obstructive. On top of that they sometimes seem to interpret and enforce legislation differently. There appear to be some general rules:

- If allowed, off-site signs must be directional and must not be intended to advertise the event.
- If allowed, off-site signs must be constructed, located and removed in accordance with strict guidelines, set out in legislation and governed by the highways authority.
- If allowed, off-site signs must be erected in accordance with strict regulations as to height, position, distance from the road edge, damage to street furniture, etc.
- If the erection of temporary road signs is allowed, the event manager will be liable under any legal action claiming that the presence of event signs caused or initiated any accident, injury or damage.
- If allowed, off-site signs and staff erecting and removing them must be covered by public liability insurance, that will indemnify the event manager and any staff from liability for any injury or damage caused or blamed on those signs or the sign-erecting staff.
- If allowed by the local authority, off-site signs may only be erected within a maximum of a five-mile radius of the event. The distance will be dictated by the Highways Authority and will be based on the distance deemed necessary to direct traffic to the event from the nearest major roads. The signs must be erected shortly before the event, and removed soon after the event.
- Generally, no signs will be allowed on motorways or major trunk roads.
- Any on-site signs that are designed to be visible and viewed by motorists from a motorway or trunk road may not be allowed.
- On-site signs that will only be in use for a few days during an event are generally acceptable.

Government websites

Various government websites can be used to view the wording of the legislation in force, and sometimes show proposed changes to legislation. For example, the following web sites may be used to view current legislation:

- http://www.planning.odpm.gov.uk/outadvert/index.htm
- http://www.dft.gov.uk/
- http://www.hmso.gov.uk/

However, due to the extent and complexity of the legislation, viewing sections of one act may give an event manager a false view of the law relating to their proposed signs. For example, while your interpretation of the wording may make it appear that your proposed signs are permissible with 'deemed consent', that is blanket permission for a type of advertisement which is written into the law, the local authority may have a different view. They may take action against you using their powers under the 'Town and Country Planning (Control of Advertisements) Regulations 1992', and be prepared to argue the legal point in a lengthy and expensive court case. Other factors may also limit your options; for example, special rules apply in all National Parks!

The simple rule is that while investigating and planning your proposed event, you should discuss event signs with the police and the local authority to arrive at a mutually acceptable schedule, particularly in relation to off-site signs and advertisements. As public servants they *should* have the same objective as you, 'to safely and efficiently direct large numbers of vehicles to the event site, where they will be parked off road, causing minimum disruption to through traffic and local residents and businesses'.

Remember, if your proposed site is on the border between two local authorities, you may have to deal with two separate local authority planning departments, which both have jurisdiction over part of your proposed site and access roads.

Discussions with the local authority

If you are making the first contact with the local authority and do not have a named contact, I suggest you start by asking to speak to somebody in the Planning Office (temporary signs) and the Licensing Office (events). (For more on licensing, see Chapter 17, 'Permissions'.)

Be ready to explain the nature of your enquiry. Begin by saying you want to discuss temporary event signs, and then give a brief description of your event, the attractions, numbers attending, proposed dates and the exact location of the proposed site. With that information they should be able to connect you to the person who will be able to deal with your enquiry.

Though initial telephone contact will be required, to effectively discuss your event and sign requirements and proposals, you should arrange a face-to-face meeting. At that meeting you should have:

- a copy of your event objective,
- an outline of the proposed event type,
- an outline of the event attractions,
- an outline of the audience size, where they will come from and how they will travel,

- an outline of the event site (or at most two or three optional sites), and
- an outline of your public liability insurance arrangements.

With this information, an initial meeting will be fruitful. As you progress formally agreeing on an event site, with input from the police and the local authority you will be able to more accurately define and agree an event sign schedule.

Schedule of signs and locations

In early discussions with the authorities, they will indicate which signs you may be able to use. The safest course for any event is to assume that planning permission will be required for every sign you want to use. For any agreed signs and advertisements, the authorities will probably expect the event manager to produce a sign schedule. The schedule will include specifications of the construction of the proposed signs, which must comply with the law in relation to size, material, colour and lettering style and lettering size. The event manager must also provide a list showing the agreed locations of off-site signs. By law the regulations relating to temporary signs, strictly specify such things as:

- optimum distance from junctions,
- optimum height above ground or footpath,
- optimum height of poles,
- angle of sign in relation to approaching traffic, and
- background colour and lettering colour combinations.

Relevant considerations

The following sections of this chapter discuss various aspects of sign posting, for the information of an event manager. These sections give an indication of the benefits of various types of signs, their positioning construction and use. When approaching the police and local authority for advice and permission, it may help an event manager to consider which signs could be of benefit at their unique event, and what questions to ask.

Remember, these sections are to raise awareness of the use of signs and 'advertisements', but as the event manager *you* are responsible for obtaining permission from the police, highways authority or local planning office to erect and use any signs.

Sign posting – safety

When erecting and removing signs, safety is a critical consideration. You must also remember that where authorised, signs must be erected within stringent rules and regulations. As an alternative to providing, erecting and removing signs yourself, the RAC and AA both offer a service of providing signs to temporary events. You may wish to discuss your event and proposed sign-posting requirements with them, and ask for a quote to produce, erect and remove signs for your event. Remember that the erection and removal of signs creates a potential risk for several groups of people.

The sign posting vehicle

The signs must be erected at key points and junctions over a considerable area, so if authorised, it is almost certain that your sign-erecting staff would be moving from site to site, or junction to junction in a vehicle.

The proposed erection sites are probably near major junctions and roundabouts etc. – busy points and potential accident spots. The added complication of your staff stopping unexpectedly or parking dangerously on bends and junctions could be the direct or indirect cause of an accident, *for which you would be liable*.

Make sure that when they stop, your sign posting vehicle drivers are instructed to take particular care not to cause an obstruction, or park in such a way that they do not block traffic, or block the view of other motorists at a junction or roundabout etc. As elsewhere, if in doubt, consult the local authority. It is possible that for a fee you could even arrange for them to supply and erect appropriate signage.

Your staff

By definition, if permission is given, your staff members would be sign posting at major junctions and so will have to leave their vehicle and move about on or very near to the road, which is probably carrying fast-moving traffic. I suggest that if you do not want to pay the AA, RAC or possibly the local authority to erect the signs for you, and you want your staff to erect the signs:

- staff should be equipped with a fluorescent high-visibility jackets that meet Health and Safety requirements
- they should be instructed to make safety their top priority
- they should take extra care in stopping and pulling away in vehicles
- they should aim to park safely away from the junction they wish to signpost
- they should be instructed as to where to fix the signs, as directed by the local authority or police, or if not specified by them, in accordance with the legislation

- they should also be instructed in the method of fixing the signs to posts etc., which must not cause damage to any street furniture, fences etc.
- signs should not be erected in a way that causes or allows them to overhang the road, where a vehicle may hit them, or cause a high-sided vehicle to swerve around them
- event signs should not obscure or distract members of the public, particularly drivers, from any existing signs
- the signs must be erected securely so that they will not fall onto the road, or on vehicles or pedestrians etc.
- staff must only erect signs as per an agreed sign schedule, and must record where signs have been placed – for later collection.
- they must be trained in and familiar with all tools and equipment they are using
- all tools and equipment must be of an acceptable standard and quality
- when removing signs all traces of their presence should be removed, and damage caused reported to the highways authority.

Assistants to sign erector

For safety reasons any member of staff who is erecting signs should have an assistant to help them.

The assistant can watch and steady the bottom of a ladder and guide the public around any ladders or other equipment. They will also be warning oncoming traffic of the work, warning the sign erector of any dangerous traffic approaching because he or she will be looking at the sign itself. The assistant can also help to carry the equipment from a safe parking area; without an assistant, the sign erection staff may be tempted to park close to a junction and consequently park dangerously.

Insurance

When enquiring about insurance, you should enquire about the possibility and cost of insuring staff for the erection and removal of signs, against injury to themselves and against the signs falling on and damaging property or people, or causing damage to street signs or fences etc., or causing accidents during erection or removal.

The public

The authorities will almost certainly insist that you or the signing organisation are insured against injury to members of the public. If liable, the event manager could be liable for hundreds of thousands of pounds of damages. For this reason it is best to pay an organisation to suply, erect and remove the signs, then they carry the liability.

If not, you must insure yourself and your staff to cover the erection and removal of the signs, as well as any injury to the public, whether caused by accident or negligence. Your insurance cover should also indemnify you against claims that the presence of your signs caused an accident, by obstructing the view of an existing sign, or blocking the view of a driver at a junction for example.

The cost

The cost of making a sign can vary between minimal – if you use available materials for on-site signs – and considerable – if you are required to have off-site signs made to street sign standards.

Only you know what is involved in your event, so only you can make the decision as to whether the cost of making signs by your chosen method, to the correct legal standards, can be justified by the income to be derived. As a rule of thumb, the first couple of times an event is run, 'cheap and cheerful' is probably the best policy. If an event becomes a large annual extravaganza, then it may be worth investing in some more permanent and professionally produced signs, advertisements and notice boards. Until then, be miserly with sign-posting budgets where possible, while making sure that they fulfil the purpose for which they are intended, attracting people, indicating the route, pointing to entrances and exits, warning of danger, etc.

Remember, if you select your site carefully, with easy access routes, in close proximity to major roads and motorways, your need for off-site direction signs will be negligible anyway.

Whatever materials are used, the regulations require the signs to be simple, clearly understood and large enough to be seen and understood by drivers travelling at speeds in excess of 30 miles an hour. All signs should have lettering that is large enough to be easy to read, as specified in the legislation. Off-site, signs should contain minimal information, so that a driver only has to glance at the sign to understand its meaning. On-site, signs may contain more information, assuming that generally pedestrians will read them. The sign should also be easily identifiable, not mounted behind a bush, or allowed to become splashed with mud or dirt so as to be unreadable.

Advertising

Signs can also be used to advertise the event before the actual date on which it is to take place. With local authority permission and possibly permission from the owner of the land where you want to erect the signs, you can put up a substantial sign advertising the forthcoming event. These are particularly effective on a main road, where larger numbers of people will see that sign. You must however still abide by legislation and the rules relating to advertisements and signs. Do not expect a passing driver to take his eyes off the road to read a sign containing a lot of information!

Remember that depending on the size, construction and location of the sign, the length of time it is expected to be on site, the content of the sign and the event it may be advertising, planning permission may be required. Consult the local authority well in advance.

If allowed, include only the bare essentials in an advance sign at the event site, e.g. event type, event date(s), event time, entry fee and possibly contact phone number.

STEAM FAYRE

Sat 12th & Sun 13th April
Entry £1
Free car parking
CALL 0123 456789

Where people are just walking past, a sign like this is very effective. However, you might get planning permission for a series of signs. So, the first large sign may say 'STEAM FAYRE', the next 'Sat 12th & Sun 13th April', the next 'Entry £1 – Free Parking' and finally '0123 456789'. Using these signs you could inform passing drivers of the forthcoming event, and the driver need only glance at the individual signs to collect all the information.

Such signs could be erected in two ways. Either erect the series of four signs over, say, half a mile of road, so the information is passed on in 'bites'. Alternatively, one fixed sign could be used, and the content changed once each week. During the first week the sign reads 'STEAM FAYRE', the next week it is changed to 'Sat 12th & Sun 13th April', etc. Ask your planning department for advice as to the advertising process they would be most likely to permit.

Site signs

At or near the selected event site (perhaps in a shop or garage window) you may wish to erect a smaller and more informative sign that gives local pedestrians more details about the event. If it is displayed as a notice at, say, the gate of the proposed site, it will require permission of the landowner and planning permission. The sign will still advertise the day, date, time and cost information, but should include more details that will provide information to local residents and those interested in having a stall or display at the event.

STEAM FAYRE

Sat 12th & Sun 13th April
Tickets £1 per person
Free car parking
Tickets and general information
Phone 0123 456789
Group discounts call 0123 565622
Stall holders call 015 356276
Gates open to set up Friday 11th 14:45
Gates closed Monday 14th by 22:30

Directional signs

Directional signs must be clearly visible and easy to read. If authorised to erect signs you should adopt a standard approach within the limitations imposed on you, so that drivers become familiar with the signs they are following, allowing them to identify your signs earlier and therefore make earlier, safer signals and manoeuvres.

Remember that you will need left-turn signs, right-turn signs, straight-on signs and possibly signs showing the exit to use from complex roundabouts. For off-site road signs, you will benefit from the expert advice and assistance of the police and local authority, and be working within the framework of strict legislation and regulations.

For events such as marathons and cycle races, route signs are very important. Though marshals should be positioned at all junctions to indicate the route the competitors should be taking, temporary signs will help with the smooth operation of the race. Simple left- and right-turn signs, or straight-on signs at intermediate junctions, will please competitors because they will be able to easily see and follow the route and avoid getting lost or taking short cuts.

At one road cycle race I attended, a lost cyclist was found by a police patrol over three miles off the route after he had missed a turn. He said he had become concerned after he had not seen any marshals for some time, but soon after that he was waved on through a road works by yellow-jacketed road works staff, so he assumed they were marshals and that he was still on the route! The police found him with his

133

head down, pedalling hard. When he was stopped and his error was pointed out he let the officers know in fairly basic language how bad he thought the sign posting, management and marshalling for the race was – and they told him to address his complaints to the event manager!

Other information

If possible, I try to include other details on the direction signs that relay important, useful and calming information to the motorist, but planners do not usually allow this additional information – even though some agree that it would be beneficial:

- *Distance* – where it is a particularly big event, I try to reassure motorists that they are getting closer to the event by printing the distance remaining, e.g. 'Air Show – 2 Miles', 'Air Show – 1 Mile'.
- *Fuel* – I might indicate that they are passing the last garage before the show site, 'Last Fuel Before Air Show', because most people want to go straight home without wasting time in heavy traffic looking for a garage where they can fill up. On your advice the garage may put up a sign!
- *Supplies* – I could indicate that they are passing the last shops where they can buy supplies. I have only done this where people may want to buy films for their cameras before they reach the site, e.g. 'Last Films Before Air Show'.
- *Directions* – I may include directional information where there are categories of traffic that need to be directed to appropriate car parks, e.g. 'All Air Show Coaches' or 'All Air Show Cars'.

Drivers are happier and more relaxed when they think an event has been organised properly, and you have to remember that for nearly all of the people attending your event, your approach signs are where they get their first impression of your event and your organisational abilities.

Tip

Make sure that you don't use a single bolt or other fixing to attach direction arrows – some fool will inevitably come along and simply spin the arrow to point in the opposite direction. Use two fixing points to prevent this.

Required signs

Depending on the event size and your agreement and approval from the police and local authority, a wide range of signs may be required. Most of the types of signs that could be required are discussed below. Broadly speaking, signs can be divided into two classifications – promotional and instructional. The following sections briefly discuss the various type and uses of signs.

Event and promotional signs

These are signs that advertise the event and which probably require planning permission so check with your local planning authority.

Event type and name

On the day of the event, large banners could be erected at the site describing and naming the event. This will have the benefit of advertising the presence of the show to passing traffic, and possibly attracting additional casual spectators on the day. It will also indicate to the public that they have reached their destination. Depending on planning permission, such banners could advertise the type and location of the event for several days or weeks beforehand.

Though most details are already shown on the handbills and tickets, adding date/time/entry fee/free parking etc. information to signs on site can have additional benefit. While sitting in the queue of cars approaching the site, the public knows from the sign that the display does not start for another hour, or that the gate fee is one pound per head. They will then know that they have plenty of time to get into the site, and they can begin to sort out their money before they arrive at the gate.

Off-site directional signs

These signs help people to get to the area of the event, or avoid it. Those attending may have to head for different gates, for example competitors or stallholders may have to go to Gate 2 only. If there are no specific direction signs at or near the event site, nobody will be getting to the right gate and your traffic management problem will be immense.

Part of the traffic management role is to sort out the arrival of traffic. With the approval of the appropriate authorities, the following signs may be required:

- Through Traffic
- Village Avoiding Show Ground

- Coaches Only
- Competitors
- Staff Only
- Emergency Services
- Keep Gate Clear
- No Parking
- Fire Exit
- Cleaning Services
- Toilet Queue Here
- Event Manager Only
- Heavy Vehicles Only
- Caravans
- Car Park
- Car Park 1, Car Park 2, etc.
- Car Park Full
- Overflow Car Park
- Disabled Car Park
- Staff Car Park Gate 4, etc.
- Judges' Car Park Gate 5, etc.
- Warning – Slow Moving Traffic
- Caution – Vehicles Turning Ahead
- Caution – Overhead Cables
- No Overnight Parking
- All Vehicles To Be Removed By 8pm
- Slow – Event Ground Ahead
- Unauthorised Cars Will Be Clamped.

On-site directional/location signs

Off-site signs are important to get stallholders, competitors and the public to the site in time and to make it easier for them to come in through the right gate. Informative and direction signs are just as important on site. They should be used where required and where possible on site, at a height of about 2.5 metres above ground level (to keep them above crowd level) so that they remain visible even when the crowds are in.

Signs will vary depending on the size and type, theme and content of the event, but the following signs are fairly common:

- Judges' Parking
- Judges Only
136   - Event Ring

- Event Manager's Office
- First In Class, etc.
- Overall Winner
- Lost children
- Drinking Water
- Toilets
- Public Telephones
- Way Out
- Main Display Arena
- First Aid
- Car Park 1/Elephant Car Park, etc.

Hold a brainstorming session with deputy managers to try to cover all possible aspects of your event. Apply common sense, though. List the signs you know you will need, and only consider making signs that the authorities approve. Do not make up signs that you may not need, or you will not be allowed to use.

> **Tip**
>
> Don't commit to ordering or making any signs until it is confirmed that the event is going ahead, and the authorities agree and confirm your on-site and off-site signing schedule.

Reminder signs

Though stallholders and judges etc. are usually given passes to allow them to enter the event ground and disabled drivers have disabled parking permits, for some unknown reason, they almost universally fail to display them.

When dealing with a constant flow of traffic, the marshals and any police officers do not want to have to stop and talk to every driver. If a car has no visible stallholder, judges' or other pass displayed, it should be assumed that the driver is a member of the public and they should be quickly and efficiently directed to the public car park. There is nothing more annoying or disruptive to traffic managers than the sleepy driver who ignored the instruction to display their stallholder's or member's sign on the car windscreen, who then insists on searching the car boot to find it!

When you send out joining instructions for your event, make a prominent note that signs and badges *must* be clearly displayed and that vehicles without them will be treated as members of the public *with no exceptions*. Make it clear that anyone who fails to comply and causes disruption will be asked to leave.

When you send the passes, make this mesage the first thing the recipient sees when they open the envelope, and repeat the message on every page you send them. Also, with the permission of the local authorities, erect early warning and reminder signs at least a mile or so each side of the entrances, preferably some distance before a lay-by to give them a place to safely stop, find and display their pass. It will help if the local authority allow you to note 'Lay-by Ahead' on the reminder sign.

If they fail to do so, they must be treated as a member of the public, or waved on to find their way around the approach roads again and come back into the circuit *with their pass properly displayed*. If it makes them late – it's their own fault. Why should hundreds of people be delayed because one driver cannot follow a simple instruction?

Early warning signs

Early warning signs positioned some distance before car park and pedestrian gates will be of great help in avoiding congestion and delays at the gates, but you will need permission to erect them. You should point out to the local authority that they will be of huge benefit to the local community, passing traffic, and people attending the event in getting event traffic off the public highway. Be prepared to propose a safe location for such signs, and draft a design that they can see and hopefully approve. These signs should warn the public what fees they have to pay and ask them to have the right change ready. Thus a sign saying 'Car Parking £1 Per Car – Correct Change Please' will give the drivers enough time to have the money ready and reduce delays and traffic jams, therefore reducing the period during which there will be any potential risks on the highway.

Signs at car park exits

It is a good idea to post signs at car park exits giving onward journey information, such as:

• All Vehicles Turn Left Only,
• M4 – Left – Then Left At Roundabout,
• A456 – Right – Then Left At Lights,
• M3 – Left – Left At Roundabout Then Follow Signs,
• Bypass – Right – Then Left At Traffic Lights.

These signs can save a lot of time, to say nothing of the voices of car park staff when they are asked 'Which way to the M4?' for the six millionth time.

Sign-writing equipment

No matter how good you are, or how many events you have arranged before, you will never have all the signs that you require. That may not be a major disaster, but the inconvenience can be considerable.

Tip

Keep simple sign-making equipment in the roving car park supervisor's vehicle and the event manager's office. Nothing fancy is required, just a few pieces of hardboard or stiff card, a pot of black paint with narrow brushes, a few nails, pointed wooden stakes and a club hammer. Any emergency signing requirements, for example 'Lane Flooded – Turn Right', can be met quickly, cheaply and simply. Check with the local authority and police to ensure that they will approve such 'emergency' signs. They may refuse permission to use anything other than scheduled and agreed off-site signs, no matter what the emergency. As stated above some local authority staff stick by the letter of the law and are willing to risk the traffic chaos that may follow if they ban the use of emergency signs.

Thank you signs

There is no harm in being polite, especially for charitable events, so consider placing a friendly sign above or at the main exit along the lines of 'The Hospice Staff And Patients Thank You For Your Valued Support – Have A Safe Journey Home'. The cost is only a few pounds, and the effect can be a warm glow in the hearts of all attending and maybe a few voluntary donations!

Advertising next year

You may also wish to place a sign above the exits along the lines of 'ACME Steam Event On This Site Saturday 25th And Sunday 26th August Next Year. Write It In Your Diary NOW!'

Progress – Chapter 16

You should now:

- be aware of the benefits of signs to you, your staff, the local community and people attending your event,
- have introduced procedures for the safe erection and removal of your signs, ensuring that their positions are recorded so that they can be removed when the event has closed,
- be aware of the use of promotional and directional signs,
- have considered any extra information you may wish to place on directional approach signs,
- have reviewed the suggested list of signs, held a brainstorming session and compiled a list of the signs you will require for your event,
- have concentrated on reminder and early warning signs that will help your event staff by easing the flow of people into your event,
- have considered and drawn up a list of exit signs that will help speed the departure of the public when the event closes,
- have decided on a method of sign production, considering your event theme, objective and budget, and prepared sign-making equipment for the event manager's office and roving car park supervisor's vehicle, and
- give a checkpoint presentation to a new group to confirm your decisions.

Product completed

- Schedule of on- and off-site signs agreed and required.
- Specification of agreed design of standard direction sign (for example yellow background with black writing).
- Designed sign schedule form to allow sign erection teams to record what signs have been erected and where, for later collection.
- Agreed list of materials and equipment needed for emergency sign production and erection.
- Agreed list of training and equipment needed for sign erection teams.
- Agreed insurance cover required for event manager and sign erection teams.
- Checkpoint review – authorisation to continue.

17 Permissions

You will almost certainly have to get permission and/or approval from several different authorities, people, organisations and groups before you are allowed to run your event. The permissions required change depending on the location, size, format, content and type of event being organised. As the event organiser, a critical part of your feasibility investigation will be to check that all interested parties will give permission for the event to go ahead. Before you commit to spending any money, you should have received formal and written approval for your event to run.

Local authority

The local authority is usually a good source of information and advice. They are also responsible for approving and licensing certain events. There are two main classes of event that *must* be formally licensed: those that include singing, dancing or music (which will probably require a public entertainment licence), and those that include contests or demonstrations of boxing, karate and other contact sports.

As a general rule most local authorities now have some sort of safety advisory group that has been formed to advise on and approve or disapprove events in their area.

You must check with your local authority, explain the details of the event you want to organise, then take advice as to which permissions are needed. They will also usually advise you in relation to the planning and delivery of your event.

Licensing and restrictions

Depending on the type of event you wish to arrange, the venue you have selected, the numbers attending and many other factors, the local authority – in consultation with the fire service and police – will make a decision on whether your event should be licensed. Don't assume that you do not need permission; the laws and regulations are complex, which means that there are some rules that could catch you out. For example, did you know that under some circumstances you may need to apply to the courts for a liquor licence, even when the only alcohol present at your event is to be given out as prizes?

If the local authority give you permission to run your event, they often issue a formal *letter of agreement* to the organiser, which outlines the conditions and restrictions that the event manager must follow. For example, the conditions may require the event manager to employ a certain number of marshals, or arrange for five million pounds of public liability cover. They may demand proof that a risk assessment has been undertaken and acted on, to comply with health and safety regulations, or that staff have been properly trained and equipped etc.

The health and safety of members of the public is a primary concern and there are many rules and regulations that may apply, depending on the site, structures, format and size of your event. For example, you may need to have certificates of safety for electrical items, power supplies, potential hazards, guy ropes, fire exits, mechanical rides, stewarding and crowd management. These vary from event to event, depending on what is being organised, so check with your local authorities to clarify which regulations you have to comply with for your event.

The local authority will also advise on other regulations. For example, where food will be sold at an event, the event manager must inform any permanent catering businesses nearby of the dates and times of the event and what on-site catering facilities are planned, all of which must be completed a month before the date of the event.

Health and safety
■ ■

The key consideration in terms of licensing and permissions is that you must consult your local authority, fire service, police and the health and safety executive for advice to ensure that everything is safe and correct. (See Chapter 5, 'Health and safety', for more information.)

Your aim has to be to make the event safe for everyone affected by it in any way. The authorities may require you to show that you have consulted the various authorities, undertaken risk assessments and acted on them, employed appropriately trained staff, and arranged for sufficient off-road car parking space etc. Check with your local authorities at your earliest convenience, stay in contact and benefit from their knowledge, skill and experience.

Electrical installations

The organisers of almost every event, regardless of the size, will need to arrange for electrical supply to be provided for the stalls, stands, event manager's office and cash office etc.

Installing electricity to a temporary site and making it tamper-proof, child-proof and weather-proof is clearly a job for a professionally qualified electrician. The security and safety that they will guarantee is worth the cost. Wherever the site is, it is worth contacting the local electricity supply company for advice and quotes for them to provide the power supply, if not give advice regarding approved local tradesmen.

Road closures

There may be a need to restrict traffic movement if you are planning to organise a street party or marathon etc. Very large events may also require restrictions and controls on traffic movement in surrounding roads, simply due to the number of vehicles concentrating on that area for the event and especially during the main arrival and departure times. Be warned that obtaining road closures and instituting temporary one-way systems is an expensive option!

Early consultation with the local authority, police and local residents, tradesmen, neighbours and their associations is essential, especially for such events as marathons and cycle races that require streets to be closed for the safe passage of competitors. The earlier consultations begin the lower the likelihood that unforeseen problems will emerge. The extent of the consultations and remedial actions will minimise the potential disruption that your event could cause.

Who do you have to talk to? The size, type, location and content of your event will dictate that. Bear in mind that even a modest event will probably disrupt the daily routine of everything within a radius of at least a mile. Take the advice of the local authority on how to inform and consult with local residents and businesses.

Though the police will take the lead in keeping local roads free from congestion, it may be beneficial if you work with the local authority to talk to local garages, shops, warehouses, offices, hotels, hospitals, sports centres, clubs, etc. Work with them; 'sell' them the event in terms of increased trade for local businesses and quality entertainment for local residents. They may have concerns; perhaps an undertaker may be concerned that traffic would disrupt a funeral booked for that date, or a local supermarket may be concerned that parking restrictions would prevent their lorry delivering fresh fruit. Listen to their concerns, and working with the police and local authority, generate an action plan that will resolve those problems. For example, the undertaker may be given a special police escort for the funeral, and the supermarket may have special permission for their lorry to park and unload for 20 minutes.

Remember that closing roads, making temporary one-way systems and/or temporarily banning right-hand turns at specific junctions, will all affect the people who live in, work in or just travel through the area. Do your best to minimise the impact.

Food and drink

Mobile food vans

Local authorities can give you advice on the licensing that mobile food vans should have, and possibly help you to select approved and licensed mobile food vendors.

As most mobile food sales outlets use bottled gas to provide the heating source, they present a fire hazard and must be risk assessed as such. For example a mobile gas-burning chip van should not be located between the go-cart fuel store and the hay barn!

Static food sales

Some events are arranged at sites where kitchen facilities are available, e.g. schools and club houses etc. If the owners approve of you using those facilities during your event, the local authority can advise you on what you need to do, to be allowed to use the facilities.

Food storage

Foodstuffs will need to be stored prior to the event opening, during the day(s) of the event, or overnight for an event running over several days. Once again there are many rules and regulations that vary from foodstuff to foodstuff concerning the storage of food. Check the local regulations and try to make sure that all food outlets abide by them.

Waste-food disposal

There are many rules and regulations that can vary from foodstuff to foodstuff and from area to area, concerning the storage and disposal of waste food. Check the local regulations and *wherever possible* negotiate for food outlets to deal with and dispose of their own food waste off-site, and under no circumstances in your bins and skips.

Drinks

Local authorities will advise about the sale of food and drinks. It is likely that the static and mobile food sales outlets will also provide drinks, but it is worth checking on your proposed or planned arrangements.

Alcoholic drinks

The local authority, police and local magistrates become involved if you decide to include a bar or beer tent. Although you can arrange all of this yourself, it is more sensible to simply contact the local pub or one of many commercial organisations that will arrange and operate the bar/beer tent for you. You can either pay the cost of staff and stock, then take the profits from alcohol sales, or get them to pay you for the right to run the bar/beer tent from which they then keep any profit on drinks they sell.

Fire and rescue service clearance

Depending on the type and size of event you wish to run, you may need approval or permission from the local fire service. At the very least you should contact them for advice about the possible risks and preparations that you could or should make to avoid potential problems.

The safety of the public and event staff must be an important consideration. (See also Chapter 14 'Event site', Chapter 22 'Security', Chapter 23 'Insurance', Chapter 24 'Emergency and normal procedures'.)

Sports

At higher levels, many sports have governing bodies who dictate rules and regulations stating how their sports should be organised. For example to 'qualify' in a national scheme a marathon may have to have a minimum of 75% of its route run on tarmac; or in rowing, the boats may have to be of a certain size and weight, and run in a current of a given speed.

Other clearance/notification/authorisation

It is surprising how much the rules differ from area to area, how different authorities apply or waive different regulations and how different rules, regulations and laws affect different event types. The following facts about fireworks displays illustrate the need to consult your local authority and emergency services before organising and running an event, to ensure that you abide by all rules:

- When organising a fireworks display at or near the coast, the organiser must discuss the event with the Coastguard and obtain clearance from them before the fireworks display is run. Apparently the 'coastal' rule ensures that fireworks are not mistaken for distress flares from ships at sea, hence the coastguard needs to know that at a certain place and time you will be firing off rockets and mortars for the enjoyment of your crowd!
- In certain locations near airports, the Civil Aviation Authority may require you and your fireworks company to sign a declaration that the fireworks to be used will not travel higher than one thousand feet. This is of course to prevent any interference with air traffic to and from the nearby airport.

Tip

Always check and discuss everything with your local authority and emergency services, governing council of sporting associations etc. before planning, organising and running an event. Continue to consult with them as your plans evolve, to make best use of their skills and experience.

Boundary complications

You may be unlucky and find that your chosen event site is on or near the boundary between two or more local authorities, police areas or police forces. I attended a half marathon, where the parish boundary followed a stream, which crossed the main road 15 metres short of the gate to the event site. To be legal and safe, as those last 15 metres of road were the responsibility of another local authority; we had to arrange for a separate road closure order through the other local authority, to cover those 15 metres.

If your proposed site straddles or comes close to various boundaries, during your early research and consultation the authorities should notify you of the problem. During subsequent investigation and research they will work with you and advise you of any additional liaison, enquiries or permissions you might need.

Police approval

For larger events, many police forces will compile a *'statement of intent'* to identify the division of responsibilities between the police and the event manager, defining the command procedures necessary in the event of any emergency.

In simple terms that is just a document stating who is responsible for what and in an emergency what responsibilities are retained by the event manager and what responsibilities revert to the police under specified circumstances.

Even if your event is particularly small, it is worth informing the police, just to let the local officers know what is happening on their patch. If the event is anything more that a small local affair, you *must* talk to the local police, to ensure that everything runs safely. Most forces have liaison officers who deal with events and they can use their expertise, skill and contacts to advise and help you to make the best arrangements for your event.

If you have never dealt with the logistics of handling large numbers of vehicles, don't try it. It is a specialist field where either training or experience can provide a working solution. If you just keep your fingers crossed and 'have-a-go', you may end up not only destroying any hope you have of making your event pay a profit, you could gridlock the roads for miles around.

Consider inviting the police to attend the event. For example the crime prevention officers or local beat officers could set up a stand. At some specialist events – for example a rural crafts show – the police 'country watch' or 'horse-watch' co-ordinators may wish to attend as well.

Land owner

In most circumstances, the event manager will not own the land where the event is due to be held. It is therefore obvious that you will need the permission of the landowner, without which there will be no event. The landowner may impose restrictions on you depending on their use of the land. For example, they may refuse you permission to run traction engines – if there is an unacceptable fire risk to a barn and crop of ripening wheat in the adjoining fields.

Electricity/water/sewage connections

It may be possible that the only available power, water or sewage pipe access for your event is in a barn on a neighbouring farm. If that is your only realistic source of power etc, you must include the landowner in early negotiations and planning.

Vehicle access and parking

Knowing the number and size of stalls, arenas and attractions, you will have calculated how much space you need. But the event ground is not the only consideration.

Assuming you have a field or site large enough to accommodate the event itself, you will have to arrange for sufficient space to park visitors' cars off the road. Calculating the space provided, arranging the logistics of entry and exit plus disabled car parking etc. is a more complex process than most people realise. (See 'Calculations' section of Chapter 14, 'Event Site'; Chapter 15, 'Traffic management'; Chapter 18 'Car parking'.)

Staff car parking space

Usually special arrangements are made for staff car parking. You don't want to alienate your staff by making them pay any parking fee, or putting them in a field 2 miles from the event, whether they are volunteers or not. Make sure you don't put staff in a huge car parking field from which they cannot escape when their shift ends because the exit is blocked by a never ending stream of vehicles coming in. Be sensible and be considerate, make special arrangement for staff.

Large vehicle access and parking

People running the stalls and attractions will need special attention as well. They will be arriving well ahead of the public and most staff. They may come in large trucks, or sometimes with trailers. They may also arrive with caravans intending to stay on the event site until they pack up and go after the last attraction closes on the last day.

You will also need to consider arranging for early access so that exhibitors can come in and set up. They will need access to the event ground for their heavy goods vehicles delivering stock, erecting stalls and generally setting up.

Some of the people running the attractions may well arrive in heavy trucks. Outside suppliers delivering and erecting toilets, Portakabins™, tents, speakers, telephones etc. will also need access to the event site for heavy vehicles, they may also need room to manoeuvre on the site before all of the small stalls and displays are set up.

When allowing for the larger vehicles, you must remember that a heavy truck needs a wide swing to get into and through a gate and high clearance to allow access without damage to the vehicle, street signs, bridges, low trees, cables, phone lines etc.

You will also want the ground to be firm, for two good reasons:

- You don't want heavy trucks getting bogged down on site – if there is any chance of that they may refuse to deliver anyway.

- You don't want them cutting up the ground, leaving it rough and uneven (and possibly causing injury to small or elderly visitors). If the public see that your event ground has been churned up into a mud bath by multiple passes from heavy vehicles, they will not be attending your event, and the farmer may be demanding compensation for damage to his field.

Many of the larger vehicles will be visiting the event ground outside opening hours. Most drivers will park while they deliver and will then leave, but some drivers will almost certainly need to park up safely for the duration of the event. If you are running a steam fair for example, large numbers of low-loader and articulated trucks that have carried displays to your event could need to park, and could give you a major headache.

Make sure that this aspect is considered and planned in detail. Though you can do a lot of the investigation on the telephone, there is no substitute for visiting the site personally, to confirm that it is suitable. You should have spoken to the landowner in depth, during your planning phase, during which you will have been informed of fields or areas that are prone to flooding, or are soft and will be turned into mud by constant traffic. Go and check to confirm what the landowner says. Ask questions and 'politely' insist on answers. Make sure that permission for trucks and caravans to be left in the farmyard or on the hard stand outside the barn has been granted.

Tip

Even constant pedestrian traffic can churn damp ground and grass into mud. If you keep a supply of sawdust or sand handy, grounds staff can lay it over areas where mud is forming to make passage easier for the public, making them more inclined to stay. (Don't use straw or hay, it is a fire hazard.)

Landowner access

Remember that the landowner may also require access at some time during the event. They may need to drive cows along one of the lanes, which will interfere with your car park access, or may need to drive a tractor through your event field to access the adjoining field. Clarify any access requirements before you agree to rent the site. A perfect event site is not so perfect if the landowner insists on driving 75 cows through your display arena twice a day for milking.

Car park access and exits

It is possible that the only sensible arrangement for entrance and exits to your event is via another landowner's fields, gate or lane etc. If this is the case, it is important that you include any other landowners in the feasibility stages, to ensure permissions will be given. You must of course also agree payment, damage, compensation, access hours etc. with any other landowners.

With any luck, the public will come in large numbers and park obediently in your car parking fields. You will need to arrange for sufficient parking spaces for those cars, but still allow for free access to early departures and late arrivals, emergency services and breakdown trucks etc.

Depending on the size and layout of the event site, car park access points, approach roads and the volume of traffic, I always try to ensure that traffic enters and exits through different gates, utilising different roads. This 'one-way' traffic flow through your car parking system will separate early departures from the heavy flow of main-stream arrivals. Making traffic leaving the site use a different road to the vehicles arriving will also prevent congestion on the highways.

If the segregated entry and exit method has a choice of a long route and a short route, wherever possible I arrange it so that all vehicles use the longest route in and of course the shortest and most direct route out. I use the long route in, to remove as many cars from the main highway as quickly as possible. If they are queued on a mile and a half of farm tracks or side roads, that is a mile and a half of traffic jam that is not blocking the main road.

With incoming queues, the hopefully minimal delays on the long approach route will be fresh in the memory of drivers. Drivers are always more impatient when trying to get out of a site and onto the road home. I find that the short exit route gives the public the impression that they have not been delayed as long as they expected and that makes them happy. Any action that will cool frayed nerves when the public is trying to get home is worth introducing.

Remember – when you involve different landowners' fields, gates, lanes and access points, you must make sure that they have all given permission to use their land before going ahead. The largest, firmest, flattest, smoothest field is no good if the neighbouring landowner will not let you use their access drive to reach it.

Neighbours

Though not strictly permission, as a courtesy you should inform the neighbouring landowners and tenants of your plans. It is important that you listen to any doubts or fears they may have for two reasons:

- They may have identified a legitimate problem that you overlooked and at this early stage can resolve quite easily.
- If you want to hold the event again next year and you have upset the neighbours, they may lodge an objection with the local authority, or put pressure on your landowner and you may not be given permission to run the event next year.

Progress – Chapter 17

You should now:

- from your knowledge and research of your event, be aware of the licences, permission and approvals you will need to obtain from the authorities before you will be allowed to deliver your event,
- be aware of any governing bodies and associations that will need to approve elements of your event,
- have approval of all landowners, where you need their permission to use gates, fields, access points and tracks,
- have discussed your plans with neighbours and minimised disruption to them and surrounding businesses and traffic, and
- have collected and collated documents and information (see Annex B, 'Approval Checklist' at the back of this book), before approaching the authorities and other governing bodies, associations or groups who must give permission, approval or licences for your event to progress.

Product completed

- Have been working with the authorities, following their instructions and guidelines, listening to their concerns and resolving issues, while working towards a proposed event and plan, which they will formally approve.

18 Car parking

Contrary to popular belief and perception parking large numbers of cars is difficult and there is considerable skill in doing it safely, quickly and correctly. Efficiently parking vehicles so that the roads are not obstructed, that the cars have the space to leave when they want to and without wasting space in the field is harder than it looks. (For advice on estimating the space needed to park a given number of cars, see the 'Calculations' section in Chapter 14, 'Event site'.)

If you are expecting large numbers of cars and if you have no experience of managing and directing them, seek advice from the local authority or the police. If you are planning a large event and are really stuck, it is best to approach a large stadium or car park operator and be prepared to pay for some advice from their traffic manager. Make sure that you are sure of the fee payable before entering an agreement, they may simply demand a flat fee, or demand a percentage of total gate money. There are also a few experienced freelance people around, so you should be able to get advice and assistance from somewhere.

Car parking is important, not only in relation to access, but also to sign posting, marshals, arrival, departure, adequate vehicle security and simply taking care of the 'pride and joy' of so many motorists.

Don't expect the owners of shiny new saloons to drive through axle-deep mud or over rough broken concrete. Don't expect them to be happy about parking so close together that they cannot open the door to get out without damaging the car next to them, or more importantly the risk of the car next door damaging theirs. Remember to be considerate with you arrangements.

Car park site

The site is normally selected for convenience, but make sure that it is suitable and big enough.

As mentioned in Chapter 14 'Event site', traffic at some events has a definite pattern. Though 9000 people are expected to arrive by car for an event, that does not mean that you will need parking for 9000 vehicles. It is possible that at a dog show for example, competitors will arrive in waves to attend heats for different breeds of dog. Losers will depart as the next wave arrives for the next heat and then more losers will depart. In this way it is possible that of our 9000 vehicles a maximum of 2000 will need to be parked at any one time.

I always like to arrange to visit the site and drive over the car park field(s) and access routes. In that way I can check that the access is wide enough, what ground conditions are (dry/wet) and physical state (smooth/rough). I can also get an idea of the lie of the ground and the size of the field and where the exits and entrances are. With that information in mind I can begin to plan how the cars will be parked.

It is important that while planning car parking facilities, you remember the event format and who will be arriving. For example if it is a canoe race, many vehicles will arrive towing trailers, or with large roof racks. Ensure that sufficient space and headroom is allowed and remember that the lanes between cars and turning circles at gates will need to be larger to accommodate larger vehicles with long trailers.

You should also check the roads, approaches and junctions, etc. This will give you an idea of where you need to erect signs. (On blind or restricted bends you or the police may have to erect warning signs.)

If possible mark out the car park lanes. The best method is to use a sports groundsman's marking wheel – the sort they use to mark out the white lines of football pitches. The marking is simple and cheap, and will wash away within a couple of weeks, so there will be no ugly marks on the grass. This device can also be used to peg out and mark up the event site, so it is worth the effort needed to find and borrow one.

Portable/temporary signs

The traffic manager and roving car park supervisor will be responsible for making sure that all entry and exit signs required are available and that when the event is over, that signs are collected and returned to the event manager.

Car park marshals are sometimes required to stand for hours in a cold/wet, or hot/sunny field, pointing left or right to direct cars. Portable signs, similar to those carried by 'lollipop ladies' (school crossing patrols), are of use to them. The portable sign is cheap; a simple 2-metre pole with a white disk of hardboard nailed to the top. To the front of that is attached a direction arrow with a simple central bolt and wing nut through it. By loosening the nut and simply swivelling the arrow, the car park marshal has a sign that points left, right or straight on! (Painting 'STOP' on the back in red letters is useful too. Cars approaching from behind should stop, and by twisting their sign to display 'STOP' to oncoming motorists marshalls can halt the flow of cars to resolve a problem.)

Tip

Remember that swivel signs only work when attended. If you construct swivelling signs and leave them unattended, some fool will change the direction and you may not realise what is going wrong with your well-planned traffic flow for some time.

Traffic cones

When considering sign posting and traffic control, the effectiveness of the humble red and white traffic cone should not be ignored. Though a sign may request a driver to follow a specified path, a row of cones effectively forces them to take the required route. Cones are widely available and can easily be moved to different positions as requirements change. Funnels of traffic cones are particularly effective in guiding traffic to the correct parking locations when large open fields first come into use and will assist the marshals in that field.

Hidden dangers

When presented with a field nominated as a car park, ask the landowner about hidden dangers. Apart from fresh cow-pats, such items as tree stumps, rusted fence posts and wire, or even ditches may be hiding in what appears to be a level grassy field.

If at all possible arrange for the grass to be cut before the event to expose any hidden dangers and contours, and where necessary have the dead dry grass removed as a safety precaution. If any dangers are pointed out or discovered, make sure that posts and tapes are used to clearly mark and fence off the areas of danger.

Don't forget that dangers can come from different directions too. An 'interesting' but unfenced river or pool is a high risk to inquisitive children. Stinging nettles and giant hogweed plants provide botanical dangers. Ants' nests are annoying and wasps swarming around decaying fruit under an apple tree are quite risky. Low branches or cables can catch some drivers unawares, as can debris hidden in long grass. You must consider everything when reviewing the proposed car park.

Get as much detail from the landowner as you can. Their local knowledge will tell
you if an area is subject to flooding 'at high tide', or in heavy rain. They can tell you

which areas become soft and muddy with even a little rain. Use their knowledge, to make your plans and arrangements.

Ask the landowner and look around the field in the planning stage. Check the field later when it is nearer the time for the event and when the wasps and giant hogweed may have moved in. Take a final inspection tour before the car parks open, making sure that existing and new known dangers are clearly sign posted and fenced off.

The traffic manager should show and brief the roving car park supervisor about existing dangers and warn them to keep watching out for and handling any others during the event.

Roving car park supervisor

For larger events, using several car parking fields as you have seen, I propose that you should appoint a roving car park supervisor (RCPS). That is the senior car park marshal who, depending on site and circumstances, should be supplied with a vehicle. The vehicle should be capable of carrying half a dozen people, it should be able to cope with wet grass and some mud, and it should be able to carry various supplies. A Landrover would be ideal, but I have seen people carriers and minibuses used for this purpose.

The RCPS has responsibility for making sure that car parks are operated safely and efficiently and that appropriate staff are trained, equipped and briefed to perform the desired functions. Being mobile the RCPS will be able to transport staff to the location where they are most needed and as has been mentioned elsewhere, may be insured to take people around to look for lost cars. The RCPS will also carry a supply of water and maybe snacks for staff, as well as carrying basic sign making equipment.

Staff – safety factors

Traffic direction and car parking is a lot harder than it looks, especially if you are going to do it properly. It takes considerable training and experience, quite a lot of physical effort and a lot of concentration. The following points should be taken into account if the job is to be done effectively and safely.

Legal

Traffic direction on private land within the site can be undertaken by anyone, but you should note that for health and safety reasons, persons under 18 years of age should not be used.

Traffic direction on the public highway can usually only be undertaken by police officers or traffic wardens. It is illegal – and dangerous – for others to direct traffic on the road.

Sufficient staff/skills

The traffic manager or roving car park supervisor should make sure that they have plenty of staff to staff the car parks. Even where parking is free of charge, when cars start to arrive you need two people on each gate and a string of marshals inside the car park. If motorists don't see a car park marshal waving them on about every 30 metres, they will simply go off and decide where they want to park for themselves.

Plan it so that drivers can clearly see the next marshal (with a portable direction sign), waving them on to the parking area.

If at all possible the marshals should be accustomed to working as a team, because if they don't co-ordinate their efforts they are a lot less effective.

If your staff is unskilled you can make up for a lack of skill with higher numbers of staff. The local police or special constabulary may be persuaded to give your car parking staff some training or advice on directing cars – if you ask very nicely – though lately there have been questions of legal liability for accidents to car parking marshals so they may have to refuse to help!

If you have to boost numbers to make up for reduced skill and experience, you *must* increase the level of supervision to ensure that traffic is being handled safely!

Proper clothing

Remember that the car park marshals will be out in the open for considerable periods, so you must make sure that they are properly clothed. If they are cold and wet, or if they are sunburned and overcome with heat stroke, they will not be concentrating on what they are doing and will therefore not be doing the best possible job.

In winter they should be warm and dry and protected against the effects of the wind. In summer they should be protected against the effects of the sun. Carrying a golf umbrella and wearing factor 30 sun lotion may damage their 'street cred' and not look too cool, but it is effective.

No matter what clothing the marshals are wearing, they should additionally have something that makes them easy to spot – preferably a reflective or fluorescent jacket, or a tabard that makes them easily identifiable to drivers. You must clearly distinguish the car park marshals and other staff members from ordinary members of the public.

I have often seen army cadets assisting with car parking, but nobody has requested or insisted that they wear reflective waistcoats. If they wear that remarkably effective camouflage clothing, it may be very military, but it is unnerving to look into an apparently empty field knowing that there are 12 'camouflaged' marshals out there. Such clothing is totally ineffective and potentially dangerous.

Chair

There will be quiet times, when some marshals do not have any traffic to direct and even times when they can do their job just as well while sitting down. Arrange for, or invite them to bring, a lightweight folding camp chair if you can. When not actively directing traffic, the marshals can take a rest by using their folding chair.

A folding chair is best because, by the nature of the job, car park marshals tend to be very mobile and should not have to carry heavy equipment around. It can be slung over the shoulder of the marshal with a simple length of rope, but I have seen a very well prepared and effective marshal with a chair strapped to a rucksack, which contained food, drink and gloves.

Signs

Car park signs should have been erected at the gates. Direction signs should be available if not already erected inside the gates for the benefit of drivers leaving the site, for example 'M4 – Turn Left'. 'Car Park Full' signs are no doubt ready inside the car park gate, ready to be erected and with appropriate signs giving directions to the next or overflow car parks. Marshals may be issued with or invited to make the portable swivelling arrow signs suggested earlier. Marshals may need additional temporary signs, so if not in the roving car park supervisor's vehicle, sign making equipment and material should be easily available elsewhere.

Refreshments

As stated above, traffic direction is a fairly physical activity, requiring skill and concentration. The traffic manager should ensure that all marshals are up to standard, i.e. not so short-sighted that they can't tell the difference between a cow and a Cortina. The traffic manager should also make sure that refreshment and relief breaks are available for the marshals.

Unless you have directed heavy traffic on a cold wet winter day, you cannot possibly know how welcome or refreshing a rest, sitting down in the warm and dry, with a cup of hot soup, can be. Depending on the size of the event, the traffic manager should ensure that the car park supervisors check on the status of all marshals at frequent intervals.

Rest break/relief

As traffic control requires such effort and concentration, rest breaks and a relief should be made available.

Staff experience and skill will vary, as will their health and fitness. Holding your arms out and waving them at traffic is very tiring, but unless you continue to do so, the poor motorists will not quite know what you want them to do.

The roving car park supervisor is ideally placed to undertake frequent patrols around the car parks, checking up on the marshals and arranging for rest or toilet breaks when necessary. (Remember that the RCPS may need to give marshals a lift from the car park to the event site, or they could take half an hour just walking in to visit the toilet!)

For the largest of events, if facilities are available, marshals on mountain bikes or, with the greatest of care, on motorcycles, could also 'slowly and safely' patrol the more remote areas of car parks and access points. The extra mobile patrols must ensure that they are constantly aware of the members of the public wandering around the car park and site. Combined with the roving car park supervisor, the mobile marshals would be an added car park security resource, which will be effective and inspire the confidence of the public. Note that marshals on motorcycles must be insured for that role and you must remind them that they must still abide by all of the rules of the road and also be sensible and safe, setting a good example on site and in car parks.

Tip

If any mobile resources are used, check that the insurance cover in place is adequate and correct and that they are properly trained, briefed and supervised.

Floodlights/torches

If the event runs late, or takes place in the winter months, it is likely that some car park marshalling will be done in the dark, or during twilight hours. If this is the case, it is even more important that marshals are equipped with reflective or fluorescent jackets.

Vehicle and pedestrian gates should be floodlit, as should the marshals at their car park points and police officers in the road, directing traffic. Where mains power is not available, floodlighting generator sets are easily hired and very worthwhile for main gates.

Car park marshals could also carry torches, so that their directions are clear. (It is likely that batteries will be a legitimate expense of running the event, because marshals will almost certainly not want to supply their own.)

Communications

I suggest that it is essential for the traffic manager and any roving or mobile supervisors or marshals and the main car park gates to be in radio contact with the event manager and each other. They are on the spot and hold a heavy responsibility for the smooth functioning of a key element in the success of the event.

If there are any problems or special circumstances they should be in radio contact to get an immediate response to the problem. Imagine that a car park marshal decides that their car park is nearly full and traffic has to be diverted to the new car park from a junction half a mile away. In the time it would take that marshal to run half a mile to the junction and ask for traffic to be diverted to the new car park, there would be a half-mile queue of cars from the junction up to the now full and closed car park gate – what are you going to do with them?

This also illustrates the need for car park marshals to think ahead and warn their controllers in advance that they can say only fit in another 50 cars before they are full – thus prompting diversion of cars to the next car park and deployment of appropriate signs.

Overflow car parks

Car parks have a known or at least estimated capacity. Car park marshals and supervisors should be aware of the capacity and the number of cars currently in the car park or more usefully an estimate of the number of spaces left.

Tip

Car park marshals should declare a car park full when it reaches about 80–90% of capacity (90% if the next car park is close by – 80% if it is further away). That leaves enough space for the vehicles that arrive before the traffic is switched to alternate car parks, and still leaves a bit of free space for late arrivals etc.

It may seem unfair that late arrivals should be allowed to park nearby when others have had to park some distance away. However, looking at the bigger picture, it is preferable that the flustered late arrival should park legally in your car park, rather than rush to a distant car park and risk having an accident, or possibly park illegally. Getting them safely off the street and into the event is the prime objective at this stage.

Car parking charges

Where land is available, off-road free parking is to be advised. That is free of charge not free for all! It quickly clears the roads and allows the organiser to direct the public to a series of gates thereby spreading the burden.

If the car parks are free of charge, there is no delay at the gates and traffic can flow in freely, follow the chain of car park marshals and be parked in one smooth continuous operation.

Charging car parking fees can create problems and additional staff will be required at the gates to collect the fee.

Consideration will have had to be made to ensure that the car parking fee selected is sensible. As described in Chapter 27 'Money', a careful and sensible selection of fee rates will ease the flow of people and cars into the site and reduce the effort and burden of calculating rates and handling of change.

Fee collection

Cash float will be required at each gate, with the appropriate denominations to allow the fee collectors to offer the correct change. Fee collectors will have to be alert to prevent a bottleneck forming at the gate and so blocking the public roads.

There is a temptation for gatekeepers to leave their point and walk towards the next car in the queue, but if they do that, before long they will be half a mile down the road. It is important that gatekeepers are instructed to *stay on their allocated point* and to beckon cars forward to make the cars come to them! If possible, paint a mark using the groundsperson's wheel, or lay down a board to remind them where they should stand.

For large events and shows where fees are being taken for car parking, I suggest that consideration is given to distributing incoming traffic inside the gates through several lanes that are marked out with posts and tapes/ropes or cones, if at all possible.

This approach requires staff to plan and set up the fee lanes, assign fee collectors for each lane and several traffic marshals to simply direct the traffic to appropriate lanes to spread the load of incoming traffic.

Once they have paid, cars from individual lanes can either be filtered back into one lane towards the parking area or, preferably, directed towards different parking areas and marshals in the same parking field.

Using different parking areas in the field speeds parking and clears the entrance faster, but requires additional car park marshals and only really works in a very large car park. Multiple entry and fee-taking lanes certainly speed access during peak arrivals.

Tip

If the authorities will allow it, where there is charged parking, try to arrange for signs to be erected on the approach to the car park gate showing the car parking fee. Better that the motorist in the queue spends time getting that fee ready before reaching the gate, than having the gate constantly blocked while families search for the correct money.

Breakdowns

Wherever large numbers of cars are gathered, there is a chance that a proportion of them will break down. Inevitably, some car-owners will leave radio or lights on so that they will not be able to start their vehicle when they attempt to go home.

If the breakdown happens on site it is unfortunate, but if a car overheats and breaks down on a major junction or in a narrow access lane they could create a catastrophic obstruction. You may be able to arrange for the motoring organisations, or local garage to be present at a really big event. They will be able to tow away breakdowns, or to assist with flat batteries etc. (They will of course make their own financial arrangements with any motorists they assist.) The local farmer could be approached to provide a tractor on site to tow broken down, or bogged vehicles to a safe area, where they can be attended to by breakdown mechanics.

Remember to ensure that any towing vehicle is suitable and that the driver is trained and insured. Drivers could take legal action if they claim that a tractor driver caused damage to their car when towing it!

Towing out of the mud

Larger events are often held in rural locations. Cars are therefore parked in fields and a little rain on wet grass can strand cars on even the gentlest slopes, particularly   **161**

Tips

From experience, the following tips may help:

- Plan ahead.
- Use experienced staff. If you don't have them seek advice or advertise for experienced staff.
- If you are short on experience make up in numbers, training and supervision.
- Visit the site in advance, note the signs, locations, staff and equipment required and make sure that it is supplied and available where and when needed.
- Make good use of warning, directions and information signs. (The car park marshal is bound to get fed up saying 'The fee is one pound per car, or free for OAPs' over and over again.)
- Gate staff must make the cars come to you. Don't fall into the trap of walking towards the next vehicle or you will soon be way out of place. Instead stand your ground and erect a notice such as 'Stop And Pay At Desk'.
- Place the fee collector *inside* the car park field, away from the entrance. If they are on the entrance and a driver without change arrives or one that suddenly realises they didn't want to come into the car park, the entrance will be blocked. Moving them into the field will clear the gate for others.
- If at all possible, plan for car parks to have a separate marked exit so that vehicles trying to leave will not block the entrance.
- If a motorist comes into the wrong entrance you will have a problem. Possibly they were directed to the 'public car park' because they failed to display their 'Judges' or other pass. No matter what the reason, make them either stay where they are and use the public car park, or have them leave via the marked exit and find their way back round again to the appropriate car park. Make sure to tell them that they should stop somewhere safe to find and display any pass (as requested on *all* of the arrival instructions), or they will end in the public car park again.
- Make sure gates are in radio contact.
- Money builds up quickly at gates. Make sure that cash is secure and arrange random cash collections, so that cash can be taken back to the

cashier's office for security, counting, bagging and banking. (Remember to keep sufficient coins for a cash float at each gate.)

- Make sure that any staff on the gates know the person who is coming to relieve them. That is simplified if the relief is brought out by the roving car park supervisor, but some sort of identification or uniform will help.

Checkpoint

With all of the research above in mind and in co-operation with other staff and supervisors, the person responsible for traffic management and car parking should make a checkpoint presentation of their findings and decisions to a small group. They should then review and discuss the research and proposals to confirm that they are correct and that nothing has been missed.

Progress – Chapter 18

You should now:

- understand that safely and efficiently parking large numbers of cars requires skill, stamina and practice,
- accept that the event manager and or traffic manager, if there is one for your event, must visit the proposed car parks and question the landowner as well as closely inspect the sites for condition, access/exit and hazards,
- have rejected unacceptable car parking property and coned off and clearly marked and fenced any identified hazards in the fields that you will use,
- recognise the benefit of temporary and or portable signs and traffic cones in managing traffic flow in car parks,
- understand the roles and have nominated or appointed a roving car park supervisor and marshals where appropriate,
- be aware of and willing to supply the required training, clothing and equipment,
- be aware of the importance of rest break, relief and refreshments to car park marshals and ensure that they get them,

- understand the importance of communications and ensure that selected car park staff are able to communicate effectively, by radio or mobile phone,
- have identified and specified procedures required to allow your staff to safely operate the car parking facility for your event,
- know the problems and benefits associated with free and charged parking and, after consultation and review, have selected your chosen option,
- have reviewed the problems you might encounter and have ensured that procedures are in place and staff trained to deal with them,
- be aware of how to estimate the number of car parking spaces can be fitted into a given area and have practised that approach, and
- have made a checkpoint presentation and had all research and decisions confirmed.

Product completed

- List of staff numbers and skills required to ensure safe coverage.
- Proposed work roster for car park staff.
- Details of proposed training for car park staff, including content and schedules.
- Schedule of equipment clothing and signs required by car park staff.
- Checkpoint review – authorisation to continue.

19 Radio communications

Depending on the size of the event, the site and staff numbers, the availability of two-way radio communications could be an enormous benefit. It would at least keep the supervisors and team leaders in touch with the event manager, security, first aid and the police. If you are proposing to organise a marathon or cycle race, where road closures are necessary, and marshals will be posted at remote sites, you should strongly consider their method of communications. Though most people have mobile phones available, which they could use to call a control point, there are reception black spots that might prevent mobile phones from working. You must check phone and radio reception and ensure that all members of staff who need to communicate with each other, with the event manager and with first aid staff are able to do so.

Contact the radio hire companies and make use of their experience and skills. Explain your proposal, describe the site and event to them, and they can advise on the number and range of radio communication equipment that will be necessary, and give you an estimate of the cost. They can supply the base station, aerial, generator and training for staff as well. Depending on the amount of radio traffic expected some companies, for an additional charge, also supply a skilled and experienced base station controller, to manage communications. If the radio supplier suggests that you have a base station controller, take their advice. Operating a radio base station can be quite stressful, and it is certainly a skill that cannot be acquired over night.

Radio discipline

It is advised that everyone who is issued with a radio has some instruction on the discipline needed to make effective use of the equipment. For example, keep messages short and accurate. Don't indulge in unnecessary chatter because somebody with an emergency message may be waiting to get through. When sending messages

Emergency messages

Part of that training process should be that staff know how to make an emergency radio call and that other staff know what to do when an emergency call is being made.

For example, all staff could be taught that when making an emergency radio call they prefix that call with 'Urgent, Urgent, Urgent'. They will learn that on hearing those words, they should stop trying to make their own calls and listen to the emergency. If they are not involved in the emergency they should refrain from using the radio, unless they are called to do something by managers and supervisors. (Note: to avoid confusion, radio procedures have been included in Chapter 24, 'Emergency and normal procedures'. That chapter also covers the use of an emergency radio log.)

Tips

- Always test your radio before leaving the issue point.
- Always obey what the radio controller tells you to do (for example 'Everybody keep quiet' or 'Repeat the last message').
- Keep messages short.
- Do not talk over other messages.
- Think before you talk.
- Start a call by saying who you are calling and who you are.
- Wait for them to reply.
- If they don't reply after three attempts, call somebody else.
- Make sure emergency messages have a known prefix.
- Everybody should give way and listen to emergency messages.
- End a message with the word 'Over' to show you are finished.
- Use code words and messages – such as broadcasting a message on the public address system for 'Mr Winston Churchill' to relay private messages to security staff (see Chapter 13, 'Accommodation and services' – section on 'Emergency PA messages').
- Don't overcomplicate – if Car Park B is full, say 'Car Park B is full.'
- If your radio appears to have a fault, report it immediately to the person who issues radios.

Progress – Chapter 19

You should now:

- be aware how valuable radios will be on a large site or at a large event,
- have researched among the commercial radio hire organisations to establish the numbers required, base station, cost, etc.,
- have requested at least three quotes, including charges for delivery, set up, on-site base station operator, possible generator, possible training, collection and removal,
- have asked the suppliers to include availability in their quote and to confirm that they can supply your requirements for your proposed dates,
- have designed a radio issue administrative procedure to keep track of issue and return (if the suppliers don't have one),
- devise and introduce a method of sending emergency messages, and
- have identified those members of event staff who need a radio, e.g. event manager, cashier, police liaison, ambulance, etc.

Product completed

- Details of any radio equipment supplier.
- List of staff and liaison staff (police, ambulance etc) who will be issued with a radio.
- A radio issue administration procedure if not provided by supplier.
- Emergency radio log defined and produced.
- Required training session content and schedules where required.
- Checkpoint review – authorisation to continue.

20 Staffing

To run an event you need people. People to take money at the gates, people to make sure drivers park their trucks and cars where they are supposed to and even people to clean up afterwards. *But* – the more people you have, the bigger your problem.

Organising and managing staff for anything but the smallest event could be a significant task. The following sections offer some advice and guidance on selecting, organising and managing event staff.

The right people

Staff are a critical component of your event. The smallest primary school event can probably be arranged and run by a couple of teachers in their spare time and other than a little help from the caretaker will probably need no additional staff input. Most events, especially where fundraising or profit is the main objective, will have considerable staffing requirements, because to generate high financial returns, you have to attract and deal with large numbers of people.

Your staff members will need specific skill sets and experience to be able to perform their tasks safely and effectively. They will also need suitable and effective supervision and management. Some staff may even need specialist clothing and equipment, or special training in the tasks assigned. As event manager you will be responsible for organising that.

What staff are required?

There are many questions you need to answer regarding your staff. What skills do you want for this event? What staff do you have to have to safely run your event? How many staff do we require?

Your event is unique, so some potential staffing options may or may not apply. The staff you need depends on your specific aims, event objectives, event type, specialist requirements, risks and dangers common to your event. Do you need a qualified football referee, or a veterinary surgeon, or perhaps a reindeer herder? Only you can answer that question!

Numbers

Defining the number of staff required isn't 'rocket science'. For example, deciding on the number of gate staff you need depends on the number of public gates you have! But it can be a little more complicated than that. How long are the gates going to be staffed? Do you need one person or several at each gate? Will they be working shifts? Do you need extra cover for sickness? Will refreshment and rest breaks need to be covered? Who could you call on if the gate person was dealing with an emergency? If there is an emergency at a gate, or somewhere else on site what emergency staff do you need to have? How will they get to the site of the incident? The further you look into the 'what if' questions the more complicated the task becomes.

Roles/job types

For most general events, the roles/job types required can be drawn from the example list below. Depending on the size of the event, some of these duties and responsibilities may either be separate jobs for individuals with the appropriate skills and experience, or for smaller events several responsibilities may be combined within the job description of one suitably skilled person.

You will see that in the list below, I have included a breakdown of some of the duties/tasks assigned to each role. These may be organised and managed by one person, or for very large events, each sub task may be delegated to a different suitably skilled person.

For example there may be a deputy event manager with responsibility for traffic management and another deputy event manager responsible for accommodation, where responsibility for accommodation is subdivided into tents, Portakabins™ and furniture.

Remember that one person may take responsibility for a particular segment of the arrangements, or the individual duties may be delegated to different people with particular knowledge of tents or furniture etc. It all depends on your event size, objective and scope, and the skills, knowledge, experience and availability of your staff.

Standard jobs and responsibilities

- Event Manager (one and only one – all roles below report to the event manager who alone has the authority to make decisions)
- Deputy Event Manager (as many as needed)
- Local Authority Liaison
- Emergency Services Liaison
- Health and Safety Executive Liaison
- Site Planner
- Catering
- Personnel
  - Staff recruiting
  - Staff scheduling
  - Staff supervision
  - Staff/work roster
- Site/Route Marshal
  - Plans and control site layout
  - Directs arrival and set-up of attractions
  - Plans and locate toilets and other facilities
  - Manages problems during the event
  - Manages strip down after event
- Security
  - Cash security – liaise with cashiers/marshal etc.
  - Overnight cash security
  - Oversee control of 'valuables' e.g. tickets/prizes
  - Perimeter security
  - Gate security
  - Fire security – watch for fires and dangerous acts
  - Beer tent security
  - Night site security
- Accommodation
  - Tents
  - Portakabins™
  - Furniture
- Services
  - Electricity (mains or generator)
  - Water
- Advertising
- Ticket Sales
  - Ticket purchase/printing

- Pre-event sales
- Day of event gate sales
- Signs/notices
  - Printing/purchase
  - Distribution/erection
  - Removal/storage
- Cashiers
  - Cashier's office (bag and count income)
  - Cashier – make outgoing payments
  - Cash collectors (circuit of site taking cash to cashier's office for counting and bagging)
- Accountant(s)
- Communications
  - Phones
  - Radios
  - Messengers/runners
- Transport
  - Moving people
  - Moving money
  - Moving equipment
- Traffic Manager
- Car Parks
  - Roving Car Park Supervisor
  - Gate Controller
  - Parking Charge Collector
  - Car Park Marshals (teams)
  - Car Park Security Patrol
- Site cleanliness
  - Toilets and attendant (if not organised by supplier)
  - Litter
  - Food waste
- Supplies Officer (may be included as part of other jobs)
  - Toilet rolls
  - Air freshener
  - Buns/drinks
  - Charity cash-collecting buckets
  - Gate tickets
  - Receipts
  - Black bin bags for litter collectors
  - Gloves for cleaners and litter pickers

175

- Etc. etc. etc.
- Fireworks Liaison
- Safety Manager
- Animal welfare and movement
- First aid/medical services

As can be seen from the list above, a wide variety of different skills could be required to manage and run your event. The range of duties that need to be filled means that most events will need to find and employ some staff. In a sizeable event, you will require a considerable number of staff with a variety of different skills and those staff members must be located, hired, organised, scheduled, controlled, possibly trained, briefed, managed and most important of all – available at the right time and place.

Make a note that some of the decisions you make here may complicate your staff management and scheduling problems even further.

List the roles

You must identify and list all of the roles/job titles that you need to fill. Don't forget that the list of roles above is a guide only and that specialist events will probably need specialist roles that are not listed here. For example a shooting event may require safety officers, weapons officers and range officers. An animal show will probably require the presence of a vet and perhaps a blacksmith/farrier. Does a racing pigeon show need a meteorologist to check the weather conditions and confirm that winds and an approaching storm front are favourable for a release? You know your event, target audience and requirements, so you must compile a list of necessary roles and staff.

Define the numbers

When you know the roles you have to fill you need to know how many of each role you will require, for example 'gateperson' is a role, but you will require as many gatepeople as you have gates, plus some reserves.

Review the roles against staff you have available. Bearing in mind the size of your proposed event and the work involved, you also have to decide if roles can be combined into one job description for a suitably qualified member of staff, or if perhaps a single role needs to be shared and so requires two job descriptions. For example, though there are common elements to their jobs, the morning gateperson has different responsibilities to the afternoon gateperson. The morning gateperson concentrates on arrivals and taking money, while the afternoon gateperson probably focuses on getting people off the site when the event closes.

Remember that at this stage your event planning is still a work in progress and requests and advice from the authorities may require you to revisit this task to define new roles, merge roles, or simply drop roles.

Reviewing the list of necessary roles and knowing the size and scope of your show, you can allocate those roles to different jobs. Thus, for your specific event the two roles of 'traffic manager' and 'roving car park supervisor' *may* be combined into one role – 'transport manager'.

I suggest that appropriate supervisors should define and write an extended job description for each role before moving on to the next.

Job descriptions

For each role/job you need to fill you should generate a job description. Defining a job description will take some thought and familiarity with your proposed event objective, requirements/classifications, attractions and site.

When I am defining staff requirements I compile an 'extended' job description, which has four parts:

- a person specification,
- a job description (list of tasks required in that role),
- a training schedule, and
- an equipment schedule.

The person specification

The person specification is simply a list of the abilities, skills and experience that an applicant must have to fill a given job. It is a 'shopping list' of attributes that will help you to select a suitable candidate for the role. You might for example specify that a car park marshal needs the following attributes:

- a mature and sensible person,
- previous car park marshal experience *if possible*,
- if not experienced, available/willing to train before the event,
- healthy, active and able to stand for at least 4 hours at a time,
- good eyesight with or without glasses,
- willing to work in any weather,
- strong willed and able to deal with conflict.

The person specification allows you to plan and propose the attributes required for a given job. For some roles you may need to specify some attributes as mandatory and others as simply desirable. Depending on the candidates available, you may have to employ somebody who does not have all of the attributes required. If you do, you have an obligation to introduce training and closer monitoring and supervision as control measures to reduce or remove any risk associated with employing them.

Note: Remember that this is an illustration only – you must define your job descriptions based on your own unique event and requirements.

The job description

Next you have to define the role. To follow through with our car park marshal example above, the job might be described as follows:

- A uniformed role – where the marshal has to wear a reflective jacket and perform physically demanding traffic control and direction for up to two hours at a time in all weathers.
- The marshal will guide and control moving vehicles by use of clear hand and arm movements as will be demonstrated and practised during the familiarisation/training course to be held on 25th July at 1400hrs at the club house.
- The marshal will be required to see coloured badges fixed inside the windscreen of approaching cars and then direct them to the appropriate entrance and parking area (so must not be colour blind).
- Working shifts of either 0800hrs to noon, noon to 1600hrs, or 1600hrs to 2100hrs as directed or agreed.
- Working in accordance with their training, in small teams or independently, away from supervision and using their own initiative.
- Informing the roving car park supervisor of any problems, including lack of space in the car park in use, persons reporting lost cars and anything that may cause damage or is a risk to members of staff or the public.
- Where required to do so, remaining as car park monitor when a car park is declared full. While doing so to maintain order in the car park, ensure that late arrivals park safely, in designated areas and act as an additional car park security patrol.
- Where required to do so, transferring at the request of the roving car park supervisor to direct traffic in any new or overflow car park that is opened.
- At all times to act in a manner that promotes the safety and security of themselves and everyone else.

The training schedule

178 Excluding the detailed briefing they will receive before they begin their shift, this schedule lists the training the candidate may need if they do not already have the desired experience. For our car park marshal this may be:

- the selection and wearing of protective and visible clothing,
- the use and construction of a portable traffic direction sign,
- the clear and efficient direction of traffic by recognised and standardised hand signals as illustrated in the highway code,
- the identification and classification of vehicle passes and badges issued to different people attending the event and their access rights,
- the safe and efficient use of an event radio,
- the collection and storage of cash from car park fees,
- familiarisation with the risk assessments related to the job, and
- familiarisation with normal and emergency procedures related to the job and to the appropriate risk assessments.

Though the member of staff should be trained in the skills required to perform their job and be fully briefed, they should also be supplied with some documentation. They need a copy of their job description (required tasks), training and equipment schedules, site maps and the clothing and equipment required to do the job.

The equipment schedule

This schedule should list any equipment that is required by the candidate to perform the role. For the car park marshal the list would include:

- a portable vehicle direction sign,
- a reflective jacket,
- a secure money-collection container,
- cash float,
- a torch and or floodlights,
- emergency sign making equipment,
- relevant emergency procedures,
- a site map, and
- an event radio (one per gate).

Event manager's manual

Where possible I create a reference sheet for each job, collating the person specification, job description, training schedule and the equipment schedules together.

There will be a reference sheet for each job/role and copies of all job reference sheets will be retained in the event manager's manual.

Employment law and regulations

The rules are complex. You must check on the status of your 'staff', because if they are classified as employees, a whole new raft of legislation applies. If you employ people for work, then you must abide by complicated tax, National Insurance and pensions legislation. Employees then come under the Europan working hours directive, and with 'employees' you must also abide by the workplace fire precautions regulations. The workplace regulations require the 'employer' to carry out a risk assessment and act on any findings.

To illustrate the complexities, I am told that the following is true:

> If an indoor event is designated public entertainment by the local authority, they will require you to apply for a Public Entertainment Licence (PEL). In such a case the relevant and specific fire safety requirements imposed will depend on the venue, event type, size etc. *But* if a PEL is not required and people are employed to work at the event, the Fire Precautions (Workplace) Regulations 1997 (amended in 1999) – which are enforced and managed by the local fire authority – will apply. However, this set of regulations would technically also apply if a PEL was in force even though the PEL regulations would probably be classed as 'the most appropriate' to apply.

Is that clear? No! Join the club!

Tip

Seek expert advice from the local authority, fire service, police and health and safety executive. As usual, check with the appropriate authorities and experts, to ensure that you are complying with all appropriate regulations, laws and rules.

Using volunteers

Using volunteers may further complicate potentially high staffing levels. You may need two or three volunteers (working for a couple of hours each) to cover a single shift and it is possible that volunteer staff may not always turn up on time every time.

Managing, motivating, recruiting and controlling volunteers has its own problems, some of which are discussed below. Splitting shifts among volunteers reduces your demand on their time and makes it easier to get volunteers, but it also significantly increases the number of staff required and exponentially increases the management problems.

Recruitment

Where do you get the volunteers? In some instances your club, school, or league could supply the staff (see 'Members of your organisation' section below). However, it is likely that for anything other than the smallest event, additional staff will have to be found. Some possible sources of volunteer staff are:

- your school, club, staff,
- other schools/clubs (the idea being 'you help us and we'll help you'),
- cadet forces, scouts etc. (especially if you give a modest donation to their funds) – but bear in mind legal restrictions as to the 'work' that can be carried out by minors,
- local and associated charity volunteers,
- territorial army (especially if there is a charitable aspect or some training value, such as orienteering they can get out of the event, or if you allow them to set up a recruiting stand),
- appeals in local press or radio,
- last of all, family and friends.

Reliability

You cannot and should not wholly rely on volunteer staff unless you have close links with them and previous experience of their reliability and commitment. With all due respect and apologies to volunteers, I realise that a lot of voluntary organisations are managed very efficiently and the volunteers themselves are trustworthy and committed. Unfortunately, I have experienced the disasters that occur when voluntary staff are not as reliable as promised.

The main problem is that as the event manager you have no leverage to control volunteers. Though this should not strictly be necessary, if the success of the event relies on ten people at the gates collecting money, the whole event is a costly disaster if the event was superb, but there was no one at the gates and the public walked in for free.

Paid staff know that if they fail to turn up they will not be paid and may well lose their job. I was called in to arrange emergency cover at an event when a group of volunteers had accidentally double booked themselves and simply decided not to turn up to one of the events. They didn't even bother to tell the event manager that they weren't coming. He found out early on during the day of the event when he called their leader to ask when he and his team were going to arrive for the final briefing!

At another event, the weather on the day was very cold and wet and 11 out of 16 volunteers simply decided that they had better things to do than to stand around in a cold wet field that day. The event had to be cancelled.

On another occasion a club member generously promised eight people. During briefings he assured everybody that 'his team' would be there on the day. Unfortunately, 'on the day' *he* arrived – with just his rather disgruntled wife. It transpired that he simply could not deliver what he had promised and dragging his wife along had been a last-ditch effort to bring some staff and save face.

Tip

I always insist on having the names of the volunteer staff in advance and, if at all possible, hold a briefing meeting a few weeks before the event to make sure that they exist, that they know they have been volunteered and that they will actually come. This also gives me the opportunity to check on the quality of staff I am getting and I can select team leaders etc.

The moral of these stories is that generally you cannot rely 100% on volunteer staff, unless you have considerable previous experience of them, or close links with them.

Numbers

It is acceptable to expect paid staff to work their full eight-hour shift with a pre-scheduled break for lunch. Unfortunately, volunteers are not often sufficiently committed to invest that much effort. One of the attractions I have used is that in some areas I double up on volunteers, they share one job and while one works the other can enjoy the event – for free. (They may have got in free but they are spending money at the event so I have an added audience member.) I also use these extra 'resting' staff as a pool of reserves in case somebody else doesn't show up. A suitably desperate plea, with a suitably grateful acknowledgement that they have 'saved the event', usually persuades them to make the extra effort.

Whatever you do, make sure that you have enough staff to fill all the critical posts that you need to effectively and safely run the event. If at all possible, always have a few spare staff in reserve as well.

Tip

If you nominate 'reserves', *always* use them. They will not be best pleased if they attend and sit in a tent all day waiting to be needed. At least every couple of hours, get some of the reserves out to do a security or safety review tour of the site and make them feel wanted and valued as well.

Selecting a team leader

If you get any number of people working together, one of them has to have some degree of authority, to control, supervise and co-ordinate the work of the rest. Some organisations have built in rank structures (cadets for example); other groups naturally select their own leaders. On some occasions, however, you (or the deputy event manager responsible for that element of the event) will have to select and appoint team leaders yourself.

Ask them if they have a leader. If not, ask if any of them should be the leader, this usually results in the group pointing out somebody they look up to, so you can consider making them the leader. If there is no leader or their nominated leader is for some reason unacceptable to you, you will have to appoint one. Your selection can be based on previous experience, but with staff of equal ability, depending on age and maturity of staff, it may be sensible to appoint a more mature person as team leader for each group.

Using simple questions such as 'Anyone handled gate money before?', and with common sense and observations, you should be able to nominate a leader. If the team members know each other and you are in doubt about who to pick, it is useful to watch their reaction when you 'think aloud' about somebody. If you mumble 'Maybe Bert would make a good leader' and they all groan or laugh and three of them say they are going home – Bert may not be the best person for the job. Watch them during the briefing; if they all turn to Maria for an opinion, Maria is probably their natural leader. Remember though *you* are ultimately responsible. Good leadership is based on organisational and motivational skill, not popularity, so remember the most popular team member will not necessarily make a good leader.

Briefing

As in any organisation, distribution of work and devolution of responsibilities is a problem in itself. The larger the work force, the larger the problem. With larger staff numbers, it is likely that the work force will have to be divided into teams, with team leaders appointed purely to simplify the task of giving instructions and briefings.

Remember that briefing and issuing jobs to a group becomes increasingly difficult as the size of the group increases. Consider breaking staff down into teams, brief the team leaders and leave them to brief the team members.

Where staff will be at a remote point, for example marshals on a marathon or cycle race route, they should all be very thoroughly briefed. In addition, when the marshals are dropped off at their remote and sometimes isolated points, their supervisor should orient them by telling them where the racers/runners will come from and go to. Their supervisor should make sure remote staff know where their closest staff contacts are and that they have a copy of the route map, event timetable etc. If at all possible I give remote staff an estimated time of arrival of the race or procession etc. at their point. If road closures are to be enforced, they should also be informed of times and closure points in their vicinity.

At a time when most people have mobile phones, remote marshals if not equipped with an event radio should have the contact numbers for the event manager, first aid and their supervisor.

Tip

I suggest that if there are more than 15 staff, you should consider breaking them down into teams. The teams should be divided 'naturally', for example 'pedestrian gate staff' and 'vehicle gate staff', or 'arena staff', 'road staff' and 'mobile staff'. Brief the team leaders and allow them to cascade the information down to their team members in separate briefing sessions later.

Debriefing

At strategic points during the day, at the end of each day and certainly at the end of the event, you should have debriefing sessions. Depending on the number of staff involved, this should either be with the whole staff, or with team leaders who have previously debriefed their teams.

Although you have debriefed team leaders, always hold a follow-up session for anyone who feels they have something important to say – you never stop learning yourself! Though frequently there is little to say at a debrief, it is possible that some critical oversight may be brought to the attention of the event manager or team leader that could save the day, or make tomorrow go a lot better.

It is infinitely better to have a fruitless debrief, than not to hold one and miss something important. A debrief session also reinforces the teams' perception of your need and respect for the team leaders and staff. Don't be shy about standing up and thanking them all during a debrief, and if a member of staff or team leader has come up with a cunning plan to resolve a major problem, sing their praises as well. It motivates that person and also motivates others to look at their role or sector and gives them the encouragement to make their own suggestions.

Communications

Ensuring that lines of communication are open and working is an important responsibility of the event manager. Cascade briefing and debriefing will help to make sure that communications lines are unclogged and effective, but a few more factors should be considered.

As the size of the site increases, the number of staff and the communications problems increase. The event manager must make absolutely certain that at all times there is a way for staff to communicate quickly with him or her, or at least with the event manager's office – which itself will be in immediate contact with the event manager.

The most remotely located staff member with the most insignificant responsibilities could be the first person to become aware of an emergency, such as a fire in the car park, or a member of the public collapsing following a heart attack. It is therefore vital to make sure that all members of staff know how and where to contact key event managers and that they know how to summon appropriate assistance without delay.

Staff selection

You may be able to staff the whole event with members of your football club, Round Table or whatever organisation is running the event. However, you must always remember that the common sense, skills and abilities of the people selected must match the task they will be given. An inactive person with failing eyesight is not the best person to select as a car park attendant, no matter how eager and enthusiastic they may be!

Members of your organisation

Using members of your organisation has advantages:

- You know them and their skills, strengths and weaknesses.
- They may do the jobs without pay or reward.
- They are readily available and have a vested interest.
- You can call in their family and friends as well (arm bending).
- Fancy titles can persuade them to take on roles.
- You have some leverage and control over them.

Unfortunately, there are also potential disadvantages:

- The right skills may not be available.
- If there are not enough of them available you will have to pay others to help. Your volunteers may resent the inequality with paid staff and start looking for free refreshments and travel expenses etc.
- They will probably not be willing to work long shifts (e.g. over four hours).
- You have no real control over them; they may walk off the job if they get bored or cold and wet, possibly without telling anyone.

Paid staff

Using paid staff means that the above disadvantages are instantly eradicated. The only real problem is that you actually have to pay 'paid' staff. Arranging for the appropriate number of paid staff with the right skills and experience could prove to be a very expensive exercise.

Part-time/job-share staff

For the duration of the event, part-time staff who share the role can fill most posts.

For example, for a two-day event, two people could share a job, one doing mornings, the other doing afternoons.

Ticket-sellers, gate-money collectors, car-park attendants and similar positions can be filled by anyone who is available at the time! That is, as long as they are sound of life and limb have the appropriate skills and are properly briefed. The problems grow because the more part-timers and 'shifts' you utilise, the greater the scheduling, briefing and logistical problems become.

Scheduling cover for 15 jobs, taking into account availability, meal breaks, preferences, skills and experience, is a complex task. The more drop-outs, sickness and emergencies etc. that we throw into the equation the more complex the scheduling becomes, rapidly reaching a point where it is impossible.

This added complication is one reason why we delegate elements of the work to deputy event managers. Their scheduling task with smaller numbers of staff are much simplified and if you have chosen wisely they can use their particular knowledge, skills and experience to make a good job of it, while you concentrate on the bigger picture.

Full-time staff

A full-time member of staff must fill some jobs. That is, they may still be a volunteer, working on the event evenings and weekends, but they should concentrate on just one role as far as possible for the duration of the event. As a volunteer, they probably have their normal everyday job to attend Monday to Friday, 9 to 5, but outside those times, you must ensure that they are available to make the fullest commitment to some roles, such as deputy event manager.

Committee

Never try to arrange anything but the very smallest event by a loose committee of people with equal authority; it won't work. It is widely believed that a camel is a horse that was designed by a committee and that perfectly illustrates the sort of problems that can occur using this approach. The camel looks vaguely like a horse, it's got a head, a body and the right number of legs, 'but a horse it aint'! Using a comittee to design your horse, you could even get a camel with four front legs, because there was confusion about who was doing the back legs!

Delegation

While delegation is necessary and acceptable, remember the Golden Rule – 'Delegate   **187**

... but not too far!' Delegation eases the burden at the top, allowing deputy event managers to schedule their own staff, and converts one huge problem into several smaller and simpler problems. However, it can also create a lot of new problems.

As an illustration of how simple decisions can radically complicate matters, consider organising a member of staff to do one vital job for an eight-hour shift. If we make the decision to allow that job to be shared and split into four, two-hour shifts, we suddenly have at least six problems (and with a little consideration you can probably easily add a few more to this list).

- Who is going to locate and recruit those extra three members of staff?
- Who is going to organise a reserve to cover sickness?
- Who is going to ensure that all the selected staff have the right skills and training?
- Who is going to organise their briefing and debriefing?
- Who is going to manage and supervise them to make sure one of them is doing the job for the whole eight hours?
- If there is an emergency, who will take responsibility for knowing who is doing the job at any given time?

And that's just the sharing of one job. Imagine what would happen if this was allowed to happen through the whole event, and visualise the disaster that would emerge if all problems were multiplied by 600% or more.

Professionals

Professionals must perform some tasks. This may be for safety reasons or to ensure that best practices are followed and accurate information is being used.

For example if you want electricity connected for the event manager's office, you must use a qualified electrician to undertake the work, to ensure the safety of staff and the public. If you want to provide walkie-talkie radio sets to event marshals, ask a professional to advise you and supply the equipment. They know the range and frequencies that can be used legally, battery life etc. They may even provide a base station operator to act as control.

Police presence

If you are organising a particularly large event, in consultation with the police, I suggest you consider requesting on-site police presence. From the earliest opportunity, you should consult and work with the local police, in planning and organising your event. Take advantage of their advice and their skills in for example undertaking a risk assessment of the event. Listen to what they tell you and act on it.

If you require police presence on site, you will probably be charged a significant fee. Depending on the event type, scope objectives, audience, size and location you may think it worth investing in a small police presence.

When holding negotiations and discussions with the police, investigate the possibility and cost of police cover. Consider the possibility of requesting the attendance of members of the Special Constabulary in the UK. They have full police powers, but are volunteers and so unpaid. (In 2004 payment in some form was being discussed – though no general change is expected for several years.) There may be an administrative charge for their presence, but as salaries are not involved (yet) fees should be significantly lower.

If you do use members of the Special Constabulary, for anything other than the smallest event and certainly for any event where money will be taken at the gates, remember what Specials are. The Special Constabulary in the UK is a disciplined but voluntary and unpaid police service. Take very good care of them. Breaking my own rule I suggest you consider supplying free refreshments and possibly complimentary tickets for their partners and children. A burger and chips, plus a ticket or two so Specials bring their families along rather than leave them at home on a Bank Holiday Monday is not too high a price to pay for eight or more hours of professional police cover. You should remember that if you upset or abuse the good will of Specials you may never get them again, and regulars come at a pretty high price!

If police cover is arranged, make sure that the event manager is in radio contact with them. As a minimum, provide a police officer with an event radio, to act as event liaison and help direct them to any trouble spots.

Police liaison officer

Most police forces have a liaison officer, who will discuss and advise on event arrangements. Take advantage of that opportunity at the earliest opportunity and stay in close contact with them during your planning and delivery of the event.

Police and road traffic

In most police forces, under-resourcing means that the police will probably not want to provide a presence on the event site and may well discourage you from running the event if it means risking major traffic problems.

One thing is almost universally accepted and that is that traffic flow on the public roads is a police responsibility, so they will usually look at monitoring and controlling traffic on the public highway at a major event.

Staff tracking

If you have more than half a dozen staff you need a process to keep track of them. I suggest that all staff must report to the event manager's office to sign on duty and sign off duty. This has many benefits; for example you have a ready record of which staff are working on site at any time. In an emergency you can tell the police, fire and ambulance crews who was working at the time of the incident. If somebody calls and needs to urgently trace a member of staff, the event manager knows if they are on site working and can contact them.

Duty schedules

You have seen that supplying the right number of people with the right skills can be a problem. Don't compound that problem with lax management. To ensure that you have scheduled enough staff to fill required roles for the length of the event, you should also provide a duty schedule – that is, a chart showing who is on duty at what time for which role.

The schedule will be a benefit to you, especially if you have delegated different elements of staffing to deputy managers. You will bring all of the staffing resources together on one schedule. This will allow you to see problems, such as gaps, or where one person is assigned two roles at the same time, and allow you to quickly locate spare staff if somebody reports in sick.

For larger events with a mobile work force, I try to obtain a dry wipe-board to record key staff assignments and radio call signs. If no wipe-board is available I have used a sheet of hardboard painted with white gloss paint. I still maintain the duty schedule, all staff still have to report to the event manager's office to sign on and off, but the deployment of senior and key staff is also recorded on the 'at-a-glance' wipe-board.

If details are written clearly on the wipe-board as illustrated below, the event manager can see at a glance who is currently filling each role and what their name and call sign is. As the members of staff who are on duty change, the details on the board are simply wiped and rewritten to bring them up to date.

Event manager	Cashier	First aid	Police
Dave Smith	Sarah Jones	St John	Sgt Davies
Radio – Event 1	Radio – Cash 1	Radio – Doc 1	Radio – Police
Etc.	Etc.	Etc.	Etc.
Etc.	Etc.	Etc.	Etc.

Roving car park supervisor Chris Smith – Radio Roving 1

Elephant Car Park	Oaktree Car Park
Gate Ben Jones – Radio Park 1	Gate Brian Jakes – Radio Park 2
Marshal Tom Williams – Radio M1	Marshal Tim Blood – Radio M4
Marshal Joe Gordon – Radio M2	Marshal Jane Seymour – Radio M5
Marshal Dave Waten – Radio M3	Marshal Sue Black – Radio M6

Progress – Chapter 20

You should now:

- accept that staffing can be a major problem,
- realise that you need the right people with the right skills to fill roles and you may have to train some of them,
- identify the roles and numbers that you require for your event,
- produce a person specification, job description and training and equipment schedule for each job,
- be aware of the complications that employment, tax and pensions legislation may impose on you and be ready to seek expert advice for your staffing needs,
- have evolved a staff selection, recruitment, briefing and debriefing process and a method of selecting or nominating team leaders,
- have an idea of where the staff required can be found,
- have considered your need for police presence on site,
- have established a management method, possibly using a dry wipe-board to display staff positions, names and call signs, and
- have begun to identify potential staff and have recruited anyone who will not cost you anything.

Product completed

- List of staff roles that are required for your event.
- Created a reference sheet with the extended job descriptions which includes person specification, job description, training schedule and equipment schedule for each role.
- List of staff numbers for each role required for your event.
- Possibly have created a dry-wipe duty and status board for the event manager (include a diagram and description of its use).
- Documented risk assessment for each role. Note: do not try to copy them all into the proposal pack. Simply refer to them in the proposal pack, take them with you and be prepared to produce them during your presentations to the authorities while formally asking for licensing and written permission to run the event.
- A schedule of duties to ensure that adequate cover is available when required.
- Checkpoint review – authorisation to continue.

21 First aid

You need first aid cover. No matter what the format, audience size or location, where more than a few people have gathered together, serious consideration should be given to arranging some first aid cover.

Requirements

Our example small primary school fête or sports day can probably make do with the first aid skills of the teachers. However, a larger event will require a more formal first aid presence. In fact, your insurers may insist on a stated minimum level of first aid cover.

Working with your first aid organisation, you should undertake a specific first aid risk assessment. During this assessment you will consider every aspect of your event, including the number of people present, the activities undertaken, specific high-risk activities and situations. In doing this you will identify the hazards and risks and be able to identify the level of first aid cover required.

First aid staff

First aid staff at an event should not have other duties and responsibilities; their time should be dedicated to providing first aid cover. To make that completely clear to you, 'your first aiders must not be marshals or ticket collectors, or have any responsibility and assignment other than being a first aider'.

Qualifications

Not everyone with a first aid certificate is qualified to act as first aider at an event;

for example holders of First Aid At Work certificates are not necessarily qualified to perform first aid duties at a public event.

First aid staff have to meet some regulations, including being over 16 years of age, be trained and equipped, be identifiable and be fit to carry out their duties.

In the UK approach one of the three first aid organisations (St John Ambulance, British Red Cross and St Andrew's Ambulance Association) and be guided by their expertise and experience.

Organisations

Most events and shows call upon the services of one of the three first aid organisations. Each organisation relies on the services of skilled volunteers, though arrangements can be made for paramedic attendance with support from St John (however, fees will be charged for their presence at an event). Remember that the first aid organisations have limited resources, so book early or risk having to move the date of your event because there are no first aid services available.

The local authority will probably insist that you have some cover from one of the voluntary services, supported where necessary by doctors and paramedics. You must not simply rely on dialling 999 or calling out paramedics or ambulances to treat any injury or accident victim.

Radios and equipment

If radios are in use, as a minimum provide the first aid control point or senior medical officer with a radio, so that they can be contacted quickly in an emergency. There would be a benefit if all first aid ambulances and patrols were in radio contact with the event manager's office.

Where radios are used, you should agree a simple and easily identifiable and remembered call sign such as 'Ambulance' or 'Red Cross'.

Ensure that they have a map and thorough briefing on the layout of the site, so that they are able to attend the scene of accidents as quickly as possible.

First Aid staff must be equipped to do the job and that requires more than a couple of packs of plasters and a bottle of aspirins. Don't get involved in this. Leave it to the experts and negotiate with one of the first aid organisations to provide cover. That cover will include the provision of first aid kits, ambulances and first aid tents etc.

Depending on the site being used, it is likely that the first aid staff will work out of their ambulance or bring and set up their own first aid tent. If possible provide them with a substantial first aid room, with running hot and cold water and electricity. If the site is particularly remote, do the best you can, as long as you meet their stated minimal requirements. Remember to try to provide a separate toilet facility, solely for the use of first aid staff.

Casualties

At all times remember the privacy and dignity of any casualty, and train staff to screen the casualty from bystanders and help first aid staff to remove them to a private treatment area as soon as it is safe.

Recording details

I create an accident report form and take advice from the insurers and local authorities as to what details to record. I generally include an associated risk assessment form to accompany the accident recording form, because the fact that there has been an accident tends to point to an unprotected or unknown hazard somewhere.

If there are any accidents or reported injuries, you should be collecting as much information as possible and noting the name and address of the casualty, anyone involved but not apparently injured and any witnesses. If possible obtain a short statement from witnesses for yourself and for your insurer.

Where there has been an accident or injury, your duties when responding to it are:

- to provide medical assistance to any casualty,
- to obtain details of the casualty,
- to record details of the accident,
- to record details of the circumstances leading up to it,
- to record details of witnesses and obtain a short statement,
- to report the incident or accident to the landowner and your insurer,
- if possible to take pictures or video images of the scene,
- to risk assess the area and equipment etc. involved,
- to take remedial action to prevent further incidents or accidents, and
- to record the detail of the risk assessment and remedial action.

It is vital that a member of staff should protect the scene while the casualty is being removed for first aid treatment and to await the arrival of a supervisor who has been trained in risk assessment. Where possible as long as there is no immediate risk to anyone, before anything is touched I would try to take photographs or video images from all angles to show the site and circumstances of the accident or incident for later inspection.

The risk assessor should have been given details of the accident/incident and the full circumstances and should then perform an immediate and detailed risk assessment.

You should be aware that similar equipment or circumstances elsewhere on site may be faulty and should be attended to. For example if a public address tower has collapsed, injuring somebody, event staff should immediately be sent to protect people around other masts that may have the same defect. Those other masts and similar equipment should be checked as soon as possible and/or fenced off if there are doubts as to safety. You should also note that if it was contractor's equipment such as masts, tents or temporary fencing that has failed and caused the injury or incident the representative of that contractor and your insurer should be informed immediately.

Your second duty is to everyone else on site, so you should undertake an immediate risk assessment of the location and circumstances and if necessary take remedial action to ensure that there are no other accidents or injuries caused by the same problem.

Your third and final duty is to report the incident to your insurers and the land-owner with as much information as possible.

Accident form

You may wish to devise an accident form to record appropriate details. The form outlined below contains the details I would expect to record for any accidents or even incidents that do not actually result in injury! This form will take the place of the 'accident book' that most people are familiar with from their work place.

SOUTH BUDLEY STEAM EXTRAVAGANZA	
Accident form	
(circle as appropriate) Paying public – Staff member – Volunteer – Contractor – Exhibitor Other (please write in) Casualty name Age Date of birth Address Phone number	
Date of incident	Time of incident
Date reported	Time reported
Exact location	

Exact circumstances			
Was there any faulty equipment/defect involved?			
Equipment details (including supplier, erector)			
Were photographs taken? If yes, give details		Yes	No
Did casualty seek first aid treatment on site?		Yes	No

If yes, fill in details:

Name of first aid organisation

Contact phone number

Name of person who treated casualty

Explanation of injury

Details of injuries apparent on examination

Injuries suspected due to symptoms and examination

Deployment of casualty, e.g. sent home or transported to hospital – if sent to hospital details of hospital and result of examination

If no, fill in details:

Why did they not seek treatment on site?

When did they seek treatment?

Where did they seek treatment?

Diagnosis after examination

If witnesses available, list details below:

Note status – Staff member – Volunteer – Contractor – Exhibitor – Other

If more than four witnesses, continue on plain paper and staple to this form.

Witness 1			**Witness 2**		
Name			Name		
Address			Address		
Phone number			Phone number		
Status			Status		
Statement taken?	Yes	No	Statement taken?	Yes	No

Witness 3			Witness 4		
Name			Name		
Address			Address		
Phone number			Phone number		
Status			Status		
Statement taken?	Yes	No	Statement taken?	Yes	No

Form completed by
Name
Date
Time

Accident/injury reported to insurer
Name of contact taking report
Date
Time

Accident/injury reported to landowner
Name of contact taking report
Date
Time

NOTES – for example cars and other property left on site and arrangements for their removal by relatives or breakdown services etc.

Associated accident/incident risk assessment form	
Was incident covered by existing risk assessment? Yes No	
If yes, which existing risk assessment?	Who performed the incident/accident risk assessment? Name
Was accident foreseen in any existing risk assessment?	Results of risk assessment Hazards identified
Were control measures in place?	Have circumstances changed since original risk assessment?
Could accident have been avoided?	
How could accident have been avoided?	What measures were taken to remove the hazard or reduce risk and impact?

Your insurers or other authorities may require you to record specific information following an accident or incident. The above outline form supplies all the information I require:

- details of the casualty,
- details of the accident or incident,
- details of the location and circumstances,
- details of on-site first aid given,
- details of organisation/person giving that treatment,
- reason why on-site first aid was not requested,
- diagnosis details of injury suspected from examination,
- details of treatment given,
- details of person completing the form,
- details of when landowner and insurer informed,
- details of immediate risk assessment of accident site,
- details of any existing risk assessment,
- details of findings of new risk assessment, and
- details of measures taken to remove hazard risk.

Disclosure

The details you take are for your own records. You should not disclose details to outside parties. For example the local press may ask for the name and home address of a casualty, or you may get a call from somebody claiming to be a close relative of an injured party. Keep all details of the casualty, their accident, their injuries and their treatment confidential. If in doubt – say *nothing*.

Emergency helipad

As mentioned elsewhere, in considering emergency helicopter evacuation, seek advice. If the event you are organising is likely to generate serious injuries (motor racing, horse riding/racing/jumping etc.) you may wish to set aside an area to be used as an emergency helipad for helicopter paramedics and evacuation of anyone who is seriously injured. Discussions with the appropriate authority will guide you as to size, location, fences, power lines etc. that will need to be considered.

Progress – Chapter 21

You should now:

- be aware of any mandatory first aid cover requested by your insurance company and have investigated availability and cost,
- have planned a visible first aid centre at or near the main vehicle entrance for ease of transfer of any casualty in ambulances or other vehicles,
- have planned for the issue of maps, radios and any other equipment required to first aid staff,
- be ready to brief first aid staff on the radio, its use, their call signs and details of the site, including gates and other landmarks and any hazards disclosed by your risk assessments,
- be ready to issue first aid staff with site maps and lists of event managers and radio call signs etc.,
- have agreed what details will be passed to the event manager if there are any injuries or accidents, and
- have an accident book or accident/incident forms available for use.

Product completed

- Agreed minimum first aid requirements with the authorities and your insurance company.
- Have received quotes for that insurance cover – including accidental injury to staff and visitors etc.
- List of first aid staff required for your event.
- List of equipment and supplies that you must supply to allow them to perform the first aid function.
- Checkpoint review – authorisation to continue.

22 Security

Generally for smaller events, the only security you will need is the vigilance of your staff. The larger the event the greater the need for a dedicated security presence.

There are many aspects of security that should be considered in relation to a larger event and broadly speaking the security presence can be divided into two classes, police presence and private security.

The police

Don't expect the police to provide uniformed car park attendants for you! The police are a public service and they are there to help you, but unfortunately their resources are stretched so they cannot waste resources on car parks.

The police do have a duty to keep traffic flowing on the public highway and most forces accept that if there is an event or show in their area, they will need to allocate sufficient officers to keep the traffic flowing smoothly.

As early as possible in your investigation and planning process, you should be consulting your local police; include security in your discussions. They have vast experience with planning and handling large events, and are keen to keep disruption to a minimum. Where possible, you should get their co-operation. Apart from the obvious advice as to traffic flow and car park entrances and exits, they are a useful source of information regarding conflicting events. Organisers of other events have almost certainly been in contact with them to help plan and arrange their events, so the police liaison officer can let you know if other similar or conflicting events have been arranged in the area for your proposed date.

Traffic

Even the smallest event may attract the passing attention of the local area beat police officer, which itself can be appreciated by junior school fêtes etc.

Larger events will attract considerable numbers of vehicles and, because the police have a duty to keep traffic flowing, they will advise and may attend the event. After consultation with you during the investigation and planning stages, they will probably have assigned sufficient officers and supervisors to ensure that the roads remain open as far as possible. This may include erecting 'Slow' signs, but they are less likely to be involved in the distribution and collection of no parking cones etc. Depending on circumstances, the police may station police officers on traffic points at major junctions etc.

For very large events, the local traffic and highways authority may also arrange for temporary traffic regulation orders modifying local traffic regulations, that allow the police to enforce temporary one-way systems, no right turns and parking restrictions etc. If this is required, it needs to be included in the earliest discussions and planning. Take advice from the local police and traffic and highways authority.

Police 'security'

The police have a duty to prevent crime and will always respond to thefts and fights etc., as long as resources and priorities allow (if police are dealing with a murder, a call about a shoplifter will almost certainly have to wait and a car park obstruction won't even be considered).

Therefore, if problems develop on the event site and the police are called, depending on resources available and their workload at that time, it is likely that they will arrive and deal with the problem, though it is not guaranteed.

As a courtesy, try where possible to provide on-site facilities for the police assigned to the event, making a rest room/tent, parking area and separate toilet facilities available near the main entrance for ease of access.

Paid police cover

By prior arrangement almost all forces will allocate police officers to provide cover on site at a large event, but the event organisers will have to pay the appropriate rate for that presence. This can be quite expensive.

You are probably wondering why you would need police attendance at an event ground, where the weather is going to be fine and members of the public will be in a happy carefree mood. There are two functions that the police can fulfil: deterrent and reactive.

The presence of police officers on site acts as a deterrent because criminals are less likely to be active with a uniformed police presence. Also, on-site police can react immediately; they are are ideally located and are trained and equipped to deal with any incident that may occur.

Special constabulary

At many events and shows, it is likely that police forces will rely on the services of members of the Special Constabulary to provide most (if not all) of the manpower to cover your event. Special Constabulary officers are part-time, unpaid volunteers, with full police powers and authority. Though they are volunteers, they nevertheless have considerable experience at policing events.

All Special Constabulary officers have full-time jobs and perform their voluntary duty in their spare time. I suggest you remember that and make sure that you look after them while they are on site.

Though I have cautioned elsewhere against the free distribution of complementary meals and drinks, unless funds are severely restricted I always try to arrange for meals and drinks to be supplied to police officers on duty at the event, particularly for Special Constables.

Private security

Hiring private security will most certainly be cheaper and easier to arrange than police presence, but security staff are usually limited in number and often have less training, ability, power and equipment.

They could be used to cover the same points and whilst their presence will be a deterrent, it will not be as powerful as police presence. You may wish to raise the matter of security while discussing plans with the local police force, which may be able to advise you.

Problems for police/security

Why would you need any security or police presence? Apart from the deterrent effect, which can be worth any fees paid in itself, a selection of other problems that police/security might need to deal with at an event are are listed below. An ordinary member of your staff would not be equipped or have the powers to deal with most of these, and simply be too scared by a few of them. Again the type of event you are organising will dictate the relevance of this information. The primary school sports day will almost certainly not be under threat of most of these problems and so will not require the presence of police or security staff.

Theft

The most common problem encountered at events, is theft. The sections below briefly discuss the areas which thieves are likely to target.

Equipment

An event site is potentially a self-service store for thieves. It is usually located in a rural area and almost certainly there will be a range of expensive equipment and tools lying around with little supervision and a lot of confusion. People and vehicles are coming and going at odd hours. Nobody would notice a couple of lads loading a generator into a van – until the owner of the generator comes to turn his lights on!

Vehicles/trailers

You picked your site with easy access in mind. Every person and piece of equipment on site probably came by vehicle, and the vehicles and various trailers are expensive and likely to be targeted by thieves.

Stalls/stock

Stalls are frequently set up and stocked early, or even the day before the event starts. Sneak thieves may try to raid these stalls and steal some of the stock.

Cash theft

Thieves can target cash on site, either on the stalls or rides, or at the pedestrian or car park gates. Considerable sums of money build up quite quickly at these points and they are soft targets. You may think that the sums involved are too small to bother with. I strongly caution against complacency. You don't have to look too far through the newspapers to read of armed raids on post offices and building societies, where the stolen money amounts to only a few hundred pounds. If they are willing to go to such lengths against quite secure targets such as post offices and building societies, imagine how sweet and soft a target like your gates could appear.

Property from cars

Theft of and from cars is a major element of reported crime in the UK. Event car parks are a tempting soft target. Some cars are left insecure, but criminals can quite easily break a window to steal bags, phones, radios etc.

Property from caravans/tents

At larger events, some people will stay on the event site for the duration of the event, either sleeping in a caravan or tent. During event opening hours, it is quite likely that the criminal element will roam around the caravan and tented area, looking for an opportunity to steal anything available.

Pickpockets/handbag theft

The public may be the subject of theft by pickpockets and/or handbag theft. Where the public gather and are likely to be carrying money/credit cards etc., and will probably be distracted, the thieves will not be far behind.

Arson

It is not unknown for tents, stalls, sheds, hedges, farm barns and stores, fields of crops etc. to be set on fire by youths, simply for the mindless and cowardly thrill of seeing the fire engines attend to deal with the fire.

Criminal damage/sabotage

Similarly youths have been known to damage or deliberately sabotage equipment for no apparent reason. This could be disruptive to your arrangements, but more importantly could be very dangerous

Disputes/domestics/drunks

Disputes are likely anywhere, but if there is a beer tent, disputes will be more common due to the influence of drink. If the weather is hot, people have a greater thirst, more alcohol is consumed and the likelihood of drunken disputes increases.

Counterfeit currency

At any large public gathering, criminals are likely to attempt to pass counterfeit currency. Cashiers, gate staff, stallholders etc. should be warned to look out for counterfeits.

You are reminded that counterfeit notes and coins have no value and that it is a criminal offence to attempt to pass on a forged counterfeit note or coin. Just to make sure you understand that – if you take and accept a forged £50 note, then realise it is forged and try to pass it on to avoid the loss, you are now committing the criminal offence! When found, all such notes and coins should be surrendered and the police notified.

Animals in distress

While security staff are patrolling car parks and the event site, particularly in summer, they should also be aware of the potential problems of pets or event animals left in cars. It is possible that car park patrols could find dogs or other animals locked in unattended cars and in distress. It is very easy for a dog, or anything for that matter, to die in a locked car, without too much sun at all. If an animal is found in distress, I suggest that you broadcast a message with the vehicle details over the public address system, requesting the owner return to the vehicle immediately, and inform the police and/or the RSPCA and any on-site vet.

People left in cars

On a large site, it is not unusual for elderly or young people to be left alone in a vehicle, to rest while the rest of their group continue to enjoy the events. It is worth briefing your security patrols to check anyone in a vehicle. They may just be asleep, waiting for their partner to return, or they may have had a heart attack, or they may be stealing the car radio!

Progress – Chapter 22

You should now:
- have a clear idea of the composition of your event and have identified your security needs and the sources of that security, having either made do with event staff, paid for police presence, hired private security staff, or a combination of the above,
- have read and understood the possible security threats and have reviewed potential specialist security threats for your event,
- have identified, risk assessed and specified procedures required to allow your security staff to maintain order at your event, and

- have held a checkpoint meeting to review and discuss security issues and resolved them in consultation with the police.

Product completed

- Agreed list of security issues relating to your event.
- Agreed list of security staff required to secure your event.
- Details of the source of security staff, police, private security or your staff.
- Documented risk assessments of security issues.
- Checkpoint review – authorisation to continue.

23 Insurance

With increasing litigation, the event manager should ensure that all staff, exhibitors and the event as a whole are covered by insurance. When you have a basic idea of scope, type and size of your event, you should seek expert advice.

Types of insurance

Public liability/injury

Some local authorities, police forces, landowners, organisations and groups insist that an event be covered by insurance. Whether they insist or not, you should as a *minimum* consider taking out public liability insurance.

I suggest that the event manager should always insure themselves against accident or injury to anyone on or near the site resulting from the erection and removal of event signs (see Chapter 16, 'Sign posting'). As you may be subject to claims that road signs obscured the view of or distracted members of the public the Highways Authority may insist that full insurance be taken out, and demand to see the certificate of insurance before they will grant permission for signs to be erected.

Employee public liability/injury

Depending on the status of your staff, you may need to arrange for employee liability cover as well. You must consult the experts and establish the status of all members of your staff, to ensure that you are not in breach of any rules or regulations.

Contractors/attractions insurance

All contractors and sub-contractors working on the event will also need to have public liability insurance cover. It is a duty of the event manager to ensure that they can produce a copy of their insurance certificate to prove that they are insured. The event manager may wish to present a copy of that certificate to the insurers to check the scope and validity of that insurance.

Rain/storm insurance

Even with the best investigation, planning and organisation, if there is a heavy storm on the morning of the event, it is possible that the site will be flooded and/or the attractions wrecked. Even if the site remains safe, the public may decide to stay at home in the dry.

It is possible to insure the event against the effects of a storm or similar problem, but it can be expensive. Investigations as to cost and cover should be part of your investigation phase. The larger the event and the more money laid out in advance for exhibits, accommodation and services, the more likely it is that the cost of insuring against cancellation and other problems becomes viable.

Almost any problem can be insured against. However, I doubt if it would be worth insuring against an alien invasion of the event site (unless of course you wanted to use that as an advertising gimmick, to get the general press to give you coverage).

Remember though that insurers may insure you against financial loss due to freak weather or fire, but nobody will insure you against financial loss due to your own oversights or incompetence.

You *must* check everything and check it again, before you commit to spending *one* penny on your event. Only go ahead if you are really sure, that your investigations and plans are sound and that you will achieve your objective. Don't spend anything until you get formal approval and licences to run your event.

Tip

Talk to your insurance broker at the earliest opportunity. Discuss the insurance possibilities, cover and costs. Note the requirements and advice of police and the authorities and take out any required insurance. Take their advice about displaying and printing disclaimers on tickets and signs, such as 'Caravans, vehicles and their contents parked entirely at the owner's risk'.

Restrictions/requirements

Your insurer may well impose requirements and restrictions on you and your event. For example they may insist that all staff are over 21 years of age, or that anyone driving a vehicle has a clean driving record with no convictions for speeding or other driving offences. They could demand that you arrange for a safety inspection of all electrical and mechanical installations and provide them with a copy of the safety certificate issued before your event opens to the public.

Even though you have adopted safety as a key priority, you must listen to and abide by any restrictions or requirements imposed on you by your insurer.

Progress – Chapter 23

You should now:

- be aware of the importance of insurance cover,
- have established the minimum cover that the authorities and or governing bodies may require you to arrange,
- have decided what optional insurance you are considering (e.g. roving car park supervisor carrying members of the public while looking for lost cars), and
- have consulted several insurance companies or agents and asked for at least three quotes for the cover you have identified above.

Product completed

- Details of the insurance cover the authorities required you to have for your event.
- Details of selected insurer.
- Details of any proposed insurance cover, plus any restrictions and limitations the insurance company may impose on you (such as, all drivers must be over 21 and hold a clean driving licence – which will feed into staff requirements and job descriptions).
- Checkpoint review – authorisation to continue.

24 Emergency and normal procedures

You could describe a procedure as a cross between a series of instructions and a checklist. It will ensure that even in a crisis nothing is forgotten and that the right people do what they should, at the right time and in the right order. 'Procedures' allow your staff to operate effectively and efficiently, as well as forcing you to investigate and understand in advance what you will need to do under a given set of circumstances.

For the primary school Easter Hat Show, normal school procedures will be sufficient, but the larger the event the greater the need to research and define event procedures.

Defining procedures

At the investigation and planning stages, in consultation with the police, fire and rescue, St John or Red Cross and the local authority, you should define the procedures, which you will need to generate. You should be able to define most of the procedures required by simply asking each deputy manager to individually generate a list of procedures required for their area of responsibility. They can produce those procedures and hold a checkpoint review to confirm that the procedures are understandable and adequate.

When drafting procedures, you must be realistic and accept and recognise the restrictions and limits imposed on you. For example if you only have one qualified electrician, you cannot draft an emergency procedure that calls for the presence of three qualified electricians! If three electricians are needed to safely run the event, that has to be fed into the staff requirements!

When the individual managers have completed their checks, I like to pull them all together and hold a desktop run-through of the event, to check all aspects including procedures.

Desktop review

The desktop review checks procedures but also checks that all other aspects of the event, plans, arrangements and staffing will actually work together to safely deliver the planned event.

I invite all managers along and have copies of all planned arrangements at hand, lists of staff members and their skills/roles, sign schedules, risk assessments and job descriptions etc.

I run through the event programme, while following it through on the site plan. From early exhibitor arrival to final clear up, as each member of staff is assigned to a task, we check the relevant planned activities and procedures. This run through is quite labour-intensive, as it requires somebody to check through the procedures, somebody else to check the sign schedule, somebody else to check that risk assessments have been completed and somebody to check that staff with appropriate skills are available at the right time etc. This desk top review method highlights skills shortages as well as potential problems with the schedule, procedures, risk assessments etc.

What ifs

During this 'run through', I also call for and welcome 'what ifs' at any stage, such as 'What if the farmer has lost the key to the main car park gate?' 'What if a traction engine breaks down in the narrow access lane?' If possible, there and then I call on the manager with the appropriate knowledge and responsibility to answer the 'what if'. Any that cannot be dealt with immediately, or which require amendments to sign schedules or site plans etc., are recorded and where necessary the schedule and plans are amended and new risk assessments and procedures are commissioned.

The objective is to resolve the potential problems from the research, resources and plans as they stand. In the two examples raised above, I might propose that we assign the traffic manager to make sure the gates are open by 7am either with the key, a hacksaw, or bolt croppers, and as a precaution divert traction engines to approach via another route that they cannot block!

It is essential that the people who wrote and defined the procedures and job descriptions are present and able to work through the final review. Their skills and intimate knowledge of the subject may show that a 'what if' has already been dealt with, or that due to other measures in place the 'what if' would not occur.

Remember that for the event, as well as being a management and briefing tool, procedures can be a training aid for new and inexperienced staff, or for teams who are not used to working together in an unfamiliar environment.

What procedures should cover

It is impossible to say what procedures you may need for your event. There are some common procedures that should be considered, for example when there is a fire in a tent or other place, injury to spectator/staff/participant, a bomb scare, or an animal escape.

Generally pre-defined procedures should cover all emergency situations, major/critical activities and any other activity that the event manager thinks requires a procedure. I would not write a procedure for the above example where the farmer has lost the key to the gate, but I would make sure that a hacksaw with spare blades and bolt croppers were available in the roving car park supervisor's vehicle and the event manager's office.

Where the safety of staff and visitors is at risk, procedures have to be set down and staff trained to comply with them. In that way, everybody knows what is expected, what is allowed and how it should be done. By using the correct procedures, controls, checks and supervision, nothing is forgotten, left half done, or done wrongly.

In an emergency situation, it is even more vital that there are specified ways of dealing with situations. All staff do not necessarily have to have memorised the procedures, as long as the supervisor and management know what they are and have access to the checklists stating what has to be done. All other staff should know that there are set procedures for any given set of circumstances.

In most mundane situations, staff should decide how to handle the necessary activities themselves, though guidelines may be set to ensure a standardised approach – for example 'for any activity – the safety of people at the event is highest priority'. Writing procedures for 'how to take a fee from pedestrians at the pay gates' or 'how to inform control that one of the toilets has been blocked' would be a waste of time. Staff should be aware that a normal procedure, for example checking a person in a car, could turn into an emergency when they find that person is not breathing.

All staff should be alert and professional in their actions at all times and have the health and safety culture firmly established in the way they behave and operate.

Records of procedures

Defining and producing procedures is of no use if they are not actually available to be used at the event. The procedures should therefore be kept in the event manager's manual:

- The pages should where possible be laminated or protected in plastic wallets.
- The manual should contain a simple but extensive cross-referenced index (so that for example 'heart attack' could be found under 'H' for heart, 'A' for attack, 'F' for first aid and 'C' for collapse etc.) and the page reference (e.g. 21/1) should be shown to allow for quick reference – see 'Sample procedure' below.
- There should be at least three copies of the event manager's manual – with the event manager, the cashier and at the main gate. You may wish to provide a copy in the roving car park supervisor's vehicles as well as at other locations. Then if there is a problem involving the event manager's office, the manual is still available.

Sample procedure – heart attack

The sample procedure shown opposite contains the required critical information:

- *Title* – South Budley Steam Extravaganza
- *Procedure name* – heart attack
- *Procedure number* – 21/1 (ie Chapter 21, Procedure 1)
- *Actions* – list of actions to take
- *Performed by* – list of people involved
- *Problem?* – Note if any problem found during use
- *Written by and date* – name of author and date written
- *Review due and reason* – date review due and why, and
- *Checked by and date* – name of checked approver.

The sample has been simplified to illustrate the use of procedures. No two events are the same, so it is impossible to define a standard procedure format. Depending on the event you are running, you could add a list of equipment that has to be available, for the procedure to be implemented. For example at a shooting competition, a security check procedure may require a range marshal to securely lock two access gates – they will therefore need keys, locks and chains!

South Budley Steam Extravaganza 1 August 2006

Procedure – heart attack		21/1
Actions	Performed by	Problem?
1) Report *any* medical emergency to event manager immediately	Any staff locating emergency	
2) *All staff* to recognise emergency and refrain from using radio unless part of the emergency	All staff	
3) Event manager to relay emergency to ambulance service (inform police if on-site), start emergency radio/communications log	Event manager – or deputy in event manager's office	
4) Reporter to call in location, casualty sex, age, condition and other details (known medical problem – medication lost etc.)	Member of staff who located casualty	
5) Reporter to relay details to ambulance service; event manager to confirm	Reporter – event manager to confirm	
6) Staff in area to assist to shield casualty and move the public on	Staff assisting casualty	
7) Event manager to warn gate staff to clear gate for arrival of ambulance/medical aid – marshals to clear path to site of casualty	Event manager or deputy	
8) Reporter to collect additional information – does casualty have friends relatives at the event? – relay to event manager	Reporter/supervisor comforting casualty	
9) Maintain staff presence at gates and barriers, take *any action* e.g. free vehicular entry to car park, to clear roads and speed arrival and or departure of ambulance	All staff	
10) On instructions of event manager, public address (PA) to call for friends relatives to attend event manager's office	PA on advice of event manager	
11) Reporter to report arrival of medical assistance to event manager	Reporter	
12) Reporter to collect information on deployment of casualty to event manager – (recovered and gone home – taken to hospital)	Reporter	
13) Event manager to close incident and close log, open radio to normal traffic	Event manager	

Written by	Review due	Checked by
Bill Williams	June 2008	Tom Jenkins
Date	**Reason**	**Date**
24 July 2005	Procedure 3 years old	1 August 2005

215

Remember that if you include equipment in your procedures, you probably need to introduce a procedure that checks that all necessary emergency equipment is available and in working order at the start of every day.

Radio use

Normal radio traffic

Assuming your event is large enough to justify the use of a radio system, there will be a lot of normal traffic passing over the radio network during the event. The normal rules for radio use apply, so you may have a radio procedure that defines radio issue testing and use, including:

- Check the radio with a test call before you get too far from the radio issue point.
- Make sure you know what radio channel you should be using.
- When making a call, wait for a break in radio traffic, then start by saying who you are calling and who you are.
- Wait for a reply.
- Make your radio calls brief – never chatter on the radio – somebody may be waiting to make an urgent call.
- Don't try to make a call more than three times if there is no reply. If there has been no reply from the person you are calling, after three attempts try to contact any base station operator or other member of staff to relay a message.
- The base station to be monitored at all times.
- The base station operator will relay messages if there is no answer.
- The base station operator should caution users if they break the accepted rules of use.
- All staff should be trained and able to make, recognise and receive emergency calls and know what to do when an emergency call is being broadcast.

Urgent messages

When you have to make an urgent call, you must make sure that everyone knows that the call is indeed urgent and therefore takes priority over other traffic. Starting any emergency message with the words 'Urgent, urgent, urgent' should alert everyone to stop talking and to listen.

If an urgent message is broadcast, the event manager, or (assuming the event manager is allowed to go home for lunch or at night) whoever is manning the radio base station, should immediately take command of the incident until relieved by the emergency services. All radio users should stop broadcasting until or unless the incident is closed. Nobody should attempt to use their radio unless they are or become involved in the emergency (or a new emergency), or the event manager or whoever is operating the radio base station calls them to participate in resolving the incident.

The base station operator has a log handy to record any urgent transmission. Full details will not be required, but it would be useful to note the basic details of the call.

For example an urgent transmission log may contain:

Sunday 24th August 2006
10:23 *Car Park 1 Called medical emergency*
10:24 *Car Park 1 Tom Jones called in casualty details*
           Male approx. age 65 name Bobby Smith
           Collapsed suspected heart attack
           Wife says he had previous heart attack in 2002
10:25 *First aid called to attend*
10:26 *County ambulance called to attend*
10:30 *All staff warned – County ambulance to attend Car Park 1 main gate*
10:34 *Tom Jones of Car Park 1 reported casualty and wife removed in county ambulance to All Saints Hospital*
10:35 *Car park supervisor reports car of casualty to be Red VW Beetle Registration ABC 123 D will be secured on site until collected by victim's son approx. 7pm tonight*

Depending on the incident, at the earliest possible moment you should inform the emergency services that the incident is taking place.

Keep the records of emergency radio traffic because they will be a useful analysis tool when the day is over, and they may be required if there was any enquiry into the outcome or handling of an emergency.

Work out a code so that an emergency call is given priority and does not have to wait for a long rambling call. The call 'Urgent, urgent, urgent. Pay Gate 2 to control. Sixty-year-old male collapsed. Possible heart attack. Resuscitation started. Ambulance required' gets immediate attention and conveys everything that the controller needs.

Know the site

Remember that if staff do not know their way around the site and do not know which gate is which, they cannot report the location of an incident, or attend to assist at an incident that has been declared. You and your staff should not only know your way around, but make sure that all staff are familiar with agreed landmarks, car park names or numbers, gate names or numbers, road names, and key site features such as the arena etc.

If a member of the public collapses with a suspected heart attack on a vast 'steam fair' site, a radio call such as 'some bloke has fallen over near the gate' is of no use to anyone. Drill your staff, so that radio calls are precise and convey the required detail.

Reporting details

If there is an incident, whoever reports it must identify the nature of the incident with any obvious hazards, the exact location of it and the number of casualties involved, if any, and their apparent injuries. That will allow the event manager to decide what action to take, for example where to evacuate to (see 'Evacuation' below) and by what route, and allow them to pass details of casualties on to the ambulance service and local hospital, so that they know what to expect and what they have to deal with.

Anyone reporting an incident should remain available on the radio to provide any further details required by control staff and to remain available to update them on progress of countermeasures, evacuation etc. Staff at the incident must of course avoid getting injured by any hazards themselves and with the assistance of other staff, ensure that the scene is protected to prevent injury to others.

Emergencies

Fire

If there is any fire, inform the local fire and rescue service. A fire may look small but with even the gentlest breeze the smallest fire can rapidly get out of control.

Some people are loathe to report a fire 'because it was just smouldering' or 'it was so small'. If there is any sign of fire, call the fire brigade and evacuate people from the danger area before attempting to use any fire fighting equipment that may be available. If you do try to use fire fighting equipment, only use it if it puts nobody at risk. Any smoke means heat and burning, and the smallest fire can very easily become a major blaze. If it has smoke it's a fire – *call the fire service*.

Electrical problems

It is possible that an electrical fault or fuse can cause problems. An accident with a lighting mast, or a wire pulled out by accident could leave live wires in a dangerous state. If electricity is supplied to the site and there is any doubt about a problem, take action.

Arrange for staff to cordon off the problem area, making sure that those staff are informed of the risk and are aware of the precise fault. When the area is safely guarded, call for an electrician to come around and repair the fault. With any luck the fault will be repaired and you will then be able to declare the area and equipment safe to use.

Be aware that due to the nature of electricity your problem may be a greater hazard than you thought. For example if a loose wire is reported on one metal framed stall, it is possible that electricity is running through the frames of four or five stalls that have been clamped together for stability. Similarly, a faulty wire on a floodlight may be making an entire length of metal chain link fencing live and a potentially fatal hazard.

Emergency access routes

If there is an emergency, you will almost certainly need the assistance of the emergency services. Early discussions and liaison with the local authorities and emergency services organising an emergency access route will pay dividends. Stationing a mature car park marshal at the emergency exit, who is under instructions to keep the exit clear and open up for every emergency service vehicle, will speed the resolution of the emergency.

Remember that all staff, particularly team leaders and managers, must be aware of emergency procedures and access routes.

Spare staff

If at all possible, have a few spare staff available, who can be used for unforeseen eventualities. They need not be sitting around doing nothing. They can be used as additional site or car park patrols, until and unless needed. They could take it in turns to do a cash collection run so that there is never a pattern with the same people doing it each time. Some could crew the minibus with the roving car park supervisor so that they are at least out of the office and doing something.

Emergency runners

At larger events it may pay to have additional staff available, or possibly convert existing staff to messenger or runner duties. They can then be used to carry messages to other areas of the site, or if there is an incident, they can be used to go to visit and *report back* to the event manager on what is happening.

Easy identification

All staff involved should not only know their normal and emergency duties and responsibilities, key points at least should also be able to communicate with the event manager or other designated control point. They must also be able to recognise the supervisors and senior staff who will be able to direct or redirect them as circumstances require. This may require senior staff to wear armbands, yellow builders' hats or other identifiable clothing, so that staff, emergency services, and members of the public can identify the people in authority.

Evacuation

It is highly unlikely that you will have to evacuate the site, but it is possible. As a visitor, I once attended an event on a field covered in straw and stubble. The stubble caught fire, probably due to a discarded cigarette end, and the subsequent fire fanned by a fresh breeze swept through a corner of the event ground and into the car park. Two tents and seven vehicles were destroyed. It can happen, so be ready for it.

Should evacuation become necessary, there should be an evacuation procedure ready for use. The basic requirements for which are:

- Who can call for an evacuation?
- Who will inform the emergency services?
- Who will act as emergency services liaison?
- How will that evacuation be notified to staff and public?
- Who will specify where the threat is? (You don't want to evacuate towards the threat.)
- Where will the public and stallholders be sent?
- Where will the off-site control point be?
- Which staff should be at which points?
- What will happen to animals and livestock left on site?
- How can valuables left on site best be secured and protected?
- Who can declare the site safe?
- Stallholders should return first.
- Public can return when stallholders are in place.

Only a handful of event staff should be authorised to call for a full evacuation. While any member of staff can call for the more likely partial evacuation of a tent, field or building.

The event manager's office will be designated the emergency control point unless and until the emergency services take over – then they may move the control point to one of their vehicles.

If the event manager is away from their office, whoever is stationed at base control or the event manager's office should inform the emergency services of any incident or danger and act as liaison with the emergency services until the event manager returns to the office or emergency control point and takes command.

Evacuation points

Depending on size, location, vehicle access points etc., one or more areas should be assigned as rendezvous points for evacuated people. The points should be selected for ease of access, large enough to hold the number of people expected and in a position that is safe and does not interfere with the operation of the emergency services or passing traffic etc.

Alternate control point

If the event manager's office and any radio base control are located near the main entrance and away from the middle of the site, staff may be able to remain there during any incident. If not, an emergency incident control point should be identified and agreed with emergency services. The local farmhouse would be a good example, because it is easy to identify and has communications and power already available.

Where necessary, emergency control points should be equipped with plans of the site, lists of exhibitors, key people, mobile phone numbers, keys to emergency access gates, a copy of the event manager's manual etc.

Evacuation posts

Staff should know their evacuation posts, so that they can immediately attend and assist with the evacuation. Evacuation posts will have been pre-arranged and staff will have been briefed as to their duties. Key staff will have copies of the site plan and appropriate procedures, to ensure that the public are evacuated safely and quickly.

Animals

Any animals and livestock may well have to be left during the incident. If there is immediate danger to the animals, for example a fire in a display tent, when the people have been evacuated and if the animal handlers and owners consider it safe, they should be allowed to lead or drive their animals to another area of the site. It is vital that animals such as bulls or even cows, horses or pigs are not allowed to stampede through crowds, which may be attempting to leave the site.

Stallholders

As fast as is practicably possible, stallholders will be expected to temporarily secure their stalls and take any monies with them. As far as is practicably possible and where it is safe, event staff will be posted around the site perimeter to secure it if possible during an emergency.

Authorised return

The event manager should be the only person allowed to declare the site safe for a return and then only on the advice of any emergency services if in attendance.

To ensure an orderly return, first event staff then stallholders and then members of the public should be allowed to return to the site. This will be made easier if stallholders are held in a separate evacuation area, nearer to the event site than the public evacuation area.

Lost children

At any event, it is possible that young children will become separated from their parents. You should plan for these occurrences and make preparations that will reduce the effort and disruption caused.

It is suggested that staff are available at or near the public address point (usually co-located with the radio base station), where there should be facilities to hold and entertain lost children.

Many lost children are upset and crying so there is a temptation to give them sweets or ice cream to comfort them. *Don't!* You don't know what dietary requirements or allergies they may have. I suggest that a small, inexpensive but safe soft toy and liberal doses of Tender Loving Care, are all that is given to a child until the parents arrive to retrieve them. (Note – It is almost certain that when mum or dad does return, the child will want to keep the soft toy – so make sure that you have a small supply that can be given to the lost child, without taking away your only 'comforter'.)

Tip

Instruct your event staff *not* to give lost children sweets etc. The child may suffer from diabetes or allergies and a handful of sweets may cause them harm. Have a ready supply of small soft toys to give to them.

Do not broadcast details of lost children over the public address system unless asked to do so by the police. If asked to do so *only* pass on the details they wish you to broadcast.

If a lost child announcement is broadcast on the staff radios, gate staff and car park staff especially should be warned to look out for the child who may try to leave alone, or be escorted from the site by a person of questionable intent.

Gently question the person reporting the lost child covering any relevant points:

- What is the name of the lost child?
- What is the age, height, hair colour, style etc.?
- What are they wearing or carrying?
- Do they have a picture of the lost child?
- Where were they last seen?
- Were they with a group of people?
- How did they arrive at the event?
- Does a relative live nearby?
- Have they seen a relative, friend or neighbour etc. at the event? (The child may have gone off with Grandma or Auntie – if so, tannoy for them to attend the control point.)
- Ask if the child has any allergies or infirmities.
- Is the child taking medication?
- When is any medication due?
- What is the effect of not taking the medication on time?
- Is there any domestic dispute involving custody of the child?

Other questions can be added to suit your circumstances. If in any doubt call the police. If the police are on-site, inform them of the lost child as soon as possible.

People reporting lost children often want to go and search; make sure that the person reporting the lost child remains at the event manager's office. If nothing else the police will want to talk to them, but it has been known for a person to report a lost child, wander off and find the child, then go home leaving event staff still looking and calling the police. Keep anyone reporting a lost child in the office and offer them the use of a telephone to try to call friends and neighbours to trace the child.

Be careful as to what additional details you broadcast; information such as allergies, incapacity, overdue medical treatment, marital conflict should not be broadcast.

If the child came with a group of people, it is best to gather that whole group of people at the public address system tent/office, to make sure that the child is not with one of them.

If the child came in a car, or on a bus or train, when the child got lost, they may have decided to make their way towards the transport in an attempt to find the adults they were with. Search appropriate areas first.

Hand over control to any police who are on-site or arrive to help with the search. Be prepared to use car park marshals and other staff to assist with searches of the site and local area, farm outbuildings etc.

Lost property

Members of the public will want to report losing property and others will want to report and hand in property that they have found. Police do not normally deal with lost property relating to a private event ground, so the event manager's office must handle it.

Records must be kept of who found the property and what it was. Records must be kept detailing property that is reported lost. If a person comes in claiming they have lost something that has been handed in and you are happy that they are the rightful owners, you can reunite them after recording their details.

Tip

When making your records of found property *beware* of using assumed descriptions. The ring that has been handed in may look like a gold ring with a large diamond, but as you are not an expert, you should list it as yellow metal ring with white crystal stone. If you recorded a gold and diamond ring, the loser could insist that you return a gold and diamond ring, even though the one you are holding is brass and glass!

RSPCA

The RSPCA offer both a consultative and emergency service. They may attend some events if animals are involved. They could attend if invited to set up a stall to collect donations and give out information.

If animals are left in cars, they can overheat and die quite quickly. If the RSPCA and police are on-site, announce the offending vehicle details over the PA and ask the driver to return to the car immediately. Inform the RSPCA and police of the situation, so that they can take any necessary action.

Progress – Chapter 24

You should now:

- understand the need for formal documented procedures, to streamline reaction to emergency situations,
- have defined the structure and content of your procedures,
- have defined all of the procedures you require for your event,
- understand the difference between normal procedures, emergency procedures and radio usage,
- have introduced an emergency radio log or emergency log if no radios are to be used at your event,
- accept the need for all staff to be familiar with and know the site, so that they can explain the location of any problem they discover and attend to assist at any location they are instructed to attend,
- know how you will deal with emergencies,
- have defined any emergency access routes you need for your event,
- be aware of the need for caution when dealing with lost children, and
- have understood the problems involved in dealing with and recording lost and found property and animal welfare.

Product completed

- Description and explanation of agreed standard event procedure format and use.
- Schedule of all agreed procedures required for the event. (Note: do not try to copy them all into the proposal pack. Simply refer to them in the proposal pack, then take them with you and be prepared to produce them during your presentation

to the authorities when you ask for licensing or written permission to run the event.)

- Evidence of successful completion of desktop walk-through of the event, using current site plan, schedules and procedures.
- Defined and agreed alternate control point to event manager's office.
- Defined and agreed detailed priority procedure for lost children.
- Defined and agreed lost and found property forms and procedures.
- Checkpoint review – authorisation to continue.

25 Formal presentation

You must now be totally convinced that no two events are ever the same and that though they vary in purpose, objective, size, location and content, there are aspects that are common to almost all events.

This book has attempted to offer you a methodology and guidance in researching and planning your event. Though it has offered illustrative lists for your consideration and inspiration, it has frequently reminded you that as your event is unique, you should review the contents of those lists, add to them and amend them to suit your unique event and purpose.

At this point in the methodology, unless your proposed event has unique aspects that are as yet unresolved, your critical research and planning should have been completed and you should have all of the details necessary to apply for permission to run your event. (If not, from your contacts with the authorites you will know what still has to be done before your presentation.) When all issues are resolved and your plans and documentation are complete, you should proceed with this stage by making your formal presentation.

Do you want to continue?

If there was a potentially fatal problem with your proposed event, you should by this stage have either resolved that problem, or changed your objective and event type, adopted one unaffected by the fatal flaw, and reinvestigated and evolved a revised plan. It is highly unlikely that you would want to abandon the project when you have reached this stage, but there are some crucial questions that you must ask yourself before you continue:

- Are you confident that your investigations, research and planning have allowed you to accurately forecast attendance?
- Are you confident that your research and investigation have disclosed the full and realistic cost of delivering your event?
- Are you confident that your research and investigation are accurate and are you confident that you will attract the number of people you forecast?
- Are you confident that the event you have planned will attract the income required to at least cover the costs?
- Are you confident that you can deliver the facilities, services, staff, and attractions as defined in the plan?
- Are you willing to trust your planning skills and insurance cover, and be willing to accept legal liability for your event?
- Are you willing to trust your planning skills and accept financial liability for any potential losses?
- Are you absolutely sure that you are willing and able to commit to delivering your proposed event, as defined in your plans?

If the answer to all of these questions is 'yes', then read on and prepare to make your presentations, seeking formal approval to run your event.

If the answer is 'no', you have two choices. First choice is to go back and review those areas of which you are unsure, and to refine the detail to a level where you are confident that you are right, then ask yourself the questions above again. Your only other option is to walk away, abandoning the idea of delivering an event.

Confidence in your plans

During your planning and research, you have been meeting and discussing your proposals with the emergency services and the authorities. You have been listening to them and taking their advice, modifying your proposals and plans to resolve any issues that they have raised. During this time you should have been receiving support from them, as your plans were refined and revised and moved ever closer to a standard that they would formally accept.

At this stage, they should be well aware of the content of your plans and proposals, just as you should have a degree of confidence that they will accept them. You are now ready to make a *formal* presentation to the local authority, the emergency services, the health and safety executive, your sports governing body, and any other interested party, to formally request licensing and written approval to organise and run your proposed event.

Formal approach to the authorities

If you have taken my advice, without formal agreement and approval of the authorities, you will not yet have spent any money or committed to any expenditure. When formal approval and licenses are granted, if you are still satisfied with the financial viability of your event, you can start making or confirming bookings and orders, by paying deposits.

To obtain formal approval and licenses, you will be making presentations to various organisations, explaining to them the details of your proposed event and the plans that you have made. You will show that you have been conscientious in your attempt to make your event comply with legislation and regulations, as well as being successful, enjoyable and safe.

Representatives of each organisation may require you to make a presentation to them in person, or may ask you to submit your proposals and plans to a committee or small group, who will consider them in private.

The organisations you may have to contact to give your formal presentation could include:

- *local highways authority (direction signs),
- *local authority planning committee (signs/advertising),
- local environmental health (food sales and waste disposal),
- *local police event liaison team,
- local police traffic department,
- *local fire and rescue service,
- *local health authority (first aid/ambulance),
- *local first aid organisation (Red Cross etc.),
- local health and safety executive office,
- *any appropriate sports governing body,
- *any appropriate club or company senior management,
- local coast guard (fireworks or boating event),
- local harbour master (boating event),
- local environment agency office (fishing/rivers event),
- local airport (fireworks limitations), and
- various potential suppliers and sponsors.

The organisations that I have asterisked should probably be approached and contacted in all cases, and are those that you are most likely to need to approach. You may have to add to and modify this list, to include any authority or organisation that has control over unique aspects of your event.

Joint committees

In some areas, the local authorities are working together to improve their service and response to event managers. In some areas the authorities have introduced 'joint committees', where council, police, fire and first aid representatives form a single committee which meets to review and consider all event applications.

You may have to make one or many presentation to finally obtain all of the approvals, licenses and authorisations required to organise and run your event.

Approval Checklist

The Approval Checklist shown at Annex B has been designed to help you in preparing to make your presentation to seek formal licensing and approval. It has two functions:

- *Checklist* – it provides you with a checklist that you can use and fill in during your investigations and research, ticking off various items to document your progress and completion of the products required to deliver your event. (Remember – if you have to go back and revisit or revise any of your research and plans you should update the checklist too.)
- *Overview/Index* – the checklist itself provides an overview of the scope and depth of your planning and research in delivering the event and it will act as an index to the documentation you may be asked to present during your presentations.

The Approval Checklist is designed to be completed in stages as you finish each individual stage/chapter of this book.

The first part of the Approval Checklist is a Cover Sheet. For your unique event you may wish to amend the cover sheet entries. It also contains 'comment' and 'date completed' fields, with basic details of the event:

- event title,
- proposed event date/time,
- proposed event location,
- event summary,
- event manager and phone number,
- audience size expected,
- local authority liaison,
- police liaison, and
- other liaison.

The second part of the Approval Checklist is an overview and index to your research, plans and arrangements. It lists all chapters/stages of this book and requires you to sign off that you have read and understood them as you work through. Where you are expected to produce defined products in a given chapter/stage, it lists those products, with an entry that allows you to note the date each was completed and to write a page number of other reference showing where to access that documentation. Depending on requirements for your unique event, you may wish to amend this section.

Tip

When you are ready to continue, you should make a practice presentation to some of the event staff. Take steps to resolve any problems, then make your approval presentations to the authorities.

Rejection of your proposals

If the authorities reject your proposals and plans, it is invariably because you have attempted to take short cuts in some aspect of your planning or proposals, or simply not listened to or complied with the advice they have been giving you. They will usually indicate the changes you must make to your proposals to make them acceptable.

If you still want to run your proposed event, you must return to the section in this guide relating to the problem they have indicated, then perform the remedial research investigations and planning suggested by the authorities. When you have checked and confirmed all of your research, calculations and plans, you must re-submit your proposal for consideration.

If your proposals are rejected again, you have probably also missed your time slot to run the event this year. I suggest that you recruit somebody fresh to look at the problem, to help you make the appropriate changes and submit your proposals again for next year (after revisting the research and revising plans to make them relevant to next year).

You must remember at all times that any changes you make must be reviewed and checked against subsequent plans and arrangements. Remember that at this stage, even minor changes can have a serious and potentially fatal impact on subsequent plans and arrangements.

Acceptance of your proposals

When your proposals are accepted you must freeze the plans as they stand, identifying them with a specified date and even time of production, as the accepted plans and arrangements.

You still have work to do. The approval presentations are a watershed for your event. After this you are no longer working on investigation, proposals and plans; you are working towards actually delivering your event. Depending on the complexity of your event, you may still have from two to ten months' work before you actually open the gates and let the paying public in to your event. You have to start buying, booking, hiring, training, preparing, making and obtaining everything you require to deliver your event.

You will have established costs, availability and likely suppliers during your earlier research. You will have added up the costs of all of your requirements to define the total outlay required to deliver your event. You will then have reviewed the potential and estimated income you will attract, and established the financial viability of your event. Now is the time to make it happen!

Review your plans, quotes, deliverables and requirements, and start making firm orders.

Progress – Chapter 25

You should now:

- have reviewed your potential commitments and liabilities in delivering this event, and have accepted them and decided to go ahead and apply for formal licensing and written approval to run your event,
- have reviewed your investigation, research and calculations, and have sufficient confidence in the results that you are willing to go ahead and run the event,
- have collected and collated all of your plans and documents and made formal application(s) and presentation(s) requesting licensing and formal written approval to run your event,
- have accepted that you still have more work to do, while recognising that the investigation phase has ended and the delivery phase has begun, and
- when your presentation and plans are accepted and you are given the appropriate licenses and formal written approval to continue, you should start booking, ordering and arranging everything required to deliver your event.

Product completed

- Completed Approval Checklist.
- Have collated and collected current copies of all estimates, plans, job descriptions etc. that appear in the Approval Checklist.
- On successful application for approval, you should hold all appropriate licences and written approvals to continue.
- Confirmed orders for all event requirements specified above.
- Checkpoint review – authorisation to continue.

26 Event manager's manual

From the moment you decided that you wanted to organise an event, you have been making records, collating lists, collecting quotes and defining job descriptions and procedures. You have potentially researched and collected masses of information, some of which can be filed as background data and some of which has to be available to the event manager for the duration of the event.

Background material, such as quotes from failed bidders, should be retained to document the decisions that contributed to the delivery of the event, but they do not have to be available on site. This information can be in the appropriate files in the event manager's filing cabinet.

Content

Some information must be readily available to the event manager and other interested parties during set up, while the event is open and running and during strip down and clear up. I propose that you should compile an 'event manager's manual', which contains all of the information that is required by managers, staff and emergency services at the show.

All events are different, but as a guide I suggest that as a basis the event manager's manual should contain the information listed below. For specialist shows there may well be additional information that you require – for example with an Olympic qualifying race, you may have international helicopter news coverage and so may hold details of the helicopter lease companies, radio frequencies, air traffic control, etc.

- Event title, objective, governing body; last amendment and re-issue date.
- Original letter/report/licence etc. giving formal approval for the event to run, from sports governing bodies, emergency services, local authorities, etc.

- Event manager's name, address, phone, radio call sign.
- Chart showing event management structure and their responsibilities.
- Reference sheets including extended job descriptions for all roles.
- Table showing mobile phone number and radio call signs of key staff.
- Site map.
- Current (possibly recently amended or tweaked) event timetable and schedule.
- Risk analysis reports and schedule of control measures.
- Checklist to confirm that control measures are in place and functioning each day.
- Forms for reporting new risks.
- Forms for emergency radio log.
- Forms for reporting incidents where risk is identified.
- Forms for recording casualty details.
- Procedures for all significant and possible occurrences.
- Detailed cross-referenced index to procedures.

Format

Any format will do, as long as it meets the needs of the people using it. I like to produce all of the above material and pages that will be used frequently so that they will resist being torn, withstand spilled tea and rain etc., but still be readable. I do this by laminating them!

The pages can be grouped in a four-ring binder; as the document is used frequently, a two-ring binder allows too much movement of the pages and can allow even laminated pages to be torn out in error.

Though the event manager should be familiar with the manual and know its contents, the sections should be marked with clearly written dividers, so that in an emergency, the event manager or nominated deputy, depending on circumstances, can turn straight to the appropriate section.

Copies of the complete manual

You know your event and the people involved in making it a success. As a rule of thumb I tend to aim to produce three copies of the final event manager's manual.

Copy 1

This copy is for the event manager and remains in their office for the duration. If the event manager leaves the office and delegates responsibility to a deputy manager (for example at lunchtime) then the manual remains in the event manager's office and is used by the nominated deputy. If the event manager steps out of the office – for example to go into the cashier's office next door, or to present the 'Best Steam Engine in Show' award – they should take the manual with them. In simple terms the event manager's copy stays in the event manager's possession or in their deputy's possession.

Copy 2

This is lodged in the cashier's office. Should anything happen to the event manager's office, the event manager can quickly obtain a copy of the manual from the cashier's office. Should anything happen to the event manager and his office, the cashier takes responsibility and works from their copy of the manual, until relieved or replaced by the emergency services.

Copy 3

The third copy is lodged at the main gate. As above, if anything happens to the event manager's office and the cashiers office, a copy of the manual is available at the main gate. Of course the main gate is staffed the whole time the event is running, so if anything happens to the event manager and the cashier and their offices, the nearest supervisor will be able to work from the manual at the main gate, until relieved by the emergency services.

Copies of manual material

Again the choice of how many copies to make of specific parts of the manual is yours, and will depend on the scope and size of your event. My approach is described below.

Management staff chart/job descriptions/mobile numbers

I produce enough for the event manager's manuals and as many spares as I think may be required. The spares are available to be distributed to police liaison officers, ambulance staff, fire and rescue, veterinary surgeons and anyone else who may need to know which manager has responsibility for a given function.

Site maps

I produce enough for the manuals and the people listed above, and also for car park marshals, the roving car park supervisor and anyone else who may need a laminated site map.

Map detail

The level of map detail depends on the scope of your event. I show and name car parks and gates, display rings, truck parks, caravan parks etc. Within the site I show elements blocked in – for example a block named 'Fun Fair' and, at an animal show, a block named 'Horses' and another named 'Cattle'. In more detail I show the cashier's office, event manager's office, first aid point, public address point and toilets.

Event timetable/schedule

As above, I produce enough for the event manager's manuals and as many spares as I think may be required for event staff, police, ambulance staff etc.

Forms

I produce a supply of appropriate forms, which can be carried by supervisors, or be ready for use by any appropriate member of staff. A supply of the blank forms should be made available in the event manager's office too.

Procedures

I produce enough for the event manager's manuals and as many spares as I think may be required. The spare copies of procedures may be carried by supervisors and staff, as an immediate reminder on how to deal with an incident that they encounter, or even just as a reminder of how they should be performing their job.

Progress – Chapter 26

You should now:

- understand the importance of the event manager's manual as the central repository of information relevant to the event,

- be aware of the proposed content and have generated a contents list for your manual covering your event,
- have defined a format for your manual that will meet your needs,
- have defined the number of copies of the manual that you need to keep, and
- have established how many copies of maps and contact details, procedures and forms etc. that you will need to have available.

Product completed

- An agreed format for your event manager's manual.
- An agreement as to how many copies there should be.
- An agreement as to who should hold those copies.
- Sample manual complete as per that date, to be updated from now on to become the master copy of the event manager's manual.
- Checkpoint review – authorisation to continue.

27 Money

For the vast majority of events, one objective, if not the main objective, is to generate a profit. Making a profit, by offering the public some form of entertainment for which a fee is paid, will require the event manager, cashier and staff to handle quantities of money.

You and your staff will therefore almost certainly be handling cash. If you haven't done so before you may find that it can be quite a headache. There are many considerations to be made. The sections below outline the major considerations, though your special circumstances may well dictate additional considerations that must be covered.

Gate money

Gate money can provide a considerable income, but to realise that income you will need the investment of detailed investigation, forethought, planning and staffing.

What to charge

The fee has to be pitched correctly. As a rule you cannot expect members of the public to pay £20 entrance fee for an event with one dull exhibit. You must pitch the entry fee at a level that they are willing to pay – a level that will allow you to make an income but will not frighten away the public.

You should remember that the economic climate has an effect on the amount of money that people can afford to spend on entertainment. You should also remember that family size could make the seemingly acceptable entrance fee appear exorbitant if a parent ends up paying for three or four children. Although an entry fee of £5 each does not seem too high to you, you should remember that a family of four would be spending £20 just to get onto the site. Will they have sufficient money left to spend at the stalls and rides on the site, or will they simply refuse to pay that much and go home? If they do come on-site and have no money left to spend, the stallholders won't make a profit so will not come back next year and may well ask you for compensation for their losses.

A seldom considered aspect of gate fees is the simplicity or complexity of operation. It is a thousand times easier to deal with a constant flow of the public if the fee is £1 per head, than if it had been set at say 86p per head. Imagine the problem gate staff would have simply calculating the appropriate change when a family of three arrive and attempt to pay with a £10 note. Now complicate that by adding the huge quantities of each denomination of coins that they will have to have on hand to guarantee that the gate staff could give the appropriate change.

Use common sense – make sure that the fee is sensible and rounded to the point where it is easy to quickly calculate the sum due for a family and easy to give change if somebody offers a £10 or £20 note in payment.

If you insist on an odd entry fee, you will pay for your decision by needing more gate staff, more change, more cash floats and suffer more disputes at the gates over wrong fees and wrong change, not to mention longer queues and delays.

Tip

The bottom line is, keep it simple. Select an appropriate fee level, then round the gate fee to a point where it is likely that people will be able to pay the exact sum, for example £1, £2, £5 etc. Make it simple for gate staff to mentally calculate fees and change due.

Gate money collectors

You must have trusted staff to collect the gate money. It is far too easy to put every other £5 note in your pocket and not the cash box. You have to rely on the honesty of the gate staff – with a dash of supervision and control.

You should have adults collecting gate money. I don't suggest that teenagers would be more likely to steal gate funds – it is just that a criminal may be more willing to steal the gate money from a 15-year-old scout than from an adult male.

Remember security of the cash collected as well. If while working, the gate worker takes out a handful of £20 notes, or starts fiddling with a bag or pocket full of coins, they are advertising the large sums of cash they are holding and have given an open invitation to an opportunist thief.

The gate staff must be sharp enough to spot forged notes and coins and to quickly calculate the fee due for any combination of people turning up at the gate. Nobody will be happy if large queues build up while the gate staff plod through mental calculations and discount rates for each individual and group that comes along. Imagine the desperation of a tired and distracted gate worker, faced with calculating an entry fee and appropriate change for a fee of 68p per person. Worse still, when a family of eight turn up, one asking for the pensioner rate, two children under 7 (or are they?), dad saying he wants the 35% club member discount and by the way he only has a £50 note! In such cases I have seen gate staff give up and let them all in for the £1.27 that dad had available in change!

Discounts

Discounts should be considered. Group and family discounts may make the event affordable and so may be the difference between a group deciding to come or not. Everyone likes a bargain, so if you can be seen to be giving discounts, you are likely to increase your audience. As with most other things, the problem comes in getting the balance right.

Too much discounting makes the fee scale too complex, causes gate staff problems and holds up entry, possibly putting the public off. However, remember that not discounting may mean that a family cannot afford to come to the event.

Keep in mind that it is not just the gate fee you are after. Once inside, the vast majority of the public will spend money on food, purchases and rides, etc. A bargain entry ticket price could therefore boost your income in the long run.

Some possible discounts are:

- early ticket sales,
- families,
- groups,
- senior citizens,
- club members and families, and
- late arrivals (e.g. after 3pm on the last day).

Tip

As with everything, the event manager has to make the final decision. Simplicity is best. Don't make it too complicated, use common sense and don't get carried away.

Cash

Handling cash is more problematic and time consuming than most people think. Apart from the security aspect, the sheer weight and bulk of large sums of money in loose change creates problems, let alone the time and effort required to sort, count and bag it. The following sections attempt to give some guidance regarding the handling of cash.

Cash float – amount

You will need a cash float. That is, each gate person or other money-taker will have to have some change ('float') to start them off – if the first member of the public wants to pay with a £20 note, they will need to have change to give to them. This raises several problems, not least of which is where to raise the initial money to arrange for the cash float. Depending on the size of the event, the float required could be a considerable sum.

Banks, building societies and so on may be willing to give you specific advice, but as an illustration, on a site with four entrance gates, I would expect to arrange a float of at least £1500 to cover the gates and car parks etc.

The sum of £1500 in change may sound like a lot, but consider these simple calculations. Assume your event has two car park gates and four pedestrian gates. Now assume that the fee is £1 to park a car and £1 per head entry fee. The first 25 cars pay for parking with a £5 note, requiring £4 in change each. That means the car parks use £100 of change for the first 25 cars. Now assume that each car contained only one person and they each pay their entry fee with a £5 note, again requiring £4 in change each. In this not too far-fetched example, the first 25 people on your site have absorbed £200 in change from your float (i.e. 25 cars, £4 change each, then 25 people, another £4 change each).

Now assume your site is larger, there are four main car parks, five pedestrian gates, five programme sellers and a souvenir T-shirt stall. That makes 15 members of staff who need a cash float!

It is easy to see that a large event can consume vast amounts of change to start them off, but this is where sensible pricing, management and sign posting come to your aid.

From experience, given a choice few people will pay with coins, most pay entrance fees with notes. Depending on the denominations available there seem to be trends. In my experience the public currently prefer to tender a £20 note for entrance fees, even if they have smaller notes or change available. That means that you have to provide the correct change and make sure that the incoming bank notes are secure.

Tip

Make sure you read Chapter 16, 'Sign posting'. If you need planning permission for your signs and can obtain it, consider having warning signs placed well ahead of your gates, stating the price, for example 'Car Park £1 Per Vehicle – Correct Change Please'.

Cash float – breakdown

Hopefully you now accept that you have to have a cash float, but it is important that you carefully consider the denominations of the coins that you request when arranging for the supply of the cash float. If for example your gate fee is £1 per person, it is likely that most people will either pay with a pound coin or try to use a £5, £10 or £20 note. Therefore the only change required will be £5 and £10 notes and pound coins.

The denominations of the notes and coins in your float must match your plans. In the above circumstances it would be a waste of time and effort to arrange for the entire £1500 float to be supplied in 2p coins, or in £50 notes.

You must therefore carefully consider fees, discounts, likely sums to be tendered and likely change requirements. Plan ahead and get it right.

Cash handling

Each gate or stall will be handling cash. It is essential that the handling of the cash be formalised. A secure container, preferably with a closing lid, should be positioned conveniently for the staff and out of reach and, where possible, out of sight of the public. Thought must be given to the structure in use. Putting a cash box at the rear of the gatehouse isn't very secure, especially if the back of the gatehouse is composed of three flapping sheets of torn canvas! Many a collecting box has vanished while gate staff were busy and distracted, trying to calculate the fee for a family, or arguing about the amount of change given!

Credit card facilities

It is possible that large families may wish to pay entrance fees by credit card. I would suggest that for all but the very largest events, which are held at fixed venues, you should avoid accepting credit or debit card transactions.

Cash office

For any event you will need a secure location, out of sight of general members of the public, to act as a cash office. This is where the float is held and distributed; from where additional change can be obtained and where incoming moneys are collected, recorded and held for banking.

The cash office will be responsible for collecting, counting and bagging incoming cash and cheques ready for banking. They are also responsible for making local payments, for say a delivery of coal to a steam fair, or to pay the local farmer for the use of a field as a car park.

Depending on the size of the event, the gates and attractions could quickly collect quite large sums of money. A few years ago it was not unheard of for a local fireworks display to have £10,000 to £20,000 on hand, but with security in mind they now arrange for cash collection services to take it and bank it before it builds up to those levels.

To most people £10,000 to £20,000 may seem quite a large sum of money, but nothing to be too worried about. However, when you consider that criminals are willing to use sawn-off shotguns to raid a secure post office or building society to escape with a few hundred pounds, the cash that these local events may have on hand suddenly becomes a worrying and tempting potential target.

For security reasons that cash should not be left vulnerable at the collection points, so cash will have to be collected frequently. Again for security reasons, the collection times should be random, at least two people should go together in the collection team and if possible you should vary the people in the collecting team, the route and any vehicle used, to avoid them being recognised on subsequent circuits. When collecting cash, the collecting team should leave a working float at the gate and return all other funds to the cash office, making no outgoing payments on route no matter what the reason or excuse.

The collection teams should put all money collected into a secure container and identify where and when it was collected – such as 'Main Gate – collected Sat 12 Aug, 11:35'.

As a general rule, the cash office should be separated from the event manager's office, because the event manager necessarily has a lot of visitors during the day. To maintain security the cash office should allow access to a strictly limited number of people.

The cashier

Somebody will have to be nominated as having responsibility for the cash office; for simplicity I have called that person the cashier.

The cashier will be responsible for arranging the float, both the amount and the mix of coins and notes. The cashier should decide how the gates and attractions are going to hold the cash and how often the cash will be collected from each post.

In conjunction with the event manager and the person responsible for security, the cashier will arrange all aspects of cash security, including escorting cash collectors round the site and varying routes and times etc.

Analysis of cash received

As cash comes in, a record should be made of when and where it has come from, be it car park fees, gate money, attractions money etc. If the event is to be run next year, analysis of the sources of income may reveal a lot.

For example, analysis may show that a gate in the far corner of the site was a waste of time, so next year you may not need a gate there. Perhaps the analysis may show that souvenir T-shirts were a strong source of income, so next year you should consider arranging for more T-shirts to take advantage of that potential source of income, as long as it wasn't just a passing fad or fashion. Who wants to buy a 'Who Shot JR?' T-shirt now?

Cash security

The cash office must be secure. If at all possible make the cash office a solid building or Portacabin and, unless absolutely necessary, avoid using a tent or vehicle (van or lorry) as a cash office.

Make sure that all staff are aware of the location of the cash office, so that they are ready to call in to warn the cashier and event manager of any suspicious activity on the site.

Take any advice from the local police regarding the collection of cash and the siting and use of the cash office.

Depending on the sums involved, it may be sensible for the cashier to arrange occasional cash collections by a security company during the event. For a modest fee, a cash security company will arrange to collect money from the event site and will bank it for you. Spending some money on a collection fee, while assuring the security of the cash and the health and safety of staff and public is preferable to losing the entire £15,000 income to an opportunist yob, who stabs a couple of people to get the cash.

Counterfeit notes

At any large gathering, criminals are likely to attempt to pass counterfeit notes (and occasionally coins too), in an attempt to 'convert' them to legitimate money. Your gate staff and cashiers should be warned to watch out for these counterfeits. If they are being passed, the police should be informed immediately. All counterfeits identified should be surrendered. If you have taken a counterfeit note, it is a crime for you to try to pass it on – all the more reason not to take counterfeits in the first place!

Generosity

Beware of being generous. Many smaller events have found that generosity has turned an otherwise profitable event into a loss-maker.

For example don't give out too many complimentary tickets; in fact avoid giving out any at all if you can. Don't supply free meals to stallholders or staff – if you make the shifts of voluntary staff short enough, they won't need a working lunch break, and paid staff can afford to buy their own meals.

Don't be too generous with incidental expenses. It is easy to lose track of how much has been spent. It can be surprising how the smallest of sums, allocated to buy such things as marker pens, collecting buckets or sticky tape etc., can quickly add up.

Make sure that all prices for equipment and attractions are fully specified and agreed in advance and money spent recorded accurately whether it is £3500 for a fireworks display or £1.12 for a marker pen.

Cash collection – donations on exit

If there is a charitable element to your event, you may wish to station staff at the exit gates when the main crowd departs. If those staff rattle buckets and call for donations to whatever good cause, it is surprising how much can be raised from the visitors as they leave, particularly if they are in a happy mood. Many visitors simply toss a handful of change into the bucket without bothering to count it. I have found that a cheery 'Thanks, see you next year', is much appreciated and seems to increase the likelihood that they will donate something.

Tip

If using collection buckets, the cashier should issue a few pounds' worth of coins to be placed into each bucket. For some reason rattling a bucket with coins in it is more enticing than waving a silent empty bucket.

Free or charged parking

For all but the smallest local event, the majority of attendees will almost certainly come by car. The logistical problems of car parking are dealt with elsewhere (see Chapter 14, 'Event site', Chapter 15, 'Traffic management', and Chapter 18, 'Car parking'). This section discusses car parking fees.

Free parking is a major attraction to draw the public. You must remember that the logistical problems, space and resources absorbed by parking are considerable and so impose a significant cost and drain on resources. The decision whether to charge a fee for parking or to offer free parking has to be made for your particular event. If you decide to charge for car parking, you need to consider the following:

- As with gate fees, the parking fee should be a sensible rounded sum. A fee of £1 per car is easier to collect than 94p per car.
- Each car park attendant will require a cash float and collection tin, belt or bag.
- You need to instruct the attendants about cash security – you don't want them to leave their collecting tin at the gate while they help to search for a lost car! Equally,

make sure that legitimate staff either know the person sent to relieve them, or that staff carry some sort of identification. It has been known for a cheeky thief to 'relieve' a gate person or car park attendant and simply vanish with the collection tin and the contents.

- Cash collection will need to be arranged from each car park gate person and pedestrian gate person. Cash collection might also be combined with a security check in that car park, increasing security awareness in the car park and 'hiding' the cash collection run.

- Car park and vehicle security is another major consideration. If potential visitors think that there is a high risk that their car will be stolen or damaged while they are at the event, they won't come (see Chapter 22, 'Security'). Visitors would be more enthusiastic about paying reasonable parking fees at larger events if the event manager could advertise that vehicle security was catered for with advertised security patrols. As with everything, the event manager has to make the final decision. Simplicity is best. Don't make it too complicated and use common sense, possibly with a slightly higher parking fee covering the associated costs.

Other income

For larger events, independent stallholders often approach the event manager and ask if they can set up and sell their products at the event. The event manager may then charge them a set fee for the rights to sell baseball caps, ice cream or burgers etc. on the site. That potential source of income should not be overlooked, while remembering the local authority health and safety regulations relating to the sale of food.

Progress – Chapter 27

You should now:

- be aware of the problems involved in handling quantities of cash, especially loose change,
- have understood the problems associated with setting fee levels and have decided on a fee level for your event,
- be aware of the benefits and complexity of discounting and the problems that may cause to gate staff,
- be aware of the need for a cash float, with a relevant breakdown in terms of denominations,
- agree that a secure cash office is required and have proposed one for your event,

- have nominated a cashier who has been involved in and agreed all arrangements relating to cash,
- have established some cash-handling procedures, in agreement with the cashier and with the advice of the local police,
- have made preparations to analyse all cash income and expenditure,
- be aware of counterfeit notes and coins, know the legal status and know how to deal with counterfeits,
- be aware of the benefits and problems associated with free or charged parking and have decided on a policy for your event, and
- be aware of the sources of other income that you may gain from your event.

Product completed

- Schedule of fees for entry and parking etc. for your event.
- Schedule of cash float required including source and denominational break-down.
- Definition of planned secure cash office.
- Assigned or recruited a cashier.
- Defined cash-handling schedules and procedures in agreement with the local police.
- Defined cash-handling security schedules in consultation with local police.
- Scheduled random on-site cash collection rounds and routes.
- Identification cards for all on-site cash collectors.
- Schedule of cash collection from site by security cash vans during and after the event.
- Cash recording and analysis forms and tools prepared.
- Defined delegated spending limits for appropriate staff.
- Defined and established auditable separate method to collect and record any charity cash.
- Checkpoint review – authorisation to continue.

28 Accounts

As most events are run to make a profit, the manager of even the smallest club event will want to track income and expenditure to make sure that they don't lose money on the event.

It is therefore imperative that the event manager should keep detailed accounts of income and expenditure, if only to prove that all money has been accounted for and that none has been illicitly used for private purposes. This will show where outgoing funds have been spent and allow the event manager to keep a running total and control over what the event is costing.

Most clubs, societies and groups already have a treasurer who can be drafted in to keep the books. A profit-making event will require the services of somebody skilled in book keeping and I would suggest that for anything other than the smallest events, it would be worthwhile employing an accountant to manage the finances for the event and make use of any tax advantages.

All cash transactions must be signed for, whether they are receipts or payments. You should arrange it so that statements and paying-in books show in detail all deposits, cash and cheques. Just the amount of the cheque is not good enough; the name of the person or company on whom the cheque is drawn must be noted in the appropriate records. This allows for a quick and accurate check on receipts, should one be required at any stage. The fundamentals are that you obey the rules of the club or association sponsoring the event, and where there are no pre-set rules:

- only the event manager (and event cashier up to a stated value) should be allowed to authorise expenditure,
- three different written quotes should be obtained for any expenditure over an agreed figure (for example anything over £50),
- all quotes should be retained,
- don't simply accept the cheapest quote – quality, availability, guaranteed delivery,

inclusive insurance, customer support and hidden delivery costs etc., may affect the final decision,

- keep a copy of all invoices, receipts etc.,
- keep records of all income, showing how much was received, when it was received and what the source was, and
- keep the accounts up to date, making sure that at any stage, the 'trading balance' will be available.

Tax liability

Individuals or organisations may organise and deliver an event with the objective of making a profit. They may be charitable organisations, individuals or non-charitable clubs, only you know in which category you fit, so 'standard' tax rules cannot be quoted.

Anyone thinking of organising any event or show that is in any way designed to attract an income, should contact their accountant or local tax office to discuss potential tax liability.

Tip

DON'T try to avoid tax by simply not declaring the income. When the taxman catches up with you, your marginally profitable event that you have just spent months organising and delivering, could turn into a financial loss when the tax man presents his bill, or an invitation to a possible jail term!

Progress – Chapter 28

You should now:

- accept that you will need to keep documented accounts,
- have implemented strict controls on the handling of cash, income and expenditure,
- have assigned or employed an accountant, and
- have established and initiated accepted and accurate accounting methods and procedures for your event.

Product completed

- Have agreed an accounting method.
- Accept that a key target is to be able to present a profit and loss account for the event when it is finished.
- Be able to account for every penny of income and expenditure; there should be no 'incidental expenses' or other unidentifiable items shown.

29 Video diary/evidence

As video cameras are widely available and easy to use, it seems sensible to at least consider using them to assist you in the management of your event. I have listed below some of the opportunities for using a video camera and the potential benefits that can be gained.

Evidence

At the start and finish of your event, check the entire site, inside and out. Wherever possible, do so in the company of the site owner, using the site owner and their voice on the tape. This proves that the record was taken in the presence of the site owner or his representative, and allows you to take a verified record of the state of grass, gates, fences and hedges. The pictures will later help to prove if a fence the land-owner claims was broken during your event was already broken or if it was caused by somebody at your event.

Accident/incident

If there had been an accident or incident, as soon as possible I would try to take a series of pictures of the scene from all angles. An insurer may not require the pictures, but they will certainly be a useful aid to ensure that similar circumstances are not allowed to occur during the rest of the event, or in subsequent events.

Video diary

A video diary would prove invaluable if your event were going to be run each year.

Imagine the benefits video images could give. In 12 months' time, you will still have the slightly grubby, torn and coffee-stained site plans, but how do you describe things that worked well or went wrong? How do you convey to the people already planning next year's event that the caravan entrance was wrongly sited? How do you describe a complex arrangement of tapes, cones and pay tables in the main car park entrance? How do you explain the problems caused by long queues at the railway pedestrian gate? One answer could be to get them on videotape.

You still have to document the problems, but those reports or log entries could refer to a video record, so that the problem can be seen. Being able to show the site, populated with actual members of the public, ducking under signs saying 'Danger – Keep Out' is better than submitting a report (but submit the report anyway). Being able to video that layout of cones and pay tables in the car park that worked remarkably well this year will allow people to do exactly the same next year.

Training

Videotaping members of staff performing their function could be invaluable in briefing and training your staff for the rest of the event or for next year. With videotape you can show how a car park marshal should use their mobile sign and give clear hand signals to drivers, to direct traffic efficiently. You could run a videotape of a gate person directing judges and competitors to their assigned parking areas.

There are endless possibilities. While a picture may be worth a thousand words, a videotape is worth a million words and saves a good deal of your time.

Advertising

Assuming that you are proposing to run the event again, you could use stills, clips or the whole videotape for advertising purposes. Still pictures may be used on your posters next year. Video clips or sections of the whole tape may be run on the local news or cable channels as a local news item next year. You may want to run some tape for a prospective sponsor, a company considering advertising at your event, or a potential attraction owner who is thinking of signing up to your show next year.

The videotape and images from the event will hopefully prove how successful, well organised, well managed and popular your event was, and so interested parties will want to be part of it next year.

Recruiting

You may be able to use videotape as a recruiting aid. Showing potential recruits the role you want them to fill, as well as showing them how wonderful and enjoyable the day was, might help attract the staff you want.

Sales

You may be attempting to attract income for your event, either in terms of advertisers wanting to erect hoardings at your event, potential sponsors or perhaps stall and concession holders considering buying a plot for the next event. Showing them the videotape should be enough for them to see what the show was like, the numbers attracted and how much spending power you had on your site.

You must of course remember that this tape should have been taken at the peak time and not five minutes before closing and during a thunderstorm. If you want a sales videotape, make it a good one!

Progress – Chapter 29

You should now:

- understand the benefits of videotape as a tool that you can use to prove your event a success, and
- have decided if and how you are going to use videotape, planned what images you want to capture for what purposes and scheduled the collection of those images.

Product completed

- Have agreed when and where you will use videotape as a tool in managing your event.
- Have sourced the equipment and somebody capable of using it.
- Have scheduled the known occasions when the video equipment will be used – for example on the initial tour of a proposed site.
- Have defined within your procedures any occasions when the video camera will be used, for example recording complex tape and cone entrance lanes at the main gate, or as part of an enquiry following any incident or accident.

30 Setting up

■ ■

Countdown steps

■ ■

1. Early site survey

In negotiating for the site, you have surveyed it and discussed it in depth with the site owner. You have walked over the site, checking the width and positioning of gates, the surface condition, surrounding hazards, access to roads and you have probably also taken video evidence of the condition before your event. You may have asked the landowner to move cattle or sheep out of the fields you have agreed to use and also asked the landowner to cut and clear long grass. Any existing dangers such as rotten trees have been fenced off, as have boggy ground or areas subject to flooding etc. You will also have asked for appropriate gates to be closed and locked, to direct traffic onto the chosen route, and for other gates to be opened and pinned back, to give easy access to your event.

To make sure that all of this has happened, you should make an early visit to the site and if possible take one last tour with the landowner to ensure that all of the tasks they should have performed have been satisfactorily completed.

When the site is ready you can begin to prepare it.

2. Mark out/preparation

For very small shows such as a local school fête, almost all of the preparation takes place on the morning of the event. For larger events, there may be some competitors or exhibitors who are late arrivals, but to avoid a last-minute rush, which increases the likelihood of accidents and oversights, your aim will be to have all preparations fully completed by the day before you open.

As much as a week before the event, your staff will be preparing and marking out the site. Do not underestimate the time it will take to complete these preparations. Allow at least a day to mark out the site. Depending on your event and the advice of the contractors, allow at least a couple of days for tents and Portakabins™ to be delivered and set up, and power and telephone connections to be made. As it will be the focal point, remember to make the event manager's office the first delivery – and remember that your responsibilities start as soon as you have people on site.

One week before opening day

Usually it is the site preparation tasks that you will be able to start a week early. The list below indicates the sort of activities that can be undertaken without interfering with the highway or the local community:

- Erecting signs such as 'Elephant Car Park', 'One-Way Traffic' and 'Vehicle Exit' etc. On site these can be put up as much as a week before opening day.
- Measuring and marking out plots and access lanes using a groundsman's marking wheel. The white lines will be visible for the duration of the event. (If the landowner is going to cut the grass, make sure they have done that before you do the marking out – when the grass is cut the lines will vanish.) Measuring and marking must be completed before tents and Portakabins™ can be delivered and set up!
- When the locations are marked, staff will supervise the delivery and set up of Portakabins™ and tents, by arrangement with the suppliers (setting up the event manager's Portakabin™/office first).
- There may be a requirement to liaise with contractors installing power supplies, telephones, temporary barriers and other equipment, and to obtain any safety certificates required.
- Somebody has to supervise the delivery and placement of rubbish skips and toilets – then mark out the toilet queues with posts and ropes.
- The radio rental company may wish to come to set up and test their communications equipment, to make sure it works from the remote corners of the site.
- The traffic manager will want to begin measuring out or setting out tapes, barriers and cones to mark traffic lanes in the car park entrances and fields, as long as it doesn't interfere with the arrival and departure of heavy delivery trucks.
- You may need to supervise the early arrival of exhibits and attractions. Travelling fun fairs usually arrive a few days early to set up and test. Early arrivals will almost certainly be expecting to stay on site for the duration of the show, in caravans or other vehicles and trailers. Make sure they park and set up in designated areas only.

- Depending on the presence on site and your agreement, you may need to employ security staff at night to ensure the security of people and materials present.
- For a large event, with numbers of people setting up several days in advance, I suggest that the event manager or their deputy makes occasional tours of the site to ensure that all is being done safely and within the limits and restrictions set out in your agreements.
- Staff should point out to all exhibitors/attractions arriving where their plot is and remind them that caravans and trucks should be parked in designated areas. More importantly, they should be reminded of their agreement that for the duration of the event the site will be designated a vehicle-free zone and that strip down and departure must not be started until the agreed closing time. Remind them that vehicles will not be allowed on site until that time.

Tip

Don't try to measure the site and mark up with a 2-metre DIY tape measure. If you don't have access to a surveyor's tape, use marked ropes. Take a length of rope and mark appropriate measurements on it, by wrapping coloured adhesive tape around the rope. For example I might mark the rope in key lengths, such as green tape at 4 metres, red at 5 metres and blue at 10 metres etc. I then have a ready measurement for the 4 metre-wide access routes, 5 metres gap between structures and 10-metre plot depth etc. Be slightly generous with any minimum legal requirements – you don't want to be closed down because your access road is 10 centimetres too narrow!

Your event may have unique elements not listed in the illustration above. You should aim to complete your preliminary preparations to the same schedule. The early preparations should now be completed, leaving a clear day before your opening day.

One day before opening day

At larger events, on the day before opening, many of your exhibitors, stalls and attractions will arrive:

- Staff should again point out to all exhibitors/attractions arriving where their plot is and remind them that caravans and trucks should be parked in designated areas only. More importantly they should be reminded of their agreement that for the duration of the event the site will be designated a vehicle-free zone and that strip-down and departure must not be started until the agreed closing time. Remind them that vehicles will not be allowed on site until that time.

- Staff should remain to supervise the attractions staff while they erect their stalls, rides and exhibits and all must be supervised to ensure that they stay within the space they have rented and do not try to spread out and use space left for access routes and fire breaks.
- Depending on your agreement with the local authority or perhaps with motoring organisations, your signing can start. Direction signs, warning signs and reminder signs should be positioned and erected in compliance with your agreements and procedures to ensure that safety is of prime consideration.
- Off site, there will be a lot of activity as various managers and supervisors begin to rally the staff and resources they have arranged, so that they are ready for an early start on opening day.
- The event manager will be checking with their deputies and supervisors to confirm that staff will arrive on time and ready to work
- Training will have been completed, except possibly for last-minute substitutes. Reserves will be used first and substitutes trained on the day – no untrained staff will be used.
- The cashier has made final arrangement for the distribution of the cash float, possibly bagging it up and labelling it so that it can easily be distributed and signed for on the first day.
- The cashier has prepared accounting sheets, or books and forms, plus cash labels so that they are ready to issue and receive money and identify where it came from and where it went.
- The cashier may have checked with a security company to arrange for random cash collections from the site.
- 'Gate boxes' will have been set up, so that one can be issued to every gate. They might contain job descriptions, necessary equipment, a site map, phonetic alphabet cards, tickets, marker pens, cash bags and a secure cash box.
- The event manager has made a final check on the insurance cover and certificates and also checked the contractors and suppliers insurance as they arrive on site.

You must make arrangements so that everything you need to be delivered for your event is in place for the next morning. The lists above are an indication only. For example if you are running a field archery competition, you may well have to erect safety fences and build walls of straw bales to prevent stray arrows vanishing into neighbouring fields.

Everything that you cannot sensibly do early on the first day of your event must be completed and in place by the night before opening day. As event manager I like to take an occasional tour of the site to confirm that everything is as it should be and that the site has been marked out and set up safely and accurately in accordance with the site plan.

Opening day

You will make an early start. I begin with a tour of the site, checking to ensure that no exhibitors have expanded their plots overnight to take possession of neighbouring plots or access routes. Your gate staff and site marshals must be in place, sometimes as early as 5 a.m. for a large steam show for example. They will be there to guide exhibitors and staff to the right location and to remind them of the no-vehicle rule that will operate from at least half an hour before the site opens to the public.

As staff arrive, supervisors will sign them in, check that they have been trained, are properly equipped and are able to perform their allocated function and will then brief them for their day's duties.

The roving car park supervisor will have checked all assigned car parks for access, signs and new hazards before opening the first car parks and have made sure that the first shift staff are properly briefed, dressed, equipped and in place.

The staff car park will have been opened and staffed from an early hour to make sure that the staff park properly. The first public car park will be open at least half an hour before the gates open to the public. There will always be early arrivals, those that are keen to get in, or perhaps those who have come quite a distance and allowed more travelling time than they needed. Whatever the reason, the car park should be open to get them in off the road and safely parked.

3. Gates open

This is the moment you have worked for – everything is ready and the gates are open to the public – but your work continues. With the people on site, you have to ensure that all staff are vigilant and maintain safety standards. You must make sure that staff who are trained and equipped to do the job they have taken on are fulfilling all of their roles, and that they are doing their jobs conscientiously. You will maintain your management and control, but gently switch from planning and set-up mode to maintenance mode.

Progress – Chapter 30

You should now:

- have toured the site for a final inspection, risk assessment and review,
- with your staff, have measured and marked out the site ready for the delivery of tents, toilets, Portacabins and attractions, etc,
- have all work on site supervised to ensure that procedures are followed to ensure the health and safety of all present,
- depending on the size of your site and your agreements, have started operating security on site to protect staff and materials present,
- find that Portacabins and tents have been delivered and set up as agreed in your contracts,
- have ensured that the event manager's office is permanently staffed,
- have ensured that the cashier's office and first aid post are also staffed according to your plans and defined procedures,
- after set up, check that test calls have been made on the radios and the public address system, and
- on opening day, have ensured that everything is ready for the event to run and the public to attend, now that the event is open!

Product completed

- The site will be marked out and ready.
- All on-site signs will be erected and recorded for later collection.
- All agreed off-site signs will have been erected and recorded for later collection.
- All equipment and services will have been delivered and set up or installed to your satisfaction.
- Gates will be staffed and any security staff will be working as per schedules.
- The event manager's office and any first aid post will be permanently staffed.
- All equipment will have been checked and tested.

31 Site maintenance

Maintenance tasks

Once the gates open, the public will start to enter the site and you will need to have assigned resources to the ongoing maintenance and review of site and facilities for the duration of the event. Usually the people who do this are the people who were responsible for setting everything up. Their primary task has now been completed, and they know how everything should be installed and working, so it will be easier for them to identify problems.

The sorts of tasks that will need doing are outlined below; for your unique event you may have others to add to the list.

Toilets

You have provided sufficient toilets to service the needs of the expected audience. Those facilities need to be maintained – a task that you hopefully delegated to the contracted supplier. The toilets will need to be emptied of waste, cleaned and have supplies of toilet paper, soap and water topped up.

Tents

Depending on usage and the weather, there may be a need to make some changes to the tents. Perhaps strong winds have loosened guy ropes, or due to hot weather you want to open some of the side panels to increase ventilation.

Note: the qualified staff of the contracted supplier must do this work. Unqualified staff should not attempt to interfere with tents and other temporary structures, unless for example the tent supplier has made allowances for ventilation, and your staff are merely opening that ventilation in accordance with the supplier's instructions.

Litter bins

Depending on your arrangements, you may need to empty individual litterbins during the event. Remember that any vehicles used on site must have lights on, hazard warning lights flashing, certainly be accompanied by a marshal if it has to reverse, and if necessary be accompanied at all time for safety.

Litter collected after the bins have been emptied should be placed in any skips or other containers hired for the event. On no account should rubbish be disposed of locally or burned on site. Legislation, in the form of the Environmental Act 1990, and licensing and transportation restrictions imposed by the Environment Agency, rule the disposal of rubbish! Fines that can be imposed for breaches of this legislation are huge. Use the skips and rely on the skip hire company to obey the regulations.

Skips

You may have provided skips at central points for the collection of rubbish, animal manure, food waste etc. These skips have to be checked regularly. Depending on content, they should be positioned safely as indicated by local authorities. They should only be filled as far as the contractor advises and when full should be removed and the contents disposed of in accordance with the contractor's licences.

Remember: on no account should rubbish in skips be set on fire. If you burn rubbish in a skip, either deliberately or accidentally, you may face a claim for compensation for the damage that will do to the skip.

Site surfaces

Depending on a number of factors, such as the weather conditions and the amount of traffic present on site and in car parks, you may have to take remedial action with areas of grass or other surface.

Constant pedestrian use can turn grassed areas into a sea of slippery mud. Similarly, vehicle traffic through a single point can churn grass and soil into ruts and deep mud. Your staff must be on the alert and watching for the deterioration of surfaces and should report it and take remedial action as soon as possible.

Remedial action can vary from closing gates and diverting pedestrian and vehicle traffic, to spreading sand or sawdust over affected areas, or even laying matting or plywood sheets over badly affected areas.

Your risk assessment and research will have told you the hazards you face and will have been your guide as to your remedial action and resources you need to have available. Remember that though straw and hay is often used as a surface treatment for muddy paths, straw and hay are fire hazards and should not be used.

263

Signs

Signs are just as important during the event as they are during the arrival and departure phases, so they need to be maintained. As the event progresses there will be two main reasons to check and change signage.

Firstly, emergency signs may be required and they have to be made and erected as necessary. For example 'Lane Flooded – Turn Left', or 'Out Of Order'.

Secondly, as your event schedule progresses, different signs will be required for different phases of the event. Different car parks will close as new ones open, and the signs will have to be changed to reflect that. Towards the end of the last day of the event, any sign erection teams will be able to collect the signs that point to the event and check that the exit and route signs are still in place. For example 'M4 – Turn Left' or 'Footpath To Railway Station'.

Fences

Fences, barriers and gates are usually important to the safety and success of your event. You should have had them in place before the opening, but there will always be a need to maintain them and possibly to move them or erect new barriers. For example a muddy and flooded section of footpath may have to be fenced off, or a crowd barrier might need to be removed when a display is finished, to make way for a new exhibit.

Cheap fencing materials such as metal pins, wooden posts, rolls of plastic mesh and rope, plus staff trained and experienced in fence repair and construction should be available for the duration of the event.

Incident/accident

If there are any reported accidents or incidents, they will be attended and investigated by event supervisors. Site maintenance staff will almost certainly be called upon to undertake remedial work, to ensure that similar accidents and incidents are not allowed to happen again.

Progress – Chapter 31

You should now:

* be aware of the need to maintain facilities at your event,

- have tied your contracts for the supply of facilities into the appropriate maintenance cycles, and
- have appropriate maintenance supplies, staff, tools and equipment ready in case they are needed.

Product completed

- All staff will be briefed to look for and report problems.
- Maintenance teams will be on duty.
- Supervisors will be monitoring the behaviour of exhibitors, attractions and contractors.
- Sufficient supplies and equipment will be available for maintenance staff to keep the site working safely.

32 Strip down/clear up

By the time you come to consider implementing this part of the event arrangements, you will probably be elated, tired and full of new ideas for next year. But it is important that you put as much effort and care into the final phases of the event as you have put into the planning and delivery. The end is not far away, but there are some important considerations that you must address before you can put your feet up and take a well deserved rest.

Strip down

Timing

Ideally when stripping down, the gates should be closed to keep the public off the site. Many stallholders and exhibitors will usually try to begin to strip down as soon as the bulk of the public have left, aiming to be nearly completed by or before the official closing time – for a quick getaway.

I would advise for safety reasons that you make it a condition of accepting a stall or display that stallholders and exhibitors must not start to strip down until a specified closure time. You should certainly ban vehicles from the site until official closing time, say 6 p.m. on the last day of the event.

If stallholders want to make an early departure and they begin dismantling stalls and rides with members of the public still walking around, you have two problems.

Firstly, the public will see the stalls closing early and perceive that your event is 'closing' and so they will leave, prematurely closing your event, upsetting other stallholders by cutting short their selling time.

Secondly, by packing goods and dismantling their stalls, they may accidentally cause injury to passersby. While boxing stock and dismantling stalls, they may bridge fire gaps or block emergency access routes, introducing trip hazards or possibly leaving electrical feeds in a dangerous state. This problem is compounded if the stallholders who close early want to bring vehicles on site to collect their goods and display stands.

Tip

To keep staff and the public safe, inform all exhibitors and stall holders that the event site will be a strictly enforced no-vehicle zone from opening time on day one to closing time on the last day. *No* vehicles will be allowed on site!

Stalls

When the event has closed, stallholders will begin to transfer their stock to their vehicles and to strip down their stalls. All you have to do to help them is to give them easy access to the site. If you have not agreed with them that they remove all their own rubbish from the site, make sure that rubbish skips are available for their refuse. Wherever possible make stallholders and exhibitors responsible for removing their own litter from the site!

Rubbish

You must of course have marshals patrolling the stall areas to ensure that the stallholders do not try to abandon large quantities of rubbish and spoiled food – if they do, *you* will have to pay for its disposal!

Animals

Similar to stalls, simply allow the owner access for their transport and if at all possible keep sudden noise and flapping tarpaulins etc. to a minimum while the animals are being loaded. Make sure that skips are available for any manure and straw or other waste materials that are left. Make doubly sure that the stallholders are responsible for clearing up the mess and placing it in any skips provided.

Rides

Generally, fun-fare type rides are erected and stripped down regularly by their operators and because of this the crew/staff are very efficient. All they require is free access for their vehicles and a quick route out.

Tents

Again, tents are usually erected and stripped by dedicated contracted staff, who are very efficient. They may require assistance to clear lingering stallholders and event furniture and equipment, or to keep inquisitive children out of the danger area. Once collapsed, tents are rapidly rolled/folded up and loaded onto lorries. Easy access for heavy vehicles is a bonus for these teams.

Portacabins

With appropriate access, Portacabins can be removed quite simply, as long as the lorry can get in to a loading position, then they can either jack up the unit or crane it onto the transport lorry.

Tip

If a Portacabin was used for the cashier and event manager's office, I suggest that the contract or hire agreement states that they are removed *on the day following the last day of the event.* You will still be using these offices until the last possible moment on the final day of the event or even the day after closing!

Signs

Records will have been kept as to what signs were put up at which locations. As with erecting signs, when teams remove them they should make sure that they do not cause danger or obstruction to others in the process. On-site signs can be removed easily, but any approved off-site signs will be more difficult, especially if heavy traffic is still dispersing.

It is possible that you can get a head start by beginning to collect signs pointing towards the event site during the early afternoon of the last day. Anyone coming will almost certainly have arrived, so the signs pointing towards the site are no longer required. Remember to follow all safety procedures (see Chapter 16, 'Sign posting').

If the event is to be repeated next year, remember that you will have to make arrangement for the safe storage of the signs until they are required the following year.

Tip

If the organisation running the event has storage, such as a school or sport club, store signs there. If there is no group storage, the farmer who rented you the land may well have a corner where you could store the signs, possibly for an extra modest fee.

Make sure that the proposed storage is clean and secure. Signs can be quite expensive and you don't want to have to replace them all because they went missing, or when required next year they are buried under 1000 tons of cattle feed. Signs must be readable too, so ensure that they don't become so dirty in the storage available that they have to be replaced. You may consider sharing out the signs to store in the garages of the event management staff until next year – as long as you record who took what for storage, so you can recall them to use next year.

Security

Remember to maintain security at this stage. With the busy confusion of strip down, everybody is far too busy to bother with what is happening even a short distance away. It is far too easy for a truck to arrive and load up with valuables such as stock, generators, a display exhibit, or a stallholder's trailer or caravan etc. They depart with the general flow and then the legitimate owner of those goods suddenly realises that they are gone, forever.

Clear up

Litter is not just offensive to look at; it causes a number of problems too. Papers blown up against a fence on a dry day can provide or become a source of fuel for a fire ignited by a discarded cigarette. Remaining foodstuffs can attract vermin. Discarded bottles, tins, wire and string etc. can seriously harm people wildlife and farm animals.

Litter

No matter how well organised the event, there will be litter. No doubt in negotiating for the use of the site, you agreed to leave it in a tidy state after the event.

Some landowners demand a deposit from an event organiser that is returned if the site is clean, but retained and used to tidy and repair the site if that has not been done to their satisfaction.

Don't leave a mess. Aim to be tidy and look after the site as though it was your own – supplying an adequate numbers of bins and skips will keep general litter under control. Remember, you may want to come back and run the event next year, especially if it has been a success. (Yes – planning and negotiation for next year's event starts here!)

Staff usually don't like picking up litter, but you may be able to offer some cash to the local youth club, or army cadets to form a litter-picking gang.

Paper

Remember to work with the wind. If it is blowing left to right, start on the left margin of the site and work towards the right. Stray bits of litter will blow ahead of you. Don't try to work against the wind, you will forever be chasing litter that blows past you into the clean area you just picked.

Glass/tins

Make sure that all litter picking staff have stout gloves. I suggest if young people are being used, adults (car park staff for example) should supervise them, and if any broken glass or tins are found, they should call an adult who is properly equipped to deal with it. Put broken glass and jagged tins into a sturdy container and place that container carefully into the skips provided.

Manure

Animal exhibits may leave manure heaps. Perhaps you failed to ensure that you required animal exhibitors to tidy up after themselves. If there is a deposit of manure a local gardener or allotment society may just be persuaded to come and claim the manure and reduce your headache. If not and you have no alternative, put a skip near the manure and dispose of it. (If you forgot to arrange for animal exhibitors to remove their own manure, when you have finished forking seven tons of manure into the skip, you won't make the same mistake next year.)

Food stuffs

Waste food is difficult to deal with. It attracts rats and other vermin and is subject to many rules and regulations as to its storage and disposal. I suggest that if at all possible when negotiating for food outlets, you arrange for them to deal with their own waste.

If you are responsible for disposing of food waste, ensure that you abide by local rules and regulations.

Skips

You will probably have to hire some skips or other containers to collect and remove rubbish. If you do hire skips, the company will deliver them to the site and collect them when full.

Tip

Make sure that you position the skips where they are needed on the day. For example, place one in the middle of the animal pens and a couple along the downwind fence. Place one at the downwind fence of each car park and place one at the main entrance/exit gate. Then the skips are where the rubbish is, you don't want to have to transport every single piece of waste to the other end of the site, just because that is where the unsupervised or lazy lorry driver left ten skips!

Equipment collection and return

You have the end in sight, but you must make sure that in your rush to clear up and go home that you efficiently administer the collection and return of any equipment that was rented, loaned or issued. Any radios that you have been using must be signed back in and then returned to the hiring company. Any generators, temporary fencing, furniture, or red and white traffic cones that you have been using could easily be lost in the confusion. Remember to ensure your own security while you are maintaining security for visitors to the site.

Repairs – turf and fences

It is possible that some damage has been done to turf in fields. Remember to cover the subject of damage to turf, fences and hedges when organising for the loan or hire of the land, and make sure that you know who is responsible for repairing it.

Whether the damage is down to you to repair or not, you should make every effort to prevent any damage to the turf or anything else on the site. Remember that you probably want to come back again next year and you don't want members of the public falling into ruts in the grass and breaking bones.

If you do have to repair turf, the area damaged may be larger than expected. If so it could be a case of forget the rake and wheelbarrow and rent a tractor or digger. It is likely that the farmer has the equipment needed to level and re-seed a section of grass anyway, so if at all possible make turf repair their responsibility, without insisting so loudly that you frighten them into refusing to rent you the field.

Tip

If the damage is down to you to repair, you should make absolutely sure that you have briefed all event staff to watch out for damage and divert traffic from damp, muddy or damaged areas to minimise cost of repair. Even if damage will be the responsibility of the landowner, I try to minimise any damage to the site. *Don't* be inconsiderate; you probably want to come back next year.

Roll call

Just to make absolutely sure that you have not left some poor soul in some remote emergency access gate, do a roll call. Make sure that all staff have been debriefed, thanked, stood down and sent home. As Event Manager, I always make a final tour of all points to make sure that staff have gone and gates are locked etc.

Final tour

When satisfied that the site is clear, make a final tour around it yourself and when you are satisfied, contact the landowner and make a tour together to show that the site is tidy and returned to its previous state. Possibly take another video record of the site after the event and include the landowner agreeing that all is as it should be.

Progress – Chapter 32

You should now:

- understand that strip down and clear up requires as much planning care and consideration as all other stages in delivering your event,
- accept that for safety reasons you should make it a condition of entry that all stallholders and concessions accept that strip down and vehicle movement will not be allowed until a specified closing time,
- ensure that where possible the gates are closed to members of the public while the potentially hazardous strip down is completed,
- ensure that security is heightened or at least maintained during strip down, when general movement and confusion might allow greater opportunity for theft,
- remember to maintain your own security at this time, and protect your equipment, generators, traffic cones, which can vanish just as easily as exhibitor's valuables,
- ensure that your sign teams are dispatched with the schedule of signs posted to remove and collect them, paying as much attention to safety as they did when erecting them,
- have taken into account the conditions on the day and where necessary directed skips to be located at key positions, for the collection of rubbish,
- be grateful that you insisted that the food outlets, commercial concessions and animal displays were responsible for the removal of their own rubbish,
- ensure that you administer the efficient collection and return of any equipment that has been borrowed, rented or otherwise belongs to somebody else,
- perform a final tour of the site and the area, making sure that all signs are collected and that the site has been left in a tidy condition,
- double-check with team leaders, supervisors, deputy event managers, going through the dry wipeboard and duty sheets in the event manager's office, to ensure that all staff have been called in, signed off and sent home,
- undertake a final tour to check that all staff have been relieved, gates are shut and litter has been collected,
- attend the site the following day (if you took my advice), to supervise the return of any Portacabins that you had rented for the use of the cashier and event manager, and
- arrange to review the site and boundary in the company of the landowner and get them on tape agreeing that all is as it should be.

Product completed

- Clear up plan, which includes continued security presence.
- Accurate sign schedule, that allows signs to be collected and returned to store.
- Sign off sheet showing all staff have been debriefed and stood down.
- Site and site boundary reviewed and videotaped in the company of the landowner to record the hand back.

33 Final debrief

Do I need a final debrief?

Better than anyone else, you know the amount of effort that has gone into making your event a success. You were inspired with the idea of running the event; you investigated, researched and planned it all. You recruited and developed a team of managers, supervisors and staff who have faithfully undertaken their duties to deliver an event that the public loved. Along the way there were problems that you resolved between you. Some staff may even have ideas about improving your displays, car parks or other matters next year. Don't discard that experience and don't lose the benefit of listening to them – run debriefing sessions.

Who to debrief

The event manager sits at the centre of a web of information and control. It is likely and desirable that each deputy manager, section head and team leader has identified and resolved problems that the event manager knew nothing about.

All relevant information should be collected and collated for the final report. You should ensure that all levels of staff are able to record their comments, thoughts and suggestions. To achieve this there should be a series of debriefs. Section leaders debrief their members and in turn attend and feed information up to their team leader, who feeds information up to the deputy manager and finally to the event manager.

All comments should be recorded. Do not assume that the boy picking up litter at the bottom of the car park field cannot make a relevant and useful comment about something as significant as signs or traffic flow. Record it all and feed it up.

When to debrief

Firstly make sure that staff feel free to report problems encountered and how they resolved them during the running of the event. There should be some sort of log or register in the event manager's office to record these. Several times each day the event manager should review suggestions that have been made. The suggestions may highlight a potentially major problem, or be the key to resolving a problem that has puzzled supervisors for some time. Do not ask people with comments and suggestions to wait until the end of the day, or the evening of the event. Things can easily be forgotten, so lessons should be learned and implemented as soon as possible.

At the end of the last day staff will be tired and possibly cold and wet, or sunburned, dirty and hungry. They will almost certainly want to get home to have a bath or shower and put their feet up. Before any of the teams are dismissed or begin to drift off, and while things are still fresh in their minds, gather them together and ask for comments and suggestions.

It is also useful to allow members of staff the option to submit debrief information later. While cold and tired they may have forgotten to tell you something quite important. Make provision for them to submit late debriefs. Especially where an event is due to be repeated next year, make sure that there is a way for staff to report matters later. You may want to hand out addressed forms, or give them a note with your email address so that they can submit thoughts later.

I remember one late comment that came from a conversation as the car park marshals were walking to their cars. 'Did I tell you about that guy from the water board? Next year they are putting a water main through the event ground.' That little throwaway comment was a fact that the farmer had forgotten to tell us – so the hunt was on for an alternative venue for the next year.

Thanks

While talking to your supervisors and teams remember to thank them for their efforts, especially if it has been particularly busy, or cold and wet. Above all, remember to be considerate. I once worked as a paid car park supervisor on a commercial three-day event. The weather was atrocious – cold, with constant driving rain. Several staff failed to report on day two and even more failed to show on day three. The rest of us had to work harder in the horrible weather, but on the last day there was a rumour of a small consideration for those of us who had stayed with it. As the last cars left on the last day, a manager drove round to tell us to report to the event manager's office. We all walked half a mile in the driving rain, and gathered outside the manager's office.

We stood in the rain until he graced us with his presence ten minutes later – '*to thank us for staying to the end*'. Guess who practised his Anglo-Saxon insults and never went back there again? And guess which event manager just can't get any staff to work for him and can't understand why?

Act on it

You have gone to the trouble of holding the debriefing sessions and recorded valid points, suggestions and proposals. You have gone to all that trouble to avoid problems and improve delivery at your next event, so don't waste the information.

You must take those points and suggestions, evaluate them and feed them into your event documentation. If there is a good proposal regarding the site plan, draw the proposed changes onto a proposed plan for the next event and describe the changes and the benefits, showing why they were proposed. If the proposals relate to sign posting, draft a sign posting schedule and sign design for next year and explain what changes have been proposed and the benefits they will bring.

All valid proposals should be written into a section of the final report (see Chapter 34, 'Final report') entitled 'Proposals For Improvements Next Year'. The proposal should include a written description and, where beneficial, the proposal should include a drawing (for example where changes are proposed to the cones, and tapes are used to establish vehicle entry lanes). The descriptions should include a section describing how it differs to the arrangements used this year and what the expected benefits will be.

Note your star players and dunces

Team leaders and section heads should indicate in their reports which members of their staff were their stars. Be very careful about making negative comments in writing about anyone. That could be very demoralising and in the current climate might leave you open to legal action under some obscure European legislation!

If the event was a success you will probably want to arrange a similar event next year. If you make a note now of the staff who were particularly good and effective in their jobs, you have the core of a good team for next year and a ready-made team of supervisors and team leaders. Better still, they are now experienced, know the event, and you all know each other, so you have the makings of a good team.

Progress – Chapter 33

You should now:

- understand the benefits of a formal and an informal debrief and the benefit of making arrangements for the late submission of information by forms or email,
- be gracious enough to thank everyone for their efforts, and
- ensure that information received during debriefs, including late submissions, are documented appropriately, even if it is a very late covering letter on the final report noting the water board plans for a new mains pipe through the site next year.

Product completed

- Debrief schedule, outlining debrief process.
- Debrief reporting forms to record issues that need to be taken further, including a note of the person making the proposal and a phone number or address in case event staff need to contact them for clarification.
- Detailed reports, where necessary, allowing staff to make a more detailed description and drawings explaining their proposals and to state benefits they suggest can be obtained by adopting their proposal.
- Notes of staff who performed well and who you would like to use again.

34 Final report

You have investigated and planned, scheduled, managed and trained, debriefed, listened and delivered. You must now compile the important elements of all of that information into a final report, to encapsulate what happened. It will be an invaluable learning tool for you and a source of inspiration and information when the event comes around again.

Summary of useful information

When it is all over, the accounts have been finalised and the profits banked, the event manager, with the assistance of any deputies and other supervisors they require, should compile a final report.

This should contain an overall review of the success (or otherwise) of the event and any problems encountered, indicating where possible the actions or measures that have been implemented (or will be next year) to avoid or resolve those problems.

If possible, compile a comprehensive list of all professional services engaged, suppliers and equipment, with a note of their cost and efficiency. Some may be contacted again for future events whilst others may be relegated to the 'unsatisfactory' list.

This report will act as a quick and easy reference when planning future events, be they annual repeats of the event just completed, or similar events and shows.

Other supporting event documentation will be available for audit and to assist the event manager in following years. This report is a summary of the event. More than a meaningless list of names and contacts, it encapsulates how you delivered the event and any lessons you learned while doing so.

Content

I suggest that the final report should cover the following topics, though you will need to change the format structure and content to meet your own requirements and to cover your own event. Specialist events will need to amend the format to include their own flavour, for example leagues and finals for sporting events, range safety for a shooting event etc.

The well-used and possibly tea-stained and dog-eared event manager's copy of the event manager's manual should be included as an annex to the final report.

- Event name and dates
- Event objective
- Event manager's summary (see below)
- Event size
  - Type number and list of stalls in annex
  - Type number and list of exhibits in annex
  - Number of paying public (by day and total)
  - Estimated attendance
- Summary of accounts
  - Expenditure
  - Income
  - Profit or loss (small losses may be acceptable for club events)
- Problems and solutions
  - Summary of emergency (radio) log
  - Summary of accidents and incidents
- Contacts
  - Local authority
  - Fire brigade
  - Police
  - St John/Red Cross
  - Exhibitors
    - clubs/groups
    - individuals
  - Services
    - tents
    - Portacabins
    - toilets
    - radios
    - etc.
- Clubs

- Staff
  - supervisors
  - volunteers
  - paid staff
- Resources
  - signs (noting where they are now stored)
  - notices (noting who has the master document)
  - reflective jackets (noting who holds them)
- Proposals for improvements next year
- Potential problems for future years

Event manager's summary

This is your opportunity to put a one- or two-page summary at the front of the final report. The lists of exhibitors and a summary of the financial status will be included elsewhere. As the event manager, write your version of how the show went and highlight areas for close consideration next time.

For example the event manager's summary might be as follows:

Research indicated that the South Budley Steam Extravaganza would be well attended and would make a considerable profit. The event was held on 1st August 2006 and attendance exceeded estimates by 20%. All exhibitors have already booked places for next year and 37 additional steam exhibits have since written to enquire about next year (details included in this report).

The fun fair was well attended and the proprietor has committed to attending next year. The diversionary attractions that were introduced had mixed results. The radio-controlled model aircraft and cars were a hit and should be expanded in numbers and scope next year. The civil war re-enactment group took up a lot of time and space and were disruptive to the main show. Nobody was particularly interested in their exhibits or the 'Battle of Budley Bridge', and they should not be invited back.

Car parking worked very well under the Traffic Manager, Robert Anorak, and he is willing to take that role again next year. Sign posting was a problem. In the traffic congestion at the Four Corners Roundabout on the A111, motorists were confused as to the route to the event site. Next year we need to highlight that with the police and local authority; proposals for that have been included in this report.

There were no injuries or emergencies, though the radio hire company could not get their base station working until nearly 1 p.m. on the first day of the event, due to electricity supply problems.

I intend to organise the show again next year, but to double the size of the site and use five fields as car parks. I am already in negotiation for the use of the expanded site and car parks for next year.

Progress – Chapter 34

You should now:

- know what the sort of information that the final report should contain and have defined a contents list for your final report that is relevant to your event,
- have drafted an event manager's summary, and
- have attached the event manager's manual as an annex to the final report.

Product completed

- A final report.

35 Conclusion

Where now?

Finally, although this guide may have warned you that planning and running an event can be a tough assignment and it has alerted you to the tremendous amount of thought, investigation, consideration, effort and planning required before you spend any money – don't let it put you off!

You and your club or group obviously need to organise an event, and you either volunteered or were press-ganged into action, or you probably would not be reading this. Remember:

- All events are unique; only *you* know your proposed event.
- Always bear in mind your own objective and budget.
- Follow these guidelines, but modify them to suit your needs.
- Plan thoroughly throughout the operation.
- Hold a presentation of your decisions where possible or where you feel it necessary to have a checkpoint or 'sanity check'.
- Where possible, gather your managers and have a desktop walk-through, using the proposed site plan, staff work schedules, procedures etc., to make sure that they will work.
- Give due care and consideration and get at least three quotes before agreeing to any expenditure.
- Don't book anything or spend anything until you are sure you have all of the required permissions to go ahead.
- Make health and safety your priority.
- Consult and refer to the local authorities, health and safety executive, emergency services and other professionals for appropriate advice.

Your commitment, combined with motivation and help from other members of your group, should enable you to plan, organise and run a successful and profitable event. You will have the satisfaction of a job well done, as well as being able to record a higher balance in the appropriate bank account.

Good luck – and don't panic!

Annex A

Project management supplement: managing the event

What is a project?

'Projects' sound technical and complicated, but they aren't. Take an everyday activity like 'going shopping' – that could be described as a 'project'. You have to organise and schedule various things, with the objective of getting the shopping for the week. You have some limits, for example you have to budget to do it with the £50 you have in cash and get into town before the shops close. To prepare for that shopping trip, you have to check the contents of the fridge, plan the menus for next week, write your shopping list and then catch the bus into town. We also want to make sure that the buses are running and when we get to town we don't buy rotten oranges or mouldy bread.

A 'project' can therefore be described in more general terms as a collection of tasks, which have to be completed in a given order, within defined timescales, defined cost, defined quality and with specified resources.

Products/tasks/stages

On first examination, many 'projects' may appear to be so large and complex that they are viewed as being insurmountable. The simple act of dividing a large and possibly complex job into smaller, more manageable tasks makes the planning and completion of the main project achievable. Because organising their event is a part-time task, most people treat their event as a project and use a formal method to ensure that critical tasks and reviews are not forgotten. If in any doubt, I suggest that you treat the organisation and planning of your event as a project.

For the purpose of this supplement, we are using a simple example project – and that is 'the creation of a garden for Mr Smith, who has moved into a new house'. The example has been picked because it is a subject that almost everyone will recognise and understand without any specialist training or knowledge. The process remains the same, whether the project is creating a garden, planning the next Olympics, or building a passenger jet.

What if Mr Smith asks you these questions?: 'Can you tell me what products you have to deliver to complete this "garden" project? What tasks have to be undertaken to generate those products? In what order do they have to be completed? What will you charge for doing it? How long will all of this take you?'

Don't try to answer those questions yet and *don't* panic. At this stage you have little or no idea, but you will see below how a little simple organisation and analysis can allow you to confidently answer these questions. When you get to Step 14 below, remember that I promised that you will be able to easily answer these questions and more with a considerable level of confidence.

Definition: A *project* is comprised of *products* and *tasks*, which are split between *stages*.

Project

We know what the main job is, in this case to produce a garden for Mr Smith. The 'project' is then to create the garden Mr Smith wants.

Products

We know we have to deliver various things to make the garden Mr Smith wants. The individual things we have to make are 'products'. So, with a bit of thought we can sit and list the products we need to deliver to give Mr Smith his garden. For this garden project, the products may include: a level site cleared of brambles and weeds, a shed and a lawn etc.

Tasks

When we know the products we are hoping to deliver, we can look closely at each product and draw up a list of 'tasks' that need to be undertaken and completed to finish each product. So 'tasks' are the jobs that have to be done to allow you to finish and deliver the 'products' required for the project.

For the product 'level site' above, the tasks may be:

- Check the garden plan for required soil level.
- Decide and mark final soil level.

- Peg out final soil level.
- Remove high points.
- Fill in low points.
- Roll and compact soil.

Stages

When we have identified all 'products' and 'tasks' required to complete them, we have a long list of products and even longer lists of tasks that we have to perform to deliver those products.

Depending on the size of the project, those lists may be very long and unmanageable. To make it easier we can split the main project into smaller more manageable chunks, or in project talk – 'stages'. In our case after deciding on the list of products and stages, we could divide the garden project into three stages:

1. Clearing the site.
2. Building shed, patio and barbecue.
3. Planting plants.

Project management software

You may be aware of project management software and other computer tools that project managers use. They are not essential, but the larger the project, and the more stages, products, tasks and staff involved, the more useful such tools are. For our sample project we will make do with a notepad, pen, pencil and calculator.

Delivering the garden project in easy steps

This is where we start being project managers. The 14 steps below indicate the approach I would use to deliver this garden project for Mr Smith.

Step 1 – Project overview

What are we doing? The first thing the project manager must do is to understand the project by obtaining a good overview of what is required. We have to gather information, by asking questions, visiting the site, etc. What is the objective? What is required? What is the available budget? Are there any specific problems or requirements? Where do we start? What do we have to consider? What experts do we have to arrange? How much is it going to cost? From his initial request we know the *objective*: Mr Smith has moved into a new house and wants a garden. He wants a patio, some **287** flowerbeds, a shed, a barbecue, a lawn and some tools to help him keep the garden tidy. He has a budget in mind but wants to know what this will cost and how long it would take to finish it.

We don't have a clue yet but standard project management techniques can help us to organise and manage the project properly, answering these questions and delivering the required garden to the required standards of quality, to the price specified.

Step 2 – Define user requirements

The 'user requirement' is simply a document stating what Mr Smith wants! We therefore have to talk to Mr Smith, find out just what he wants and then write it down and get him to agree it.

Often after the first meeting you get a feel for the requirement, but later realise that there is still a lot of information missing. When we have finished his garden, we don't want him to turn around and say, 'Very nice, but did I mention a swimming pool?' or 'But I wanted a brick shed!'

We have to fill in any gaps – when he said he wanted a shed, did he mean brick or wood, what size, what will he use it for? All of these details will be written down and agreed by us all, so we know what to build, defining our *shed* 'product'.

What does he mean when he says 'patio'? Which material - concrete or slabs? What size should it be? Where does he want it? Again we write it all down and define our *patio* 'product'.

When he has finished answering our questions, we *must* write everything down and get him to read and sign it, confirming that what we have written is exactly what he wants. If he later asks about a swimming pool, we can show him his signed 'user requirements' and say, 'Sorry, Mr Smith, you didn't ask for one.'

When everything is written down, we go to Mr Smith and present him with his User Requirement. We read through it together, and then ask him to confirm and sign, saying that the user requirement contains exactly what he wants.

Step 3 – Brainstorm

Brainstorms sound painful, but they aren't. It's just project talk, for getting a bunch of people together and talking everything through. They are all expected to join in a group discussion, which will raise and list everything that is needed to deliver the garden defined in our new user requirement. That includes buying materials, tools needed to do the work, specialist skills required – everything. This gives you an idea of what has to be done and in what order.

As each idea is thrown up, you must write it down. Some ideas may in some sense seem to be duplicated. For example Joe may say, 'Buy a shed' and Harry may say

'Build a shed'. It doesn't matter. Don't try to sift ideas during the brainstorming session. Write down everything anyone says at this stage, we can think about it and sort it all out later.

Clearly, project managers and their brainstorming staff must have some relevant experience and knowledge of the job in hand, or they simply cannot complete it. Luckily our staff know what a garden is, so we begin with Step 3, brainstorming.

During this brainstorming session, we need to freely discuss the idea of creating the garden for Mr Smith. Listing everything that comes up will help us to move forward.

Tip

Note these things on Post-it® notes to help you arrange and sort them later on.

The brainstorm session produced the following items that the people present thought would be needed to deliver Mr Smith's garden:

- Clear site.
- Dig flowerbed.
- Lay lawn.
- Build patio and shed.
- Plant flowers.
- Level garden.
- Buy and position barbecue.

Step 4 – Review and define products

Now that the brainstorming is finished, we look back at the products we have identified and see if we have all the details. If not we talk to Mr Smith and get them and write them down!

Product 1 is 'Clear site'. What exactly does Mr Smith mean by that? Does he want the existing apple tree dug up and removed? Does he want the decorative steps removed? Does he want the existing concrete pathway torn up and grassed over?

For each of the products we need a specification of exactly what Mr Smith wants. We may have got the information from our original discussions about his overall objective or we may not. Don't be scared to go back and ask more questions. When you get an answer, record it, write up product definitions and get them agreed and signed off by Mr Smith.

For example Mr Smith has confirmed that the shed:

should be made of wood and treated with dark brown wood stain. It should have a pitched roof. It should be 15ft long and 12ft wide. It will be placed in the rear left-hand corner of the back garden. It will have a concrete floor. A glazed window will look out towards the house. The double doors should measure a minimum of 5ft wide to allow Mr Smith to get tools in and out easily. There will be a workbench under the window, stretching the full length of the shed to allow Mr Smith to prepare seeds and other plants. The shed will have a secure padlock.

Note: if you are interested in pure project management there are different product classes –

- *Management* – products/things that won't go into the garden. e.g. things that are used by managers to deliver the project such as
  - the actual plan drawn up,
  - the contract for the work, and
  - the invoices for goods and services.
- *Technical* – products/things that do go into the garden, the shed, plants etc.
- *Quality* – products/things that won't go into the garden but which help us to define, plan and control the quality of our work, i.e. the specification that the patio slabs must slope away from the house at an angle of five degrees to direct rainwater away from the patio door.

Step 5 – Consider sub-products

Consider and review products to identify sub-products. Sub-products are bits of something bigger. We have said that the shed is a product, but we now know from what Mr Smith has said that he wants his shed to have double doors, a bench, a window, a concrete floor and a padlock. All of them can be classed as sub-products of the product 'shed'.

It may be that during our review, to make it easier for us to understand what is wanted, some or perhaps all of the products we identified above can be broken down further, defining 'sub-products' to a sensible level.

These reviews may well even expose totally new products that we hadn't even considered earlier. Any new products can be added and written in to the plans at this stage, e.g.:

- purchased tools
- hand tools
  - spade
  - rake
  - fork
- electric power tools
  - hedge trimmer
  - lawn mower
- stocked flower beds
  - tulips
  - roses
- patio
  - bricks
  - paving stones
- lawn
- shed
- barbecue
  - bricks
  - ash tray

Step 6 – Define product flow

The 'product flow' describes the *flow of work* – that is, the order in which products have to be finished to deliver Mr Smith's garden.

We have a list of products, but we know that they have to be done in order. Imagine our list with loads of notes saying things like, 'Don't forget to clear the site before you lay the turf. Don't forget that you must lay the path before you lay the turf or the cement from the path will kill the grass. Oops I forgot – dig the apple tree out before you lay the turf …' etc.

A nice drawing can show that information a lot better than a list with little Post-it® notes and reminders all over it. The products must be put in order – that is, the order in which they have to be completed and delivered. It is clear that we can't plant the flowers until we have cleared and levelled the site and marked out and dug the flowerbeds. We can't lay the lawn until the site has been levelled. So we have a pretty good idea what has to be done in what order, and we can sketch out the order in which the products will have to be delivered. This is the product flow diagram. The flow runs from left to right. In our example the simple product flow looks like this:

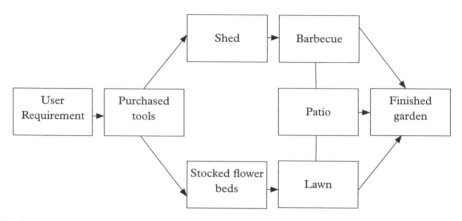

Delivery of goods

Step 7 – Define final product lists

We have been working through investigating, looking at the products and defining them. While we were working out how they have to be done and in what order, we discovered things we did not think about when we first started. All this step does is to formally rewrite and define the list of products for the record.

Thinking about and brainstorming (discussing) the project and how it will be done, has allowed us to identify more products than we had originally listed which is frequently the case. It is better to think about the products now, rather than have ten workmen standing doing nothing while we frantically try to organise some paving slabs to be delivered for them to lay! Apart from actual bricks or plants, the final products list might look like this:

Management	Technical	Quality
For planning	*Actual products*	*Quality Checks*
contract	agreed specification	inspection
plan	approved design	sign offs
control information	purchased tools	product description
stage approval	cleared site	
invoices	marked layout	
	dug beds	
	stocked beds	
	patio	
	lawn	
	barbecue	
	tool shed	
	footpath	
	finished garden	

Step 8 – Number products and tasks etc.

We are generating lists and it is easier to talk about items on a list if they are numbered. Saying 'product TP30' is a lot clearer than 'it's the middle list, third one down from the top – getting the tools or something!'

As can be seen, any reasonable project will soon generate a long list of products. For administrative purposes, it is sensible to give all products a short identifier. To distinguish between management, technical and quality products I would be inclined to give them an 'MP', 'TP' or 'QP' prefix. Adding a number to this creates a short, sensible and manageable identifier for each product. Thus a product identifier may be 'MP10' (Management Product 10), or 'TP30' (Technical Product 30). It's easier to discuss, reference, track, record and refer to product 'TP30' than 'Purchased tools'.

As we have seen, it is possible that new products will be identified and inserted into the product list at a later stage. We may discover a new product, or Mr Smith may come in and say his wife wants a bird bath in the garden. To allow for this, we build gaps into the numbering system, so the products can now be identified by numbers stepped in 10s, e.g.:

MP10 = Contract   TP10 = Agreed specification
MP20 = Plan   TP20 = Approved design
MP30 = Control information   TP30 = Purchased tools
MP40 = Stage approval   TP40 = Cleared site

Step 9 – Define tasks per product

Now that we have identified and fully defined all of the products, we have to start looking at how we are going to make, do, buy, or otherwise deliver each of them, so that Mr Smith gets his garden.

We now understand the project in some detail and the scope of the problem is becoming more manageable. We can begin to look at a lower level of detail. For example, take a look at the product 'Clear site'. Following a site visit and after reviewing the product definitions agreed, we should brainstorm what will be needed to deliver the clear site. For example:

- Cut down brambles and stinging nettles.
- Dig out roots of brambles.
- Treat soil with perennial weed killer.
- Remove existing diseased apple tree and its stump.
- Remove rubble and rubbish currently located along back fence.

- Remove cracked concrete path.
- Level remaining soil.

Using this method for all of our products, we arrive at the list of tasks that have to be done to enable us to complete and deliver that product.

This has a lot of benefits in both planning and executing this project. It is clearly helping to concentrate our minds during the planning stage. When we start work, rather than just say 'clear the site', we can give our workers the detailed instructions contained in the list above. Another benefit is that with that list it will be easier to check that the jobs have been completed to the quality we expect. Repeat this process for all products.

Step 10 – Draft task plan and effort

When Mr Smith first asked us to do his garden, we had one product and activity, 'Do a garden for me!'

By questioning him and analysing his answers we broke this down into more manageable products, from which we derived a list of fairly low-level tasks needed to deliver those products. With this list of simple tasks, we can make a fairly accurate estimate of the time required to finish each one. For example:

TP40 Clear site – Tasks and effort	
Cut down and remove brambles and stinging nettles.	1 day
Dig out roots of brambles.	2 hrs
Treat soil with perennial weed killer.	2 hrs
Remove existing diseased apple tree and its stump.	2 days
Remove rubble and rubbish currently located along back fence.	12 hrs
Remove cracked concrete path.	12 hrs
Level remaining soil.	4 hours
Total effort required	5 days

Note: if you cannot assign an estimate of the length of time you require to complete the task, it is likely that either you still don't understand part of the project, or more likely, that the stages, products and tasks are still too big for you to cope with. Look into things you still don't understand, and break down the products into sub-products, and/or break down the tasks in more detail.

In planning your project, you must go down to a level of detail where it should be quite simple for you to assign estimates of effort. This will enable you to calculate effort, resources and skills required and even finally specify a delivery date and cost.

For all products, list the tasks necessary to provide the deliverables quoted. To help you identify tasks, give each task an identifier to make it easier to refer to them later on when you have a bricklayer asking what you want him to do. For example:

Task number	Activity	Man days	Staff cost	Equip/material cost
T10	Agree specification	2	£200	
T20	Write site description	4	£400	
T30	Agree acceptance criteria	2	£200	
T40	Contract	3	£300	
T50	Approve design	4	£400	
T60	Clear site	5	£300	£20
T62	Level site	1	£80	£30
T70	Mark layout	2	£100	£20
T80	Lay patio	5	£450	£600
T90	Build barbecue	8	£600	£450
T100	Stock flower beds	3	£175	£550
T110	Lay lawn	3	£160	£175
T120	Build tool shed	2	£155	£295
T130	Creosote shed	1	£45	£35
T140	Buy tools	1	£45	£896
	Total effort in man days	46	£3610	£3521

Because we broke things down to a level we can comprehend, it wasn't difficult to generate the list above, showing the tasks and the time it will take to complete each one, based on one person doing each job. Hence checking and agreeing the specification (task T10) shows us that task T10 will take 2 days effort. (That may be one person for two days or two people for one day, etc.)

Step 11 – Task network and dependency diagram

'Network dependency diagram' is 'technospeak' for figuring out which jobs rely on other jobs being finished before they can begin!

Things have to be done in order, just like a train calling at different stations on a railway line. There is a direction (start to finish) and the train has to visit stations in a given order. Just like a railway network, tasks can be drawn in a simple 'network' diagram.

With our shed, it doesn't take much intelligence to realise that we can't put the shed roof on until we have built the shed walls. That is a 'dependency' we have recognised. We also know that we have to build the shed base before we can build the shed – another dependency. Just look at the rest of the products and identify all of the dependencies.

There is a difference between a railway network diagram and our project network dependency diagram. For our project some things can be done at the same time. A train cannot call at two stations at the same time, but our workers can do two jobs at the same time (for example Bob can build the barbecue while Harry builds the shed) and our diagram has to show that. Drawing that out is quite straightforward.

This 'network and dependency diagram' allows us to show the sequence in which the tasks have to take place. Remember, we cannot plant the flowers until the flower bed has been dug out and we cannot dig the flower bed until it has been marked, etc.

```
                    T60        T90
T10  T20  T30  T40  T50  T62  T70  T80  T100 T120 T130 T140 END
                                          T110
```

The above diagram shows the sequence in which tasks are carried out. It clearly shows that T10 must be done before T20, and that T50 and T60, and T110 and T120, can be done in parallel.

Step 12 – Stage creation

We are still in the planning stage. When we started we had one big job and now we have all these lists of products and tasks. It may be confusing because we potentially have a huge list of products and tasks. It is possible that the lists are so long that you as the project manager won't be able to grasp the big picture. We have broken an apparently insurmountable big problem, down into a lot of understandable and achievable little problems. However, the sheer number of those little problems can cause a problem themselves.

There is a procedure to follow. Look at the list of products and activities and break them down into sensible 'stages'. That is, take a red pen and draw a circle around groups of tasks and products that seem to fit together, they are then 'stages'.

Project stages shouldn't be too long, so make the stages appropriate lengths. For example, stages on a small project should not be more than a week or two at most in duration and on even the largest project you should aim to keep stages to a maximum length of three months.

A common-sense view of the tasks and products may well present a natural breakdown into stages. In our garden example, the common sense stages may be:

- Stage 1 – Plan and contract (T10-T20-T30-T40)
- Stage 2 – Approve clear and mark (T50-T60-T62-T70)

- Stage 3 – Garden (T80-T90-T100-T110)
- Stage 4 – Completion (T120-T130-T140)

If no 'natural' stages present themselves (which they almost always do), or if some natural stages are so large that they appear unmanageable, you will have to impose stages. These are the stage 'rules' that you will need to bear in mind:

- Aim to do one stage at a time.
- Do the stages in the order derived from the plans.
- When the stage is completed, perform an 'end stage review' (see 'End stage review' section below).

Step 13 – Project technical plan

'Project technical plan' is more 'technospeak' and is probably best described by referring to your holiday chart at work. Most offices show when people are on holiday or a training course using a marked-up year planner, so that everyone can see at a glance who is off at any given time. From that year planner you have an overview of who is in or out of the office.

In simple terms, a project technical plan shows stages drawn onto a year planner, except we cut off the months of the year planner that we are not using. In the example below we have shown a sample 'project technical plan'. Stage 1 starts on 3rd January and ends in March. Stage 2 can start as soon as the first two tasks in Stage 1 are completed, which means on 15th February – so these stages overlap. Stages 3 and 4 can overlap as well, and the whole project will be completed by 4 August.

```
STAGE 1   = = = = =
STAGE 2        = = = = = = = =
STAGE 3                 = = = = =
STAGE 4                         = = =
             J   F   M   A   M   J   J   A
```

Each stage should be self-contained. At the end of each stage you should aim to halt all work, to allow you to review progress and your findings to date. To do this, hold an end stage review meeting.

End stage review

The end stage review will give you a formal opportunity to check many aspects of the project. The product can be checked against the product specification. The quality can be signed off. The effort expended can be checked against the plan – for example was there a drought and the lawn turf was five days late in arriving, potentially delaying project completion? When you dug up that old apple tree did you expose an abandoned mine shaft that will cost £175,000 to fill in and make safe?

Dropping our example garden project and speaking once more in event terms, at any end stage review, the project manager invites a few colleagues with appropriate skills to sit as an end stage review panel. The project manager/event manager presents the results of their work with a short written report and possibly overheads or slides confirming those details.

It may be bad news. Perhaps a site cannot be booked, or costs have soared and the event won't make a profit. The panel may decide it is necessary to review the scope and objective of the event, or possibly abandon it.

The minimum benefit of an end stage review is that the event manager/project manager keeps in regular touch with an increasingly accurate picture of the detailed costing, plans, effort and arrangements for the event. This can at best only help to make the event a success and at worst save wasting more time, effort and money on an unsuccessful event.

As an early task, I suggest that using the lists and notes in this book, you draw up an appropriate list of products and tasks that you must complete, in order to achieve the project target of running your event. Once completed, divide these tasks up into sensible stages, so that you can monitor, manage and control progress. It is possible to assign a stage manager/deputy manager to organise and manage a given stage of the plan.

If the stage manager were to organise the event accommodation and toilets they might present a one-page written report as indicated below. The event manager can file the report and quotes and add the costs to the running event accounts and forecasts.

The event manager sits at the centre of the web of deputies, assistants, information and activity. The event manager will monitor and control and push the effort along to complete the preparations for the event, while at all times knowing exactly what needs to be done, how much time and money it will take, who is going to do it and in what order. Making sure that all end stage reviews are carried out, you will never have any nasty surprises.

A sample end stage report is given below. Depending on the size and content of the event and the type and scope of activities and products involved, the end stage report will vary. However, the basic content will remain the same. The sample below is adequate to illustrate the type of document that is required and the depth of coverage necessary.

Bradfield Social Club Fund Raiser

STAGE 3 – Investigate accommodation and portable toilets
Results

Accommodation	1 Portacabin required for manager
	1 Portacabin required for cashier
Toilets	5 suppliers agree that with the target
	10 unisex toilets for audience will suffice
Costs	Equipment booked from lowest quotes
	(all quotes enclosed for file)

Jenkins Equipment Hire Ltd

2 8ft × 25ft Portacabins	£600 Inc VAT
With 4 desks and chairs	
Including delivery and erection	
And removal	
10 Unisex toilets including	£795 Inc VAT
Delivery and collection	
Removal and attendant	
while event open	
TOTAL	**£1395 Inc VAT**

Now back to the garden project …

Step 14 – Got any awkward questions?

Back to those awkward questions I was threatening you with at the start. Remember how scary those questions seemed and how we thought that they were impossible to answer just 40 minutes ago when you started reading this supplement. I promised that you would be able to answer those questions easily and confidently. You didn't actually believe me back then – well you can apologise to me now! Mr Smith wanted to know: '…what products you have to deliver to complete this "garden" project? What tasks have to be undertaken to generate those products? What will you charge for doing it? How long will all of this take you?'

You will answer, with a smug and confident expression, liking this bit a lot because it makes you look really, really good …

'No problem, Mr Smith – we can deliver the garden of your dreams. We will deliver the project in four stages. It will cost you £9000 *(our costs from above plus a huge profit)*. It will take 46 man-days' effort, and if we start as scheduled on 3ʳᵈ January we will be finished by 4ᵗʰ August. I have here a copy of the project technical plan, user requirement, product definitions, tasks, product flow diagram, network and dependency diagrams if you care to run through them.'

Well, at that price and time-scale I don't think he will want us to do his garden. The important thing to notice is that we can now easily answer all of those awkward questions and more, with a degree of assurance that you would not have thought possible when you started reading this supplement.

Now that you understand the concept, we will leave our gardening example and returning to the event project. At this point, we have an organisation or individual that is proposing to run an event. You now need to apply the techniques outlined above to undertake a detailed investigation, planning and review process. Remembering that you can delegate sub-projects to a specific deputy manager to investigate plan and report on. Remembering too that the event is some months away, and that we have not yet received the necessary licences and permissions, we cannot book facilities, but we can certainly finalise most of the investigation and costing as soon as possible.

From that, you will be able to answer all of those awkward questions relating to the proposed event. As has been seen, diligent application of investigation, recording and management can make the delivery of your event quite straightforward.

Annex B

Approval checklist

This event approval checklist has multiple uses. It ensures that you complete and record all of the activities required to investigate, plan and arrange your event. It also helps you to compile the set of documentation that you may require to present your plans to the police, local authority and other organisations, in order to gain licences and permissions to hold your event.

Reminder: all events are unique, and though this checklist may be more than is required by the teacher organising a primary school fête, for your unique event and some specialist events, you may need to add other detail. For example, at a shooting competition you may need to present plans and arrangements for your firing range, or the supply and storage of weapons and ammunition.

Approval checklist – cover sheet	Comment	Done
Event title:		
Proposed event date/time:		
Proposed event location:		
Event summary:		
Event manager + phone no:		
Audience size expected:		
Local authority liaison:		
Police liaison:		
Other liaison:		

As event manager, you are responsible for adding any specialist products required by your unique show. Products should be listed in the product column. You may make relevant comments in the comment column – perhaps noting that a table has been created in Word or Excel format. The 'Done' date is the date when that product was completed or last revised, the page number is the page relating to a given document in this approval pack. Note: you may refer to a separate manual or document, e.g. reference sheets and formal job specifications, which are held in a separate ring binder.

Approval checklist – products	Comment	Done date	Page no.
Chapter 1 – Introduction	Read and understood		
Chapter 2 – The event manager	Read and understood		
• Have taken the role of event manager or appointed one.			
Chapter 3 – The event objective	Read and understood		
• Definition of *your* event objective.			
• Checkpoint review – authorisation to continue.			
Chapter 4 – Planning the event	Read and understood		
Chapter 5 – Health and safety	Read and understood		
• Standard meeting agenda with health and safety as permanent first and last item.			
• Completed hazard tables for the event.			
• Event health and safety policy.			
• Standing health and safety rules.			
• Checkpoint review – authorisation to continue.			
Chapter 6 – Type of event	Read and understood		
• Event outline (usually one page maximum).			
• Checkpoint review – authorisation to continue.			
Chapter 7 – When to run the event	Read and understood		
• Day, date and time when you propose to run your event.			
• Checkpoint review – authorisation to continue.			

Approval checklist – products	Comment	Done date	Page no.
Chapter 8 – Defining your target audience	Read and understood		
• Written audience profile, including age range, sex, source, interests, likely mode of transport etc.			
• Checkpoint review – authorisation to continue.			
Chapter 9 – Audience size	Read and understood		
• Estimated attendance based on at least three methods of calculation.			
• Checkpoint review – authorisation to continue.			
Chapter 10 – Advertising	Read and understood		
• Proposed advertising schedule, showing the advertisements you propose to place, and listing where and when they will be made.			
• Schedule of potential advertising income for the event showing details of the advertisers and income expected.			
• Schedule of sponsors, showing details of sponsors and sponsorship deals.			
• Checkpoint review – authorisation to continue.			
Chapter 11 – Event attractions	Read and understood		
• List of proposed event attractions, including short descriptions of the attractions, owner's name, experience, insurance cover they hold, etc.			
• Outline timetable for the event, listing the order in which competitors and/or attractions will be run.			
• Results of health and safety review of each attraction.			
• Attractions and competitors for which there is no charge, and which have been provisionally booked should be listed.			
• Checkpoint review – authorisation to continue.			

Approval checklist – products	Comment	Done date	Page no.
Chapter 12 – Event requirements	Read and understood		
• Brief report outlining arrangements and considerations required to deliver the proposed attractions.			
• Checkpoint review – authorisation to continue.			
Chapter 13 – Accommodation and services	Read and understood		
• A list of required accommodation, equipment and services, detailing known or proposed suppliers, with reference to site plan indicating location and services, etc.			
• Where provision has been made for accommodation for first aid, police, local authority liaison officer etc., list the accommodation and facilities proposed (e.g. private toilet facility), with reference to site plan indicating location and services, etc.			
• Checkpoint review – authorisation to continue.			
Chapter 14 – Event site	Read and understood		
• Details of event site, including site owner, site size, access points, usage of various areas and facilities, entry and exit plans.			
• Schedule of site transport links and expected event traffic patterns.			
• Schedule of proposed accommodation and services with reference to proposed site plan.			
• Proposed site and car parking plans and maps.			
• Proposed emergency exit and access points and routes.			
• Report of site health and safety review, listing any known hazards and proposed control measures, list vehicle-free zone times.			
Note proposed on-site sign schedule dealt with in Chapter 16.			
• Listing of event manager's, first aid, police post, and other offices and services such as public and private toilets.			

Approval checklist – products	Comment	Done date	Page no.
Chapter 14 – Event site *(continued)*			
• Be practised in estimating and calculating car parking space.			
• Report showing estimated attendance, number of cars expected, car parking calculations and arrangements.			
• Checkpoint review – authorisation to continue.			
Chapter 15 – Traffic management	Read and understood		
• Name of traffic manager, plus outline of experience.			
• Details of contingency plans and any emergency access routes agreed with police and fire service etc. Plan showing routes to be included.			
• Schedule of agreed positions of all approach and exit direction signs.			
• Schedule of all agreed car park location signs.			
• Report listing car park and traffic staff required in event car parks and on the event site.			
• Schedule of any agreed shape, design and colour for vehicle passes and badges.			
• Details of strict instructions to pass- and badge-holders instructing them to display passes and badges in their vehicle windscreen, or be directed to public car parks.			
• Summary traffic plan, including vehicle numbers, types, access routes, car parking arrangements, traffic patterns, peak flow etc.			
• Checkpoint review – authorisation to continue.			
Chapter 16 – Sign posting	Read and understood		
• Schedule of on-site and off-site signs agreed and required.			
• Specification of agreed design of standard direction sign (for example yellow background with black writing).			

Approval checklist – products	Comment	Done date	Page no.
Chapter 16 – Sign posting (*continued*)			
• Designed sign schedule form to allow sign erection teams to record what signs have been erected and where, for later collection.			
• Agreed list of materials and equipment needed for emergency sign production and erection.			
• Agreed list of training and equipment needs for sign erection teams.			
• Agreed insurance cover required for event manager and sign erection teams.			
• Checkpoint review – authorisation to continue.			
Chapter 17 – Permissions	Read and understood		
• Have been working with the authorities, following their instructions and guidelines, listening to their concerns and resolving issues, while working towards a proposed event and plan, which they will formally approve.			
Chapter 18 – Car parking	Read and understood		
• List of staff numbers and skills required to ensure safe coverage.			
• Proposed work roster for car park staff.			
• Details of proposed training for car park staff, including content and schedules.			
• Schedule of equipment, clothing and signs required for car park staff.			
• Checkpoint review – authorisation to continue.			
Chapter 19 – Radio communications	Read and understood		
• Details of any radio equipment supplier.			
• List of staff and liaison staff (police, ambulance etc.) who will be issued with a radio.			
• Radio issue and collection administration procedure if not provided by supplier.			
• Emergency radio log defined and produced.			

Approval checklist – products	Comment	Done date	Page no.
Chapter 19 – Radio communications *(continued)*			
• Required training sessions content and schedules where required.			
• Checkpoint review – authorisation to continue.			
Chapter 20 – Staffing	Read and understood		
• List of all staff roles that are required for your event.			
• Reference sheet including extended job descriptions which includes person specification, job description, training schedule and equipment schedule for each role.			
• List of numbers for each role required for the event.			
• Possibly have created a dry-wipe duty and status board for the event manager (include diagram and description of its use).			
• Documented risk assessment for each role. (Note: do not try to copy them into the proposal pack, simply refer to them in the proposal pack and take them with you and be prepared to produce them during your presentation to the authorities while formally asking for licensing or written permission to run the event.)			
• Proposed duty schedule to ensure adequate cover maintained.			
• Checkpoint review – authorisation to continue.			
Chapter 21 – First aid	Read and understood		
• List of minimum first aid requirements agreed with the authorities and your insurance company			
• Quotes and specification of proposed and agreed first aid insurance cover, showing details of supplier.			
• List of first aid staff required for your event.			
• List of equipment and supplies that will be provided for the event.			

Approval checklist – products	Comment	Done date	Page no.
Chapter 21 – First aid *(continued)*			
• Checkpoint review – authorisation to continue.			
Chapter 22 – Security	Read and understood		
• Agreed list of security issues relating to your event.			
• Agreed list of security staff required to secure your event.			
• Details of source of those staff, be it police, private security or your staff.			
• Documented risk assessments of security issues.			
• Checkpoint review – authorisation to continue.			
Chapter 23 – Insurance	Read and understood		
• Details of the insurance cover the authorities required you to have for your event.			
• Details of selected insurer.			
• Details of any proposed insurance cover, plus any restrictions and limitations the insurance company may impose on you (such as, all drivers must be over 21 and hold a clean driving licence).			
• Checkpoint review – authorisation to continue.			
Chapter 24 – Emergency and normal procedures	Read and understood		
• Description and explanation of agreed standard event procedure format and use.			
• Schedule of all agreed procedures required for the event. (Note: do not try to copy them into the proposal pack, simply refer to them in the proposal pack and take them with you and be prepared to produce them during your presentation to the authorities while formally asking for licensing or written permission to run the event.)			
• Evidence of successful completion of a desktop walk-through of the event, using current site plan, schedules and procedures.			

Approval checklist – products	Comment	Done date	Page no.
Chapter 24 – Emergency and normal procedures *(continued)*			
• Defined and agreed, detailed priority procedure for lost children.			
• Defined and agreed alternate control point to event manager's office.			
• Defined and agreed lost and found property logs and procedures.			
• Checkpoint review – authorisation to continue.			
For sample risk/hazard reporting form, see Chapter 21.			
Chapter 25 – Formal proposal	Read and understood		
• Completed approval checklist.			
• Collate and collect current copies of all estimates, plans, job descriptions, etc., that appear in the approval checklist.			
• On successful application for approval, you should hold all appropriate licenses and written approvals to continue.			
• Confirm orders for all event requirements specified above.			
• Checkpoint review – authorisation to continue.			
Chapter 26 – Event manager's manual	Read and understood		
• An agreed format for your event manager's manual.			
• An agreement as to how many copies of the manual you require.			
• An agreement as to who should hold the copies of the manual.			
• Sample manual complete as per that date, to be updated from now on to become the master copy of the event manager's manual.			
• Checkpoint review – authorisation to continue.			
Chapter 27 – Money	Read and understood		
• Schedule of fees for entry and parking etc. for your event.			

Approval checklist – products	Comment	Done date	Page no.
Chapter 27 – Money *(continued)*			
• Schedule of cash float required including source and denomination breakdown.			
• Definition of planned secure cash office.			
• Assigned or recruited a cashier.			
• Defined cash handling security schedules in consultations with local police.			
• Schedule of random on-site cash collection rounds and routes.			
• Identification cards for all on-site cash collectors.			
• Schedule of cash collections from site by security cash vans during and after the event.			
• Cash recording and analysis forms and tools prepared.			
• Defined delegated spending limits for appropriate staff.			
• Defined and established auditable separate method to collect and record any charity cash.			
• Checkpoint review – authorisation to continue.			
Chapter 28 – Accounts	Read and understood		
• Defined and agreed accounting method.			
• Accept that a key target is to be able to present a profit and loss account for the event when it is finished.			
• Be able to account for every penny of income and expenditure, there should be no 'incidental expenses' or other unidentifiable items shown.			
Chapter 29 – Video diary	Read and understood		
• Schedule defining when and where you will use videotape as a tool in managing your event.			
• Obtain video recording equipment and somebody capable of using it.			

Approval checklist – products	Comment	Done date	Page no.
Chapter 29 – Video diary *(continued)*			
• Schedule of the known occasions when the video equipment will be used – for example on the initial tour of the proposed site.			
• Definition of occasions when video equipment will be used, for example recording complex tape and cone entrance lanes at the main gate, or as part of an enquiry following any incident or accident.			
Chapter 30 – Setting up	Read and understood		
• The site will be marked out and ready.			
• All on-site signs will be erected and recorded for later collection.			
• All agreed off-site signs will have been erected and recorded for later collection.			
• All equipment and services will have been delivered and set up or installed to your satisfaction.			
• Gates will be staffed and any security staff will be working as per schedules.			
• The event manager's office and any first aid post will be permently staffed.			
• All equipment will have been checked and tested.			
Chapter 31 – Site maintenance	Read and understood		
• Schedule prepared including content of staff briefing and list of staff to be briefed.			
• Maintenance teams nominated, trained and ready.			
• Supervisors with appropriate skills and training ready.			
• Sufficient supplies and equipment available to allow maintenance staff to perform their function.			

Approval checklist – products	Comment	Done date	Page no.
Chapter 32 – Strip down/clear up	Read and understood		
• Agreed activity plan prepared, stating how the site should be cleared, rubbish removed and properly disposed of and final signs removed. Should include a definition of staffing and facilities required to perform this function.			
• Sign schedules checked to confirm all signs collected.			
• Sign off sheets checked to confirm that all staff have been debriefed and stood down.			
• Final collection of skips and other equipment arranged and supervised.			
• Final tour of event site and boundary, making videotape record as proof of state of site when event finished, while double-checking for event signs, gates closed, abandoned cars, etc.			
Chapter 33 – Final debrief	Read and understood		
• Debrief schedule, outlining debrief process.			
• Debrief reporting forms to record issues that need to be taken further, including a note of the person making the proposal and a phone number or address in case event staff need to contact them for clarification.			
• Detailed reports where necessary, allowing staff to make a more detailed description and drawings explaining their proposals, and stating benefits they suggest can be obtained by adopting their proposals.			
• Notes of staff who performed well and who you would like to use again.			
Chapter 34 – Final report	Read and understood		
• Final report outline and contents.			
• Final report.			
Chapter 35 – Conclusion	Read and understood		
• Finalise actions on the event; tidy and weed documentation and file it away.			

Index

If you want to know how … *to write a report*

'In this book you will learn how to write reports that will be read without unnecessary delay; understood without undue effort; accepted and, where applicable, acted upon. To achieve these aims you must do more than present all the relevant facts accurately, you must also communicate in a way that is both acceptable and intelligible to your readers.'

John Bowden

Writing a Report
How to prepare, write and present effective reports
JOHN BOWDEN

'What is special about the text is that it is more than just how to 'write reports'; it gives that extra really powerful information that can, and often does, make a difference. It is by far the most informative text covering report writing that I have seen… This book would be a valuable resource to any practising manager. ' – *Training Journal*

'With the help of this sensible step-by-step guide, anybody can develop first-rate report writing skills.' – *Building Engineer*

ISBN 1 85703 922 X

If you want to know how ... *to get free publicity for your event*

If your company, club, church or charity has a story to tell or something new, free or amazing to offer, journalists want to hear from you.

Getting Free Publicity
Secrets of successful press relations
PAM AND BOB AUSTIN

This step-by-step manual takes you right through from who you should target and what journalists are looking for, to practical suggestions for choosing and presenting stories that will get accepted by editors. You will discover how to write effective press releases and articles, how to deal with media interviews – and what to do if a journalist gets your story wrong.

ISBN 1 85703 972 6

If you want to know how ... *to publish your own magazine or* *newsletter*

'Great ideas, practical help, and straightforward guidance ... a must-have for anyone planning their own publication.'

Producing Successful Magazines, Newsletters and E-zines
CAROL HARRIS

This book will:

- Help you learn about printed and electronic publication
- Help you choose what kind of publication is right for you
- Show you how to set up and run a magazine or newsletter
- Explain how to attract articles and paying advertisements
- Train you on interviewing and writing
- Provide additional contacts and resources

Carol Harris has produced magazines and newsletters for a wide range of organisations and is currently the publisher and editor of *Effective Consulting* magazine. She also trains and coaches people in personal and business skills.

ISBN 1 85703 964 5

How To Books are available through all good bookshops, or you can order direct from us through Grantham Book Services.

Tel: +44 (0)1476 541080
Fax: +44 (0)1476 541061
Email: orders@gbs.tbs-ltd.co.uk

Or via our website

www.howtobooks.co.uk

To order via any of these methods please quote the title(s) of the book(s) and your credit card number together with its expiry date.

For further information about our books and catalogue, please contact:

How To Books
Spring Hill House, Spring Hill Road
Begbroke, Oxford OX5 1RX

Visit our web site at

www.howtobooks.co.uk

Or you can contact us by email at info@howtobooks.co.uk